ENCOUNTERING AMERICAN FAULTLINES

ENCOUNTERING AMERICAN FAULTLINES

Race, Class, and the Dominican Experience in Providence

José Itzigsohn

Russell Sage Foundation • New York

The Russell Sage Foundation

Library of Congress Cataloging-in-Publication Data

Itzigsohn, José, 1960–
    Encountering American faultlines: race, class, and the Dominican experience in Providence / José Itzigsohn.
        p. cm.
    Includes bibliographical references and index.
    ISBN 978-0-87154-448-3 (alk. paper)
    1. Immigrants—Rhode Island—Providence. 2. Dominican Republic—Emigration and immigration. 3. Providence (R.I.)—Race relations. 4. Class consciousness—Rhode Island—Providence. I. Title.
    JV7085.P76I89 2009
    305.868'729307452—dc22

                                                          2008050967

Text design by Genna Patacsil.

RUSSELL SAGE FOUNDATION
112 East 64th Street, New York, New York 10065
10 9 8 7 6 5 4 3 2 1

CONTENTS

ABOUT THE AUTHOR

José Itzigsohn is associate professor of sociology at Brown University.

ACKNOWLEDGMENTS

This book is the result of many years of work, during which I acquired numerous debts of gratitude. To begin, I would like to thank the Russell Sage Foundation for its contribution to all the phases of the project, from funding my research to publishing this volume. I completed a draft of this book while on sabbatical at the foundation, where the working environment, resources, and intellectual exchanges with my colleagues of the 2006–2007 cohort of visiting scholars were all invaluable to me. This book would simply not have been possible without the foundation's support.

Several colleagues read and commented on different chapters. In strictly alphabetical order, I thank Aixa Cintron-Velez, Kay Deaux, Rachel Heiman, Patricia Landolt, Tim Moran, Karthick Ramakrishnan, and George Wilson. All were generous with their time and input on different versions of the manuscript and provided important criticism and suggestions.

Over the years I have talked with many colleagues about my ideas in presentations, in conferences, or just over a cup of coffee. They have not necessarily agreed, but their conversations with me helped me think through assertions and theories. Again in alphabetical order, I thank Leticia Calderón-Chelius, Ginetta Candelario, Luis Donatello, Nancy Foner, Silvia Giorguli-Saucedo, Steve Gold, Luin Goldring, Adrianne Kalfopolou, Jean-Michel LaFleur, Jorge Malheiros, Marco Martiniello, Jason McDonald, Silvia Montenegro, Silvia Pedraza, Alejandro Portes, and Rubén Rumbaut. Special thanks are due to Eric Wanner, whose insightful criticism during the presentation of an earlier version of this work at the Russell Sage Foundation was very influential in shaping the first part of the book.

My largest intellectual debt in writing this book is to two friends and colleagues, Patricio Korzeniewicz and Jitka Maleckova. Each read more than half of the manuscript and each made fundamental contributions to it. The long conversations I had with Patricio during the time we spent as visiting scholars at the foundation were essential in helping me organize my arguments and the structure of the book. Jitka was both my friendliest and my toughest critic and would not let me get away with anything. As I read the final version of the manuscript, I can see the imprint and the value of her critiques.

I would also like to mention two anonymous reviewers. Since the acceptance of the book I have asked them to come forward so I can acknowledge and warmly thank them openly—Phil Kasinitz and Robert Smith. Phil pushed me to deepen and strengthen my analysis of the data. If my analysis is empirically solid, it is to a large extent thanks to Phil's suggestions. Robert encouraged me to further develop my theoretical framework and also offered the name: stratified ethnoracial incorporation. I owe him big time for what I consider to be one of the most important contributions of the book.

The writing of a book is not only the development of an intellectual argument. It is also a painstaking process of finding minute details, preparing the presentation of information and data, and looking for books, articles, and citations. I could not have done that without the invaluable help of the research assistants. Thanks then to Galo Falchettore, Alexsa Rosa, Orly Clerge, and Jeffrey Ruiz, who were research assistants during my year at the Russell Sage Foundation. I also benefitted from the help of current and past graduate students at Brown. Adriana Lopez-Ramirez and Mathias vom Hau each helped me develop different parts of the analysis.

I also want to thank Suzanne Nichols, Russell Sage's Director of Publications, for her constant support of this project.

My biggest debt is to the Dominican community in Providence—to all the people who talked with me, invited me to their homes, answered my survey, and invited me to be part of their lives in this country. As an immigrant myself, the Dominican community has embraced me and provided me with a sense of belonging. Participation in the life of the Dominican and Latino community in Providence has been my own path of incorporation into American life. Not only would this book have been impossible if Dominicans in Providence had not opened their doors to my inquiries, but my life would also have been much poorer without the friendship of and shared projects with so many Dominicans in Providence.

Elvys Ruiz helped me organize and conduct key parts of the fieldwork that constitute the basis for this book. He was also a constant sounding board to my questions and ideas on Dominican incorporation. My fieldwork would also not have been possible without the invaluable help of Claribel Terrero and Maria Kamara Terrero. Another friend who greatly contributed to this book is Mario Bueno. Mario introduced me to local Latino activism in Providence and for years kept asking me when the book would be completed and published. I extend also my deep appreciation to Rhode Island State Senator Juán Pichardo and State Representative Grace Diaz, both of whom generously agreed to speak with me and to let me talk about their political activities in this book. My analysis of Dominican politics would have been impossible without their collaboration.

Many other Dominicans in Providence over the years have opened their homes to me, have provided me with ideas, and have shared with me their political and cultural projects. All of them helped me complete this project. I cannot mention them all, but there are many I must acknowledge here. In strict alphabetical order, I want to thank Hugo Adames, José Alemán, Pedro Baez, Americo and Niselsa Bisonó, Marisol Camilo, Victor Capellán, Melba DePeña, Felix Diclo, Zoilo Garcia, Abraham Henderson, Dilania Inoa, Manuel Jimenez, Yuri Liriano, Councilperson Miguel Luna, Tony Mendez, Sabina Matos, Juan Mota, Francis Parra, Luis Peralta, Tomás Ramirez, Councilperson Luis Tejada, and Johanna Terrero.

I cannot finish without mentioning my parents, José Alberto Itzigsohn and Sara Minuchin Itzigsohn, who read several of the chapters, commented on them, and constantly encouraged me to complete this book.

All the people I mention helped me in large or small ways to write this book. All contributed to improve it. The responsibility for the arguments and claims, however, is solely mine. I have written this book hoping to contribute to a better understanding of Dominican incorporation and of the immigrant experience in general. I dedicate it to all immigrants, here and around the world. The hard work of immigrants helps build a better life in the places they live.

PART I

Introduction

CHAPTER 1

Immigration and American Society

What does it mean for immigrants to become American? This is an old question in American social science and public discourse that has acquired new importance as immigration has again become a central element of life in the United States. As immigrants incorporate into American society, they undergo social and cultural change. At the same time, they change the fabric of American social structure and cultural dynamics. They also have a great influence on the everyday life of the place in which they live. This book looks at the ways in which Dominican immigrants in Providence become part of American society. Through the examination of one immigrant group in one city, the book aims to participate in the contemporary conversation concerning immigrant incorporation and what it says about contemporary American society.

When I first arrived in Providence in the fall of 1994, I did not know much about the place. I knew about the role of New England in the European settlement of North America and in the formation of the United States as an independent country. I knew that the region had been the cradle of the industrial revolution in America and that it had also been a destination of European migration during the second half of the nineteenth century and the early twentieth century. I thought that to the extent that I might find an ethnic presence, it would be related to the large historical migration of Italian, Irish, Portuguese, and French Canadians to the region. I did not expect to find a large and vibrant Dominican community. I knew very well that the post-1965 migration came mainly from the developing world, but at that point I associated it with the large gateway cities of the United States, not with smaller places like Providence. In my imagination, Providence made me think of Lloyd Warner's and Leo Srole's classic Yankee City series. In *The Social Systems of American Ethnic Groups* (1945), one of a series of books on Newburyport, Massachusetts, Warner and Srole described a city with a strong presence of European immigrants and analyzed their ethnic organization and their process of assimilation.

On arriving in Providence, I came to realize that the city I had imagined had indeed existed, but only until the 1970s. To be sure, Providence's immigration history was different from Newburyport's because of the large presence in Providence of black Cape Verdean immigrants (Beck 1992; Halter 1993). The ethnic character of the city and its politics, however, was dominated by the strong presence of European immigrants—particularly Italians, Irish, and Portuguese—and their children. Yet when I arrived in the middle of the 1990s, I found a place that for the last two decades had grown through the toil of new immigrants from Latin America, the Caribbean, Asia (mainly East Asia), and Africa. Immigrants reversed the city's population decline and revitalized abandoned neighborhoods. I realized that Providence was a new kind of Yankee City, one in which minorities constituted the majority of the population. Dominicans are one of the largest immigrant-ethnic groups in town and their presence is felt in all realms of urban life.

Driving on Broad Street from downtown Providence toward the Southside, one soon notices the presence of numerous Dominican small businesses. A part of La Broa, as the street is known by Spanish-speaking immigrants, has been renamed Juan Pablo Duarte Boulevard, honoring the hero of Dominican independence. Turning right on Miller Street, edging Roger Williams Park, one can see a monument to Duarte that was built with the contributions of community members. The southern part of the city, particularly the area between Broad Street and Elmwood Avenue, is the core area of Dominican presence in Providence and the base of the growing political empowerment of Dominicans. Dominicans, however, live in most parts of town.

Encountering American Faultlines examines how race and class shape the incorporation of first- and second-generation Dominicans in Providence, Rhode Island. It focuses on two dimensions of incorporation. First, it examines the position of first- and second-generation Dominicans in Providence's socioeconomic structure and the paths of mobility across the generations. Second, it explores the identities Dominicans develop as they become part of American society, focusing in particular on the emergence of transnational and panethnic identities and the social practices associated with them. This book, then, attempts to portray a small piece of a large phenomenon in the contemporary American experience: the incorporation of new immigrant groups in new cities of immigration.

This book also joins in the theoretical debates about immigrant incorporation in the United States. Dominicans are an important group to look at in this context. For one, they are one of the largest immigrant groups in the East Coast, particularly in the northeastern states. More important, however, is how they enter American society. Most Dominican immigrants arrive with low skill levels and very few economic resources. As a result, they enter the American occupational system at its bottom. Furthermore, many Dominicans are seen as blacks by mainstream society and all are categorized as Latinos. They thus become part of racialized groups within American society (Aparicio 2006; Candelario 2007). The study of Dominican incorporation allows us to analyze the ways in which race and class shape the process of immigrant incorporation. Furthermore, analysis of the Dominican experience provides a window through which to examine the faultlines that structure American society. Based on the analysis of the process of Dominican incorporation in Providence, this volume proposes an innovative theoretical approach to looking at the contemporary forms and meanings of becoming American.

IMMIGRANT INCORPORATION IN AMERICA

Scholars of immigration use the terms *assimilation* and *incorporation* to refer to the ways in which immigrants become American. In his history of the concept of assimilation, the sociologist Peter Kivisto argued that these two terms refer to the same processes and he advocates the use of the term assimilation (2005). Kivisto was right in arguing that assimilation and incorporation refer to similar processes, but there is an important difference between the two. Classical work on assimilation suffered from two problems. First, it failed to take race into account. Second, it held on to the theoretical expectation of assimilation into what Milton Gordon called Anglo-conformity (1964).[1] It is the failure to address the dynamics of racialization that led scholars to question classical assimilation theory (Glazer 1993).

Although framed within the classic assimilation approach, Warner and Srole's analysis of ethnicity in Newburyport was an exception to the pattern of neglect of race in the study of immigrant assimilation. Warner and Srole argued that the speed with which European ethnic groups assimilated was contingent on their social distance from the American cultural mainstream and the strength of their ethnic organization. At the end of the process, immigrant groups were going to gradually lose their ethnic traits and become part of the American class order. The identity of the children of immigrants would be determined by their position in the American class structure rather than by their ethnic origin. Based on their analysis of the social distance of different immigrant groups from the Anglo mainstream, Warner and Srole presented elaborated predictions on how many generations will take to each ethnic group to assimilate. I get back to those predictions in the conclusions to this book because they serve as a cautionary tale about the risks of making predictions based on current trends in rapidly changing situations.[2] Yet it is important to point out that Warner and Srole correctly identified one insurmountable barrier in the process of assimilation—the color line. African Americans and other immigrants of color constituted an exception to the trend towards the loss of ethnic ties and assimilation into the American class order that Warner and Srole identified. Race trumped acculturation and assimilation. In the 1940s, Warner and Srole argued that racial groups "will not be totally assimilated until the present American social order changes gradually or by revolution" (1945, 292).

American society has certainly changed since their book was published. The massive popular mobilization of the civil rights movement brought a major change in the American social order and since then race and class have become much more intertwined in defining the opportunities of individuals and groups (Anderson 2001; Wilson 1978). Reflecting on these changes and previous critiques, the sociologists Richard Alba and Victor Nee reformulated assimilation theory to address contemporary migration. For these authors, assimilation referred to a process of boundary blurring through which immigrants and their offspring become closer, and eventually hardly distinguishable, from the mainstream of the receiving society along a number of important social and economic dimensions (Alba and Nee 2003). Alba and Nee did not make assumptions as to what is the end point of this process. They found evidence of the blurring of boundaries in the occupational mobility and residential integration of important segments of the immigrant population.

They argued that in spite of the pervasiveness of racialization, since the 1960s American society has become much more open and porous to the mobility of all groups. They added that because racial boundaries have changed in the past they can change in the future and become less important in the organization of social life. Their assumption was that although race and class boundaries are real and affect immigrant's lives, they are ultimately blurred boundaries that can be crossed across generations.

In spite of their optimistic outlook, Alba and Nee recognized that the color line is not disappearing. They argued that a likely scenario is the reconstruction of racial boundaries along a black-nonblack line of differentiation (Alba 2005; Alba and Nee 2003). This scenario would reshape but not eliminate the color line, and many immigrant groups, like Dominicans, would end up on the excluded side. Moreover, although Alba and Nee distanced themselves from the normative elements of assimilation theory, the concept of assimilation carries in the general public a normative expectation that immigrants, and in particular their children, will over time merge and disappear into the general American population. This normative expectation was not too long ago forcefully expressed by Samuel Huntington (2004).

Contemporary immigration, though, takes place in a context of increasing social inequality. Inequality in America has reached levels unseen since the 1930s (Massey 2007). Racialization is also a part of the everyday experience, shaping immigrants' encounters with American society (Grosfoguel and Georas 2000; Itzigsohn, Giorguli, and Vazquez 2005; Vickerman 1999; Waters 1999). The analysis of the ways in which immigrant groups are becoming Americans needs to take into account this growing social polarization and the pervasive forms of racial inequality. The argument of this book is that American society is structured around class and racial faultlines that shape the experiences of migrants and their children.

There is no doubt that immigrants are either participating increasingly in the institutions of American society or that they are acculturating. In this sense, the boundaries between immigrants, their children, and American society are indeed being blurred. On the other hand, the process of becoming part of American society is characterized by the formation of new boundaries along racial and class lines. For immigrants of color, becoming American does not mean the erasure of differences between immigrants, their children, and the mainstream, but finding a place within the faultlines of American society. For these reasons, I prefer to speak of immigrant incorporation rather than assimilation.

SOCIOECONOMIC INCORPORATION

The historical record of immigrants' social mobility in America is mixed. The first generations of European immigrants who arrived during the second half of the nineteenth century and the beginning of the twentieth century went through severe economic difficulties and deprivations. Nevertheless, within the span of three or four generations, the socioeconomic profile of their offspring was quite similar to that of other white Americans. This process of upward mobility, however, did not repeat itself with Mexican and Puerto Rican immigrants, who after three or four generations in the United States are still overrepresented in the lower income deciles and among those below the poverty line. Their predicament resembles that of African Americans, who though not an immigrant group, show persistent lower socioeconomic indicators than the white population (Bean and Stevens 2003; Grosfoguel and Georas 2000; Lieberson 1980; Massey 2007; Massey and Denton 1993; Telles and Ortiz 2008).

The question of the socioeconomic path of incorporation of the new immigrants has gathered renewed attention since the early 1990s, when the sociologist Herbert Gans first posed the question whether second-generation immigrants were experiencing downward mobility vis-à-vis their parents and joining the most marginalized sectors of American society (Gans 1992). One answer to Gans's question is given by those working within the broad framework of the new assimilation theory. These scholars recognized the difficulties of the incorporation process but rejected the idea that the second generation is experiencing downward assimilation (Alba and Nee 2003). Joel Perlmann and Roger Waldinger (1997) argued that the incorporation of the second and third generation of European immigrants was a protracted process aided by the end of the migration wave in the 1920s and the upward mobility that American society as a whole experienced after World War II, so that it is necessary to wait to see how the current process of incorporation unfolds. They added that with the exception of Mexican Americans, there is no evidence that the children of immigrants are experiencing downward assimilation (Perlmann and Waldinger 1997). Furthermore, after a close look at the available intergenerational data for Mexican Americans, Roger Waldinger and Cynthia Feliciano argued that although second-generation Mexican Americans are not experiencing upward mobility, they are also not falling back in respect to the first generation (2004).

For scholars working within the assimilation tradition, class and racial differences impose harshness in the lives of first- and second-generation immigrants, but they see a process of slow generational improvement and catching up with mainstream middle-class status. Comparing the incorporation trajectory of contemporary Mexican immigrants with that of southern and central European (SCEN) immigrants at the beginning of the twentieth century, Perlmann argued that because "the Mexican second generation is faring less well in relative terms than its SCEN counterparts, I find it reasonable to join Bean and Stevens (2003) in suggesting that Mexican economic assimilation may take more time—four or five generations rather than three or four" (2005, 124). I find this prediction problematic because it does not take into account the class and racial faultlines that shape the incorporation of immigrant generations.

A different answer to Gans's question is given by segmented assimilation theory. Scholars working within this framework argue that there are two profound differences between the contemporary American social structure and that of the mid-twentieth century, when the children of European immigrants assimilated. They claim, first, that the contemporary labor market is shaped as an hourglass. Well-paid manufacturing jobs that allowed for large segments of the second and third generation of European immigrants to achieve a middle-class life style have disappeared. Higher education is critical today to achieve upward mobility, but for the children of poor and low-skilled immigrants who go to school in the inner cities, college is generally out of reach. The second assertion is that the new immigrants belong to racialized groups; hence, in addition to poverty, they experience the burden of pervasive racial discrimination (Portes and Zhou 1993; Portes and Rumbaut 2001).

Proponents of segmented assimilation argue that immigrants are indeed assimilating but into different strata of American society. Those who arrive with high human capital or with financial resources follow the mainstream path of assimilation into the middle class. For those who do not have human capital or financial resources, the key variable is the strength of the ethnic community. Immigrant groups that have ethnic communities with high degrees of institutional completeness and the ability to enforce social norms can pass the immigrant ethos of hard work and upward mobility to their children. For these groups, the ethnic enclave becomes a springboard to the middle class. Immigrant groups without strong ethnic communities and without economic or educational resources suffer the full impact of poverty and discrimination. These groups, proponents of the theory argue, assimilate into what is often called the urban underclass, developing attitudes that reject American mainstream norms and expectations and give up on their parents' hopes for realizing the American dream (Portes 2006; Zhou and Bankston 1998).

In spite of the polemic tone of the debate between scholars identified with these two approaches, years of accumulated empirical research have led to a convergence of sorts in the findings concerning the new second generation. In a recent article, Alejandro Portes, Fernandez-Kelly, and William Haller recognized that not all immigrants who do not experience upward mobility become part of the underclass, and that some become part of what the authors call marginal working-class communities. Portes and his colleagues concluded that "it is evident that most of the new second generation is not joining the bottom ranks of society, but that a sizable minority is poised to do so" (2005, 1032).

This picture is not that different from the one Roger Waldinger and Cynthia Feliciano drew of second-generation Mexican Americans (2004). Although Waldinger and Feliciano would probably refrain from using the term *marginal working class,* they agreed that large segments of the second generation are not joining the middle class. Similarly, although Alba and Nee argued that their analysis of the socioeconomic position of the second generation shows an overall improvement over the first generation, they accepted that downward mobility indeed affects some groups: "The segmented assimilation notion that one form of incorporation will move individuals into a disadvantaged minority status is part of the reality of the future. This is especially likely for individuals with combinations of family background features—low levels of parental human capital, certain racial appearances by North American standard, and illegal status—that make it difficult for them to perceive realistic opportunities to advance in U.S. society" (Alba and Nee 2003, 289).

This convergence in empirical findings between scholars using different theoretical approaches is seen also in the results of a comparative study of second generations in New York City conducted by the sociologists Phil Kasinitz, John Mollenkopf, Mary Waters, and Jennifer Holdaway (2008). Their book, *Inheriting the City,* is an important reference for this analysis because it includes the most updated and thorough analysis of the Dominican second generation in New York City. It finds that members of the second generation are doing better than their parents. Moreover, the second generation of racialized immigrant groups is doing better than comparative native groups: second-generation Dominicans are doing better than Puerto Ricans and second-generation West Indians are doing better than African Americans. At the same time, second-generation minority immigrants in New York City are not doing as well as native whites—second-generation Chinese Americans being the exception to this pattern. For most minorities in New York City, second-generation and native alike, the most common occupations are as support workers, as service workers, and in retail sales. For native whites, on the other hand, the most common occupation is in a professional field (Kasinitz et al. 2008).

Significantly, the New York City study found that the arrest rates of second-generation minority immigrants are similar to those of native whites, showing that the former do not adopt values or behaviors contrary to mainstream culture, at least no more than those born into the mainstream do. Thus, although some children of immigrants do experience downward assimilation, the phenomenon does not affect the second generation any more than it does other groups in American society. On the other hand, Kasinitz and his co-authors argued that second-generation minority immigrants do face differential treatment from the justice system, often receiving harsher penalties than native-born whites (Kasinitz et al. 2008).

This convergence in empirical findings between scholars working within the new assimilation and segmented assimilation approach is the starting point for the arguments developed in this book. I go further by proposing a different theoretical framework in which to interpret the findings. I argue that the study of socioeconomic incorporation should focus on the forms of class and racial stratification that affect immigrant groups. This theme is strongly emphasized by the segmented assimilation approach (Portes and Zhou 1993; Portes and Bach 1985). Scholars working within this framework, however, tend to focus on differences between groups rather than on within-group stratification. I argue that it is necessary to focus on the patterns of stratification within the immigrant generations and compare them to the overall pattern of stratification in American society.

There are two additional important differences between the theoretical argument proposed in this book and the segmented assimilation approach. First, the segmented assimilation research focuses on the part of the second generation that joins the so-called underclass (Portes and Rumbaut 1996). This is understandable because this group experiences the most marginalization. However, to understand the incorporation trajectories of low-skilled immigrants, it is necessary to refocus analytical attention on the predicament of those people working in low-skill, mostly service jobs—the majority of the second generation according to several findings (Kasinitz et al.2008;

Waldinger and Feliciano 2004)—a sector I call the new services working class. Working-class immigrants have generally been considered part of the middle class or on their way to middle-class status, but this an unexamined assumption. The working-class positions into which most unskilled immigrants incorporate constrain their mobility opportunities and those of their children. Moreover, the lives of the working class and the marginalized sectors are intertwined.

Second, the segmented assimilation approach argues that upward social mobility for low-skilled minority immigrants depends on the presence of an ethnic enclave. In making this claim, the segmented assimilation approach overstates the positive effects of ethnic enclaves and misses other available paths for intergenerational mobility. The Dominican experience suggests that second-generation mobility takes place in and through the institutions of mainstream society. Looking at the internal class stratification in immigrant and ethnic communities, at the predicament of working-class immigrants, and at the mechanisms of mobility in American society provides a fuller picture of the socioeconomic incorporation experiences of immigrants, of their children, and of the social structure of contemporary America.

INCORPORATION AND IDENTITY

The identities of immigrants and their children have been a central preoccupation in the study of immigration. The large numbers of immigrants who maintain a differentiated identity and social presence has been a source of anxiety for mainstream society and continues to generate nativist responses (Higham 1955; Huntington 2004). In Gordon's classic elaboration of assimilation theory, identity assimilation—in other words, the erasure of ethnic identities—marked the completion of the process of change immigrants undergo (1964). Gordon proposed seven stages in the process of assimilation. First, immigrants acquired American cultural and behavioral patterns (acculturation). Then—the key stage—they became part of the social networks and institutions of mainstream society. After this, immigrants experienced high levels of intermarriage and developed a sense of self based on the identity of the receiving society. The ultimate outcome of assimilation was the disappearance of ethnic identities and allegiances and the emergence of Anglo-conformity as the dominant attitude among immigrants and their children. Gordon proposed three additional stages—the absence of prejudice, the absence of discrimination, and the absence of value and power conflicts—but these referred to changes in the attitudes and behaviors of the receiving society rather than to changes in immigrants' practices and beliefs.

This classic view of assimilation was based on the experience of the children of European immigrants, for whom ethnicity became a matter of choice. Ethnicity became a form of symbolic identification expressed occasionally in a number of public events, a marker that can be worn on special occasions and left aside in most daily interactions (Alba 1985; Alba 1990; Waters 1990). The new immigrant groups enter a society that marks them as nonwhite. For minority immigrants, ethnic choices are limited by racial classification boundaries. As immigrants of color acculturate to American society one of the paramount things that they learn is that they are seen as racial others. In fact, first- and second-generation immigrants of color construct their identities around the acceptance or rejection of the American racial categorizations (Halter 1993; Vickerman 1999; Waters 1999).

In her study of first- and second-generation West Indian identities, Mary Waters posited a relationship between race and class in the identity of immigrants and their children. She showed that second-generation working-class West Indians tend to adopt a black identity whereas middle-class people tend to adopt an immigrant or an ethnic identity. Waters asserted that those who identify as black have a very skeptical attitude towards the mainstream themes of mobility through study and individual effort. She found that those attitudes hurt mobility opportunities, but she argued that they reflect the experiences of low-income immigrants (Waters 1999). On the other hand, a recent study of New York City second generations—Waters is one of the authors—indicated that adopting a black identity may allow for access to institutions that promote mobility, such as unions or black studies programs (Kasinitz et al. 2008). These institutions were developed in response to the African American struggle for rights and inclusion and now also serve minority immigrants. Furthermore, the anthropologist Ana Aparicio has showed that adopting a black identity can be a springboard to mobilize and empower Dominicans (2006).

I follow the findings of these authors in arguing that the process of incorporation to a racialized society generates ethnoracial differentiation. American society expects immigrants and their children to assimilate, but the process of acculturation leads in fact to new ethnoracial identities and communities. These identities and communities do not indicate a failure to assimilate; they are the result of the process of incorporation. They constitute a form of positioning minority immigrants in a society that sees them as members of racialized groups.

Although the process of incorporation into a racialized society leads to the creation of ethnoracial identities and groups, the particular forms and characteristics of those identities and groups are not predetermined. In choosing their identities and in undertaking group practices based on those identities, immigrants and their children forge a place for themselves in American society. They act within the overall constraints of the American system of racial classification, but through their actions they can also change it.

STRATIFIED ETHNORACIAL INCORPORATION

We have considered the limits of new assimilation and segmented assimilation theories. Both capture important elements of the immigrant experience and in that sense contribute to our understanding of incorporation. Yet both also miss relevant aspects of immigrant incorporation. The new assimilation theory does not pay enough attention to racialization and the internal class stratification of the immigrant communities. The segmented assimilation approach does not account for the mechanisms that make the mobility that takes place within these communities possible.

The theoretical approach proposed in this book—an approach I call stratified ethnoracial incorporation—aims to address the complex and sometimes contradictory character of immigrant incorporation. This approach emphasizes class and race as dynamic social forces that shape the trajectories of immigrants and their children. Consequently, to understand the patterns of incorporation it is necessary to examine the stratification and mobility trends that structure American society. The study of incorporation is the study of the immigrant encounter with the American social and cultural faultlines.

A key element in the study of socioeconomic incorporation is the analysis of the internal class stratification of immigrants groups. In this endeavor I draw on the works of Erik Olin Wright and John Goldthorpe, who rework and adapt classical themes in Marxian and Weberian sociological class analysis to postindustrial societies. Class, as used in this book, refers to social positions based on the social organization of production and distribution of goods and services (Wright 2005b). To produce and distribute the goods and services we consume, people enter occupations that convey both different degrees of power and control over the labor process as well as different rewards. The powers and rewards attached to occupations are the result of the institutional organization of work (Erikson and Goldthorpe 1992; Goldthorpe and McKnight 2004). As Wright aptly put it, class position determines what a person gets and how that person gets it (2005b).[3]

The advantage of this conceptualization is that it brings social relations, human agency, and power to the center of the analysis of stratification. Class stratification is always the result of contentions over how to organize the production system in general and the labor process in particular. In the United States, most people think of themselves as being part of a broad middle class defined by access to mass consumption and, on the face of it, there is no class politics. But decisions that affect the distribution of the power and resources attached to different occupations are ultimately the result of class politics. Although in the United States there are no class-based parties, each party has a distinct class base of support. And though the class base of support of Democrats and Republicans has changed over time, at any particular point in time the class composition of the party voters is different, and these differences affect their policy choices (Brooks and Manza 1997; Hout, Brooks, and Manza 1995). More than once in my research I met first-generation Dominicans who referred to the Democratic Party as the party of the working class, the party of working people, or the party of those who have less. Regardless of whether this perception is right or wrong, this idea anchors the support of many Dominicans for the Democratic Party.

A second element that the stratified ethnoracial incorporation approach emphasizes is the pervasiveness of racialization. By this I understand the structuring of social relations and social classifications to be around racial categories. Here I draw on racial formation theory (Winant 2004). Race is historically constructed and subject to change, particularly as a result of political contestation. But racial categories have also proved to be resilient, and though they have changed they have not disappeared. In the United States, race is institutionalized in labor market, educational, and residential practices (Anderson 2001; Grosfoguel 1997; Massey 2007; Massey and Denton 1993). Racial categories also guide processes of social classification and identity formation (Kibria 2002; Waters 1999).

From this perspective, the question is not whether class or race is more important in determining life chances, identities, or outlook on social life. The question is how class and race intersect to shape the lives of individuals and groups at different times and in different places. Focusing only on class would miss the racialization of the American social structure. On the other hand, focusing only on racialization misses class stratification within ethnoracial groups. Racialization affects everyone in the United States, but class position mediates the effects of racialization on individual lives. Class position also affects the outlook on American society that minorities hold (Hochschild 1995; Kibria 2002; Kwong 1996; Lacy 2004; Wilson 1978).

Taking the intersection of class and race and its effects on the socioeconomic incorporation and identities of immigrants as a starting point, the stratified ethnoracial incorporation approach argues that in the contemporary United States the process of becoming American for low-skilled minority immigrants is characterized by three trends: first, the incorporation of immigrants into a racialized class structure in which people of color are overrepresented in its lower ends; second, the development of internal class stratification within ethnoracial groups; and, third, the formation and perpetuation of ethnoracial identities and communities.

In studying the formation of ethnoracial identities and communities, I emphasize the link between the identity labels that immigrants choose and the individual and group practices that they engage in based on their identity choices. The study of the individual identities of immigrants and their children is at the same time the study of group formation. This conceptualization draws from the multidimensional model of identity elaborated upon by the social psychologists Richard Ashmore, Kay Deaux, and Tracy McLaughlin-Volpe (2004). The analysis also relies on the work of the anthropologist Richard Jenkins on collective identity formation (1997). Jenkins pointed out that everyday experiences of individuals always transcend the accepted boundaries of collective identities. As a result there are always different interpretations over the boundaries and cultural meanings that define the group.[4]

In assessing the identities that Dominicans build, I pay particular attention to two issues that have generated considerable debate among immigration scholars—transnationalism and panethnicity. It is well established that immigrants engage in practices that link them to their countries of origin and that this is not a new phenomenon. A century ago, European immigrants also established transnational linkages with the places they left behind (Foner 2005; Portes, Escobar, and Radford 2007). The contemporary forms of transnational involvement range from sending of remittances to family members to intense participation in economic, political, or cultural projects in the country of origin. These different practices are rooted in identities and understandings of belonging that transcend national boundaries. In the second part of the book, I assess the extent to which first- and second-generation Dominicans use a transnational framework in building their identities and I examine the types of transnational practices that they embark on.

I also address the construction of panethnicity. In the United States, immigrants and their children are categorized by state agencies and by civil society as members of broad panethnic groups. These identity labels, however, do not correspond to the forms of self-identification that immigrants bring with them. As a result, many in the first and second generations reject these labels because they lump together groups with different histories and cultures. On the other hand, many embrace panethnicity as a new form of identity that guides common social, cultural, and political projects. Places like Providence, where there are a large number of ethnoracial groups, none of which is numerically dominant, favor the emergence of panethnicity.

Analysis of the incorporation of first- and second-generation Dominicans shows that they invest in the construction of transnational and panethnic identities and organizations. It is worth repeating that from the perspective of the stratified ethnoracial incorporation approach proposed here the construction of these identities does not indicate a failure to assimilate. These are the forms of identity that Dominicans use to carve a place for themselves in American society and the way in which they mobilize to make claims on the American political system.

CASE STUDIES AND THEORY BUILDING

The methodological approach of the book is guided by the logic of the case study: it analyzes one immigrant-ethnic group in one city. The strength of case studies is that they allow for in-depth knowledge of the particular case and its social and political context. Their obvious drawback is the difficulty in generalizing from one instance. How can the researcher know that what he or she sees is not just a particular set of circumstances that are different from every other case? A case study can overcome this limitation and contribute to theory building in two ways. The first is through an intense engagement with existing knowledge and theory. Rather than aiming toward generalization, the case study brings existing theories to bear in one case, permitting the mechanisms implied in different theoretical propositions to be examined closely.

Through the constant weighing of research findings against theoretical arguments, the case study contributes to expand our general theoretical knowledge (Paige 1999). At the same time, cases studies also help us to understand the contextual limits of particular theories. The Yankee City studies were written in this spirit and much of the cutting-edge knowledge on contemporary immigration, race, ethnicity, and urban issues comes from theoretically informed case studies (Foner 2001; Kasinitz 1992; Kasinitz, Mollenkopf, and Waters 2004; Portes and Stepnick 1993; Waldinger and Mehdi 1996; Waldinger 1996; Waters 1996). In this book, I use the case of Dominicans in Providence to examine the validity of the claims of the stratified ethnoracial incorporation approach presented above.

The second way in which a case study can transcend its own limits is through comparisons. These can be implicit, such as references to the relevant literature on parallel cases, or explicit, when the case is openly compared to others to examine their commonalties and particularities. Through these more or less implicit comparisons the researcher can locate the particular case in a larger universe and in this way assess the extent to which the findings are generalizable. In this book I conduct a number of such comparisons, using the existing literature on the social mobility of Mexican Americans and African Americans to investigate the structure of opportunities open to minorities in American society and thus to assess the likely mobility trajectories of future generations of Dominicans. I also conduct explicit comparisons of Dominicans in Providence with other ethnoracial groups in the city as well as with Dominicans and white Americans elsewhere in the country. These comparisons allow me to establish the scope and limits of the theoretical assertions I derive from it.

The analysis of the incorporation of first- and second-generation Dominicans in American society is based on different sources of information and different techniques of data gathering. This is what is known today as a mixed methods approach. In this volume I rely on several sources of information. First is secondary quantitative data, the main source of which is the 5 percent Public Use Microdata Sample (PUMS) of the 2000 Census, which give us a rather thorough snapshot of the socioeconomic position of Dominicans. Even though this picture is probably somewhat outdated today, a thorough look at the 2000 data provides a baseline we can use later on to observe trends.[5] I also use Rhode Island state government data to provide a background to the educational situation of Latinos in the state.

Another source of secondary data is the Latino National Survey (LNS), a national random survey that explores the education and employment situation as well as the social and political views of Latinos. Conducted during the winter of 2006–2007, the New England portion of the survey interviewed 1,200 Latinos in Massachusetts, Rhode Island, and Connecticut. From it, I have selected the subsample of Dominicans in Providence that includes 101 respondents. Ninety were first-generation Dominicans and eleven from the second generation. Given that most respondents are Dominican-born, I use the Latino National Survey primarily to compare and confirm first-generation findings.

Second, I rely on a survey of first- and second-generation Dominicans in Providence that I conducted between the fall of 2002 and the spring of 2003. I organized this survey with the help of a group of first-generation Dominicans from Providence who assisted me both in writing the questionnaire and in conducting the interviews. The sample is not random because there is no list of Dominicans in Providence from which to draw a sample. My goal was to survey the second generation. To do so, we created a list of 400 second-generation Dominicans by asking people in the community for the names of second-generation individuals they knew. From this list we randomly selected 150 names. We soon realized that some of these people had in fact been born in the Dominican Republic and had arrived in the United States at a young age. I decided to interview them nevertheless and to include also a sample of first-generation Dominicans for comparative purposes. This second sample was reached in part through the list and in part through multiple referrals, starting with those we first interviewed. The final sample included 100 second-generation and 81 first-generation respondents. This survey offers a wealth of detailed data on socioeconomic incorporation, identity, political participation, and transnational practices. I rely on it for an in-depth examination of the class stratification and intergenerational mobility of Dominicans in Providence and for the analysis of their identities and worldviews.

Third, I rely on thirty-four in-depth interviews, eighteen first generation (nine women and nine men) and sixteen second generation (ten women and six men). I conducted the interviews—conversations that lasted from one to four hours—between the fall of 2002 and the fall of 2004. Many were taped and transcribed, and in other cases I took detailed notes after the end of the interviews. During these in-depth interviews I gathered information on respondents' experiences growing up, on their education and employment histories, on their forms of self-identification and community participation, and on their transnational engagement. The interviews allow me to look at individual histories and experiences to better understand the meaning of the identities and everyday practices of both first- and second-generation Dominicans. I also interviewed two Dominican elected officials, State Senator Juán Pichardo and State Representative Grace Diaz. Both provided very valuable insights on local Latino politics and other aspects of local community life.[6]

The last but not the least source of information was my own participation in Dominican community life. Being an immigrant myself—I am Argentinean—finding a Dominican community in Providence was a very pleasant surprise for me. People in this community welcomed me and became a source of friendship and support. Through my immersion in the local Dominican and Latino community, I became a citizen of Providence, a citizen not in the legal sense—though I did become a naturalized American citizen—but in the sense of a person who participates in the public life of the city in which she or he lives. My own becoming part of American society took place amidst the Dominican and Latino community in Providence.

Yet, because my participation was from the privileged position of an academic, I do not make any claim of being an insider. In my interactions I always made clear that I was a researcher and that I was going to write a book about Dominicans in Providence—a book that took so long that most people I know began to doubt that it would ever materialize. Furthermore, studying community formation, I know too well that communities are fragmented and that close access to certain groups and individuals often precludes knowledge of others, to the point that one identifies with the particular view of those with whom one is close. Nevertheless, participating in community life does provide a close knowledge of some of the main actors and insights into the social processes at work (Burawoy 1998).

No degree of closeness, however, can provide an objective and unbiased view. Social life is too complex and any understanding of a situation is mediated through the analytical lenses of the researcher. Furthermore, any representation of a situation carries the imprint of the biases and agendas of the writer, who exercises an arbitrary authorial power. My own biases will become clear to the reader. They are there for everyone to see. The choice of class and race as the key analytical concepts and the critical look at the class stratification and racialization dynamics of American society gives the reader a sense of my own understanding of social life. Still, I believe in the social science project and I hold that though every representation is necessarily partial, arbitrary, and biased, not every representation is equally so. I believe in the validity—partial and fragile as it is—achieved through careful, theoretically informed, empirical work.

Equipped with these different sources of information, I aim to analyze the experience of incorporation of first- and second-generation Dominicans in Providence and what it tells us about the structure of American society. Immigrants incorporate into a society stratified by class and race. To understand how incorporation works, we need to understand how race and class shape the opportunities and the experiences of all people in this country. The study of the immigrant's experience helps us further understand America's faultlines. Ultimately, this book argues that the study of immigration is as much a study of American society as it is a study of particular groups within it.

CHAPTER 2

Dominican Providence

Providence has been historically an immigrant city. Irish, Italians, Eastern Europeans, French Canadians, Portuguese, and Cape Verdeans built it and populated its mills during the second half of the nineteenth century and the first half of the twentieth century (Conley and Campbell 2006). Dominicans, together with other Latino, East Asian, and West African immigrants, are settling in the places vacated by previous waves of immigration. These new immigrants, however, do not find employment in the mills but in service occupations. They are janitors, hotel workers, municipal employees, teachers, nurses, and social workers. Some are lawyers, doctors, engineers, and business managers. These new immigrants are building a new type of city—one that will become increasingly common in America—a city in which minorities, immigrant and native, are the majority of the population. It is in this new context of reception that Dominicans are incorporating into the social and political structure of the city and, in doing so, are also changing its everyday life.

DOMINICAN MIGRATION TO THE UNITED STATES

Large-scale Dominican migration to the United States started in the second half of the 1960s, a result of the political events that unfolded after the fall of Trujillo, the dictator who ruled the country for three decades until he was shot to death in 1961. The end of the Trujillo regime was followed by five years of political contestation that ended with an American military intervention in 1965. In 1966, Joaquin Balaguer, the candidate supported by the U.S. administration, was elected president and went on to become a hegemonic figure in Dominican politics for the next three decades. The first twelve years of his rule, from 1966 to 1978, were characterized by a heavy repression of political opposition. During this period, many opponents of the Balaguer regime found their way to exile in New York City, a move facilitated by the U.S. administrations of the time, interested in alleviating the political pressures in the island. From the 1980s on, Dominican migration became mostly an economic-based phenomenon, the result of recurrent economic crises and the failure of development policies (Hernández 2002).

The Dominican population in the United States is concentrated in New York City. The trend in the last two decades, however, has been toward dispersion to other states, such as New Jersey, Florida, Massachusetts, and Rhode Island, and toward smaller cities, such as Providence in Rhode Island, Patterson in New Jersey, and Lawrence in Massachusetts (Torres-Saillant and Hernández 1998). Table 2.1 shows that the proportion of first- and second-generation Dominicans in places other than New York City grew between 1990 and 2000.[1] In fact, Rhode Island has the largest proportional presence of Dominicans. The absolute number is small, because the state has a small population, but the proportion of the total state population—2.4 percent—is larger than in any other state. At the time of this writing Rhode Island and New York are the only states in which Dominicans have been elected to the state legislatures (two in each state) and New York City and Providence have two Dominican representatives each in their city councils.

THE MAKING OF DOMINICAN PROVIDENCE

Providence is an interesting place for a migration study. Table 2.2 shows that the population of the city declined from the 1950s until the 1980s, when immigration reversed the trend. Since then, the immigrant population has changed the city's economic, political, and cultural landscape. Table 2.2 also shows the historical importance of employment in manufacturing in both Providence and Rhode Island. The percentage was always higher than the national average, although it has suffered a continuous decline as it has in the rest of the country. Providence has evolved into a service economy.

Table 2.1 Dominicans in Selected Places in the United States

	1990			2000		
	First Generation	Second Generation	Total	First Generation	Second Generation	Total
New York City	253,394	100,213	353,607	368,466	160,789	529,255
% 1st and 2nd generation	71.70	28.30		69.60	30.40	
% Dominican population	67.90	67.80		59.20	58.50	
% city's population	3.56	1.41	4.97	4.71	2.06	6.77
New York State	16,650	7,738	24,388	34,160	18,635	52,795
% 1st and 2nd generation	68.30	31.70		64.70	35.30	
% Dominican population	4.50	5.20		5.50	6.80	
% state's population	0.16	0.08	0.24	0.32	0.18	0.50
New Jersey	42,665	15,783	58,448	86,422	33,539	119,961
% 1st and 2nd generation	73.00	27.00		72.00	28.00	
% Dominican population	11.40	10.70		13.90	12.20	
% state's population	0.57	0.21	0.78	1.05	0.41	1.46

	1990			2000		
Florida	28,252	10,333	38,585	63,794	28,643	92,437
% 1st and 2nd generation	73.20	26.80		69.00	31.00	
% Dominican population	7.60	7.00		10.20	10.40	
% state's population	0.22	0.08	0.31	0.41	0.18	0.59
Massachusetts	22,877	9,467	32,344	44,977	21,988	66,965
% 1st and 2nd generation	70.70	29.30		67.20	32.80	
% Dominican population	6.10	6.40		7.20	8.00	
% state's population	0.39	0.16	0.56	0.73	0.36	1.09
Rhode Island	6,296	3,177	9,473	15,761	7,769	23,530
% 1st and 2nd generation	66.50	33.50		67.00	33.00	
% Dominican population	1.70	2.10		2.50	2.80	
% state's population	0.65	0.33	0.98	1.63	0.77	2.40
Connecticut	2,824	1,161	3,985	8,842	3,624	12,466
% 1st and 2nd generation	70.90	29.10		70.90	29.10	
% Dominican population	0.80	0.80		1.40	1.30	
% state's population	0.09	0.04	0.13	0.27	0.11	0.38

Source: Author's compilation based on the 5 percent Public Use Microdata Sample (PUMS) (U.S. Bureau of the Census 1990 and 2000).

Table 2.2   Population and Employment in Manufacturing

	1950	1960	1970	1980	1990	2000
Population						
Rhode Island	791,896	859,488	946,725	947,154	1,00,3464	1,048,319
Providence	248,520	207,498	179,213	156,804	160,728	173,618
Foreign Born						
Rhode Island	14.32	10	7.49	8.87	9.48	11.38
Providence	15.87	12.54	9.64	13.5	19.62	25.31
Manufacturing*						
United States	25.9	27.1	25.9	22.4	17.7	14.1
Rhode Island	44	39.3	32.5	35.1	22.7	16.4
Providence	38.5	34.5	31.7	33	24.1	18.3

Source: Author's compilation (U.S. Bureau of the Census, various years).
* Percentage with respect total employed sixteen years and older.

Dominicans started arriving in Providence in the late 1960s, initially from New York City, but, after a local community was established, directly from the Dominican Republic. What attracted them was inexpensive housing and an abundance of well-paid manufacturing jobs. Employment chains soon led to a growing presence of Dominicans in the city. Immigrants who arrived from the 1960s until the early 1980s remember a city where manufacturing jobs in which a person could start as a low-skilled laborer and move up to a higher wage skilled or supervisory position were readily available. The decline of employment in manufacturing is noticeable in the narratives of immigrants who arrived most recently. These tell a story in which entry-level jobs are found mostly through temporary employment agencies and do not offer good wages or much opportunity for mobility.

According to my estimations from the census data, in 2000 there were 24,984 Dominicans in Rhode Island, making them the second-largest group of Latinos in the state after Puerto Ricans. In Providence, Dominicans have the highest visibility. Whether we look at small businesses, local media, political mobilization, spatial landmarks, or public events, the presence of Dominicans is strongly felt in the urban landscape and the public life of the city.

The 2000 Census indicates that 84 percent of Rhode Island's Dominicans live within the municipal boundaries of Providence. Another 9.1 percent live in towns north of Providence, mainly in Central Falls, which is the smallest and most ethnically diverse town in the state. It is also one of the poorest. Central Falls and Providence are distinct municipalities, and in a small state like Rhode Island short distances feel longer than in larger states. Still, Providence and Central Falls are part of the same urban continuum—unless a person is familiar with the place, he or she would not know where Providence ends and Central Falls begins. Furthermore, the lives of Dominicans in Central Falls are not separated from those of their counterparts in Providence. Because these are the two largest concentrations of Dominicans, and together the two cities encompass 93.1 percent of the Dominican population in the state, I include both urban areas in all the analyses of the census. Although for the sake of convenience I talk about Providence, I include Central Falls in my analysis.

Table 2.3 presents demographic data on Dominicans in these two towns and comparative data from New York City. Several aspects of the comparison are particularly significant. First is the large weight of the Dominican population within the Providence municipal boundaries: 12 percent, almost twice that of Dominicans within the New York City population. If we take Providence

Table 2.3   Dominicans in Providence, Central Falls, and New York City

	Providence	Central Falls	New York City
Number	20,995	2,286	546,002
Percent of total population	12.0	1.3	6.8
First generation	14,447	1,520	381,603
Mean age	35	30	38
Second generation	6,548	766	164,399
Percent of Dominican population	31.2	33.5	30.1
Mean age	11	12	23
Percent twenty-four years or older	8.9	15.5	14.5

Source: Author's compilation based on the 5 percent Public Use Microdata Sample (PUMS) (U.S. Bureau of the Census 2000).

and the towns north of it together, the combined weight of the Dominican population is 6.6 percent, the same as in New York City.[2]

The table also shows that the second generation constitutes close to 33 percent of the Dominican population in both Providence and New York City. It shows too that the second generation is very young. In Rhode Island, the mean age is eleven years. Across the board, the young adult and adult populations are only a very low percentage of the second generation. That is, we are looking at only the beginning of the process of incorporation of second-generation Dominicans.

Figure 2.1 shows that the Dominican population in Providence is concentrated in the southern neighborhoods of the city, an area delineated by Broad Street and Elmwood Avenue. In the figure, these streets are the thick lines that define the borders of the Elmwood neighborhood—the neighborhood that includes census tracks 2 and 3. Elmwood Avenue separates from Broad Street close to downtown, forming a triangle of sorts. Elmwood Avenue is the western limit and Broad Street the eastern. Between these two streets and on their sides—in parts of Upper and Lower South Providence to the east of Broad Street and on the sections of the West End adjacent to Elmwood Avenue, Dominicans make up between 20 and 30 percent of the population.

Broad Street is the center of Dominican life in Providence. Driving down this street one soon notices the presence of Dominican businesses—mainly bodegas, hair salons, restaurants, dancing clubs, and service agencies. Some

Figure 2.1   Dominican Population in Providence Neighborhoods

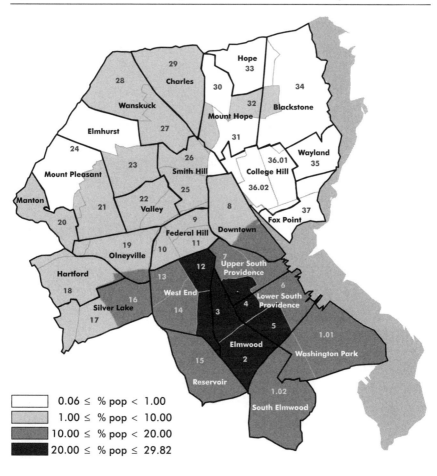

0.06 ≤ % pop < 1.00
1.00 ≤ % pop < 10.00
10.00 ≤ % pop < 20.00
20.00 ≤ % pop ≤ 29.82

Source: Author's compilation based on the 5 percent Public Use Microdata Sample (PUMS) (U.S. Bureau of the Census 2000).

businesses have been there for several years, but the turnover rate is high. During the warm weather months, one can also see fruit and vegetable sellers offering their merchandise in the street, which is alive with the sounds of merengue, bachata, and reggaeton. Doris, a nineteen-year-old second-generation Dominican who was born in New York and came to Providence with her mother as a teenager describes it this way: "I love it. I love it when the horns are, you know, beeping everywhere, everyone is going crazy. I just love that. Yeah?

Yeah. You like that kind of . . . the noise, the commotion, everything. . . . It reminds me a lot of New York."

During the long winter, the street is empty and people gather inside the bodegas and hair salons. Even during these months, however, one can see a characteristic Dominican feature, the *chimis* (food trucks) parked on the street selling Dominican food.

Every August, thousands of Dominicans march down Broad Street in a parade toward Roger Williams Park, where they celebrate the Dominican Festival, a day that marks the presence and achievements of Dominicans in the city and that has been celebrated for the last twenty years. Most local politicians show up at the festival in recognition of the increasing political power of the community. In January, they congregate in St. Michael church, in Oxford Street, off Broad Street, to celebrate the Virgen de la Altagracia, the patron saint of the Dominican Republic.

Even though Broad Street is the heart of the Dominican presence, Dominicans live in most neighborhoods across the city. As figure 2.1 shows, they make up between 10 and 20 percent of the population of the other neighborhoods in the southern part of the city and have a small but growing presence in the northern part, with the exception of the East Side (the area marked as College Hill, Fox Point, Blackstone and Wayland in the map). The East Side is home to the Rhode Island School of Design (RISD) and Brown University, and is mostly a white upper-middle-class area. The reason for the wide dispersion of Dominicans across Providence is twofold. On the one hand, upwardly mobile Dominicans simply look for quieter and more upscale neighborhoods, whether in the northern parts of town or in the neighboring towns of Cranston and Warwick. On the other hand, some working-class Dominicans choose other working-class areas away from the Broad Street area. This is the origin of the Dominican population in Central Falls.

Central Falls, a small town adjacent to Providence in the north, is part of the Blackstone Valley, which was the cradle of the industrial revolution in the United States. During the nineteenth century, the town grew around textile mills attracting immigrants from Ireland, Scotland, and Quebec. In the second half of the twentieth century, upward mobility led ethnic whites to leave the mills and the town. Mill owners resorted to recruiting Colombian workers, particularly from Medellin, a city that was then also home to a concentration of textile mills. This was the origin of the Latino population of the city. Today the Colombian population has mostly moved away from Central Falls, but their influence is felt in the local social and political mobilization of Latinos, which was spearheaded mostly—though not only—by Colombian activists. The mills have also left town but the availability of cheap housing has led new immigrants to settle there. These immigrants come mainly from other parts of Latin America, particularly Mexico and Guatemala, but also the Dominican Republic.

Latinos are the majority of the population in the southern neighborhoods of Providence. As shown in figure 2.2, Latinos make up between half and two-thirds of the population of the areas around and between Broad Street and Elmwood Avenue. In addition to Dominicans, there are mainly Puerto Ricans, although the numbers of Guatemalans and Mexicans are increasing. These latter two groups have grown proportionally faster over the last two decades. Their main areas of concentration, however, are in other parts of town. Guatemalans are mainly concentrated in Olneyville, in the western part of the city. Saint Theresa's Church, on Manton Avenue, is where they congregate for significant religious celebrations. Mexicans concentrate mainly in the Smith Hill neighborhood, north of downtown, and use Saint Patrick's Church on Smith Street. All immigrant groups attend all types of churches, Catholic and non-Catholic. In fact, one characteristic of immigrant neighborhoods is a strong presence of small evangelical Christian churches. Yet, in the same way that Saint Michael's Church is associated with the Dominican community, Saint Theresa's is associated with the Guatemalan community and Saint Patrick's with the Mexican. It is at these churches, for example, that they congregate to celebrate the day of the patron saints of their countries—Virgen de la Altagracia for Dominicans and Virgen de Guadalupe for Mexicans.

The southern neighborhoods of the city, where Dominicans concentrate, have historically been an area of migrant settlement and have seen a succession of different groups (Conley and Campbell 2006). In the nineteenth century, it was the Irish. Irish immigrants, for example, built St. Michael's Church. In the first half of the twentieth century, the area was populated by eastern European migrants—Polish, Armenians, and Jews among them. After World War II, white ethnics moved to other parts of town or left the city. This movement left the area with many empty and abandoned houses.

During the 1960s, African Americans moved into the area, particularly into upper and lower south Providence, the neighborhoods between Broad Street and the waterfront. As figure 2.3 shows, in parts of these neighborhoods, particularly in lower south Providence, blacks constitute between 35 and 40 percent

Figure 2.2   Latino Population in Providence Neighborhoods

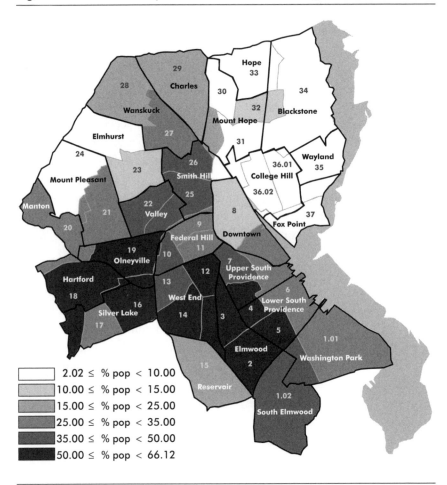

Source: Author's compilation based on the 5 percent Public Use Microdata Sample (PUMS) (U.S. Bureau of the Census 2000).

of the population. This area has been the base for the emergence of African American community organizations and political mobilization (Conley and Campbell 2006). As the maps show, Dominicans and African Americans share parts of south Providence. This has led to tension, given that the political empowerment of Dominicans has come, to a certain extent, at the expense of African Americans.[3]

Figure 2.3 Black Population in Providence Neighborhoods

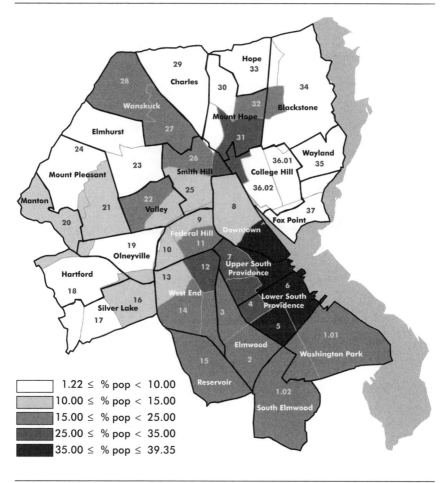

Source: Author's compilation based on the 5 percent Public Use Microdata Sample (PUMS) (U.S. Bureau of the Census 2000).

South Providence is not a completely segregated area. As figure 2.4 shows, whites also have a presence in the southern neighborhoods of the city as well as being the majority in the upper-middle-class East Side neighborhoods and the northern parts of the city. The southern presence is the result of three trends. First, some working-class ethnic whites never moved away from the area. Second, new European immigrants—particularly Portuguese—settled in

Figure 2.4   White Population in Providence Neighborhoods

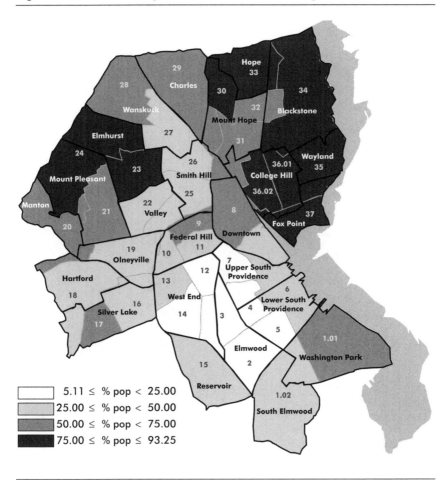

Source: Author's compilation based on the 5 percent Public Use Microdata Sample (PUMS) (U.S. Bureau of the Census 2000).

southern neighborhoods. Third, there has been a measure of gentrification in parts of the south side.

During the late 1980s and early 1990s, the Broad Street area was considered a bad neighborhood. When I arrived in Providence in the mid-1990s, I was warned by several people not to go to the south side because it was full of criminals and drug dealers. I did not follow the advice. What I found was, and is, a working poor area, admittedly with its share of crime and drug dealing,

Figure 2.5   Poverty Levels in Providence Neighborhoods

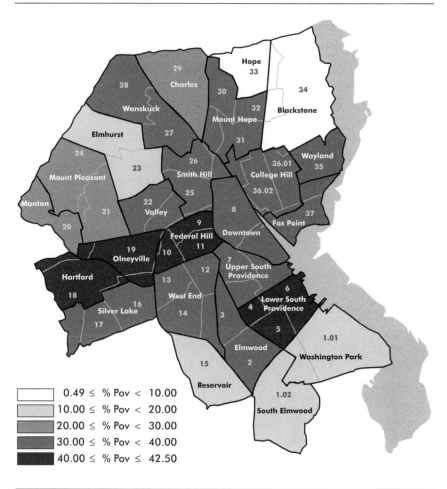

0.49 ≤ % Pov < 10.00
10.00 ≤ % Pov < 20.00
20.00 ≤ % Pov < 30.00
30.00 ≤ % Pov < 40.00
40.00 ≤ % Pov ≤ 42.50

Source: Author's compilation based on the 5 percent Public Use Microdata Sample (PUMS) (U.S. Bureau of the Census 2000).

which are issues of great concern for residents of the area, but also with a dynamic small business economy and people working hard to improve their lives and community. Nevertheless, in spite of the work immigrants have done to revitalize the neighborhood, it is still a poor area. As the map in figure 2.5 shows, the rate of poverty in the Elmwood area is above 30 percent. In parts of lower south Providence, it is higher than 40 percent—William Julius

Wilson's threshold for areas of extreme poverty. The map shows that in fact Providence has high rates of overall poverty. In most neighborhoods the rate is above 20 percent. The service employment base of the city, then, yields a large proportion of working poor.

State Senator Juán Pichardo, a young Dominican whose district includes the neighborhoods of Elmwood, South Elmwood, Reservoir, and West End, described the area:

> The district is very diverse in terms of its people. Obviously, the majority of the population are Latinos; of Latinos, the majority are Dominicans, and we have Guatemalans, Salvadorans, and some Mexicans. There are people from many countries that are part of that district and it is because they are comfortable being in the area, is more affordable economically. More so in the West End, which is a very low-income section of the area and housing is more affordable. You have Elmwood, which has on both sides very low income and then a little bit more moderate, in the South Elmwood section and the Reservoir Triangle. So, economically, when you look at it, it is still a very low-income, working-class immigrant population.[4]

Senator Pichardo explained that until recently the socioeconomic situation of the district was changing for the positive because people "were taking advantage of the fact that they were working hard and were realizing the American dream that was to be able to purchase a home instead of paying rent to somebody else." But, he added, the district was hit hard by the housing crisis and the West End section of the district has one of the highest foreclosure rates in the state. Senator Pichardo is particularly distressed by this because even in 2003 he had warned about predatory lending and had introduced legislation in the state house to prevent it.

Of course, the picture painted in this chapter is not static. State Representative Grace Diaz is a first-generation Dominican who represents district 11, a district that includes the Elmwood neighborhood—the area between Broad Street and Elmwood Avenue where Dominicans are concentrated—and a small adjacent part of the West End. The population of her district, she said in an interview, is changing. The cost of housing in the Providence urban area rose very fast since 2000 and as a result many Dominicans moved out of the state. They realized, she explained, that they could sell their houses and move to areas of North Carolina or Pennsylvania where housing is cheaper. They can buy a house there and still have some money left to open a business. She thinks such a move is a mistake, because although housing costs are cheaper in the new places incomes are also lower, and because in those places Dominicans do not have the recognition and empowerment they have achieved in Providence. Nevertheless, she knows many families in her district that have made that move, including some of her close relatives.

At the same time that some Dominicans are moving out, some middle-class whites rediscovered the revalorized old Victorian houses in the neighborhood, particularly bordering Elmwood Avenue, triggering a process of reverse ethnic succession of sorts. As a result, Diaz estimated that the proportion of non-Latinos in the district rose from a quarter to more than a third of the population since she was first elected in 2004. She noticed the growth of the white population in the calls she received from her constituents. Particularly in the summer months she received a growing number of calls from new white residents complaining that their Latino neighbors are too noisy or that they have too many large gatherings.

Historically, Diaz pointed out, the district state representative always reflected the ethnoracial composition of the district population. From 1910 to 1989, the state representatives from this area—the number and boundaries of the district changed over the years—were white, most of them male, with the exception of Elizabeth Morancy, who held the seat for ten years beginning in 1979.

African Americans began settling in the district in the 1960s. Since 1989 the district has sent two African American representatives to the state house—first, Joseph Newsome, from 1989 to 1995, and then Marcia Carpenter, from 1996 to 2001. During these years, however, the Dominican and Latino population in the district grew by leaps and bounds. Latinos also came to understand the importance of political organization and participation. As a result of these trends, Carpenter was defeated in 2000 by Leon Tejada, the first Dominican elected official in Rhode Island. Grace Diaz unseated Tejada in 2004 and was reelected in 2006. Tejada today represents this area in the Providence city council. Diaz speculated that if the present trends of change in the composition of the population of the district continue, in the future the representative of the district may very well again be white.

These urban changes pose the question of the validity of a picture of a present that is continuously shifting. Is the story told in the following chapters valid if the situation of Dominicans in Providence changes constantly? I believe it is. It is true that Dominicans are indeed a group on the move. People constantly arrive in Providence from New York or the Dominican Republic and constantly leave, mainly to North Carolina, Pennsylvania, and Florida. Overall, however, the number of Dominicans in Providence and in Rhode Island is growing. The 2006 American Community Survey estimated 31,965 Dominicans in the state. The number of second-generation Dominicans has more than doubled since 2000, reaching 13,937 people, 43.6 percent of all Dominicans in Rhode Island. The average age of the second generation is 14.7 years, still a very young group.

Dominicans have achieved a very strong and visible presence in the city, one that is not likely to change in the short term. Whether we look at politics, culture, media, or community organization, we find Dominicans in leading positions. Moreover, Dominicans have an overall good opinion of Rhode Island. Asked by the Latino National Survey how they assess the attitude of the public in Rhode Island towards Latinos, an overwhelming majority of both first-generation respondents, 74.1 percent, and second-generation respondents, nine out of eleven, answered welcoming or very welcoming.

This volume tells how Dominicans have incorporated into the city's economy and built both identities and communities. It presents a snapshot of an American experience that is repeating itself across the country. Because the incorporation of an immigrant group is a constantly evolving process, the situation of Dominicans in the city is eventually bound to change. But even if this is—as the hallmark of the incorporation process—inevitable, the theoretical mechanisms analyzed in the text transcend the limits of the place and time of the case study and help us understand the ways in which immigrants become Americans.

THE INCORPORATION ROAD

These first two chapters of the volume make up part I and have set the theoretical and methodological approach and introduced the case study. Part II analyzes the socioeconomic incorporation of Dominicans in Providence.

In chapter 3, I examine the location of first- and second-generation Dominicans in the American stratification system. I compare the socioeconomic status of Dominicans in Rhode Island to other ethnoracial groups in the state and to Dominicans and white Americans in other states. The analysis highlights three elements that characterize the process of Dominican socioeconomic incorporation: First, the second generation is doing better than the first. Second, there is a bifurcation in the occupational trajectories of the second generation between those who join management and administrative jobs and the majority who works in working class jobs in the service sector. Third, first- and second-generation Dominicans are part of an ethnoracial system of stratification.

Chapter 4 examines the encounters of young second-generation Dominicans with mainstream American institutions, specifically, with the education system. The analysis focuses on the importance of social networks for upward mobility and the limited scope of the networks of the children of working-class immigrants (Stanton-Salazar 1997). The investigation relies on and analyzes the narratives of young Dominicans growing up in the United States to study the mechanisms of social mobility and the reproduction of class inequality. The narratives illustrate how the experience of schooling, an experience influenced by class and by race, affects the trajectories people follow.

Chapter 5 analyzes class stratification within the Dominican first and second generations. Using a modified version of John Goldthorpe's class stratification model (Erikson and Goldthorpe 1992; Goldthorpe and McKnight 2004), the chapter examines intergenerational class mobility and how class position affects Dominican perceptions of American society. The chapter shows a measure of intergenerational upward mobility, but also that the main mobility trend is away from manufacturing and toward the services working class. Furthermore, the chapter indicates that those who are more incorporated to American society have, at the same time, a more critical view of their life in this country. The three chapters in this part of the book show the importance of analyzing the ways in which class and race affect the incorporation of immigrants into the American social structure.

The third part of the book studies the identities that Dominicans construct in the process of incorporation. In chapter 6, I look at the labels that Dominicans use for self-identification. The analysis shows that the main identity choices are the panethnic Hispanic label and the ethnic-national Dominican. Dominicans assign ethnic and racial meanings to these identities. Because of this, I speak about ethnoracial identities and groups. Chapter 6 reveals that Dominicans do not adopt the label American because they understand it as a racialized term. In their eyes, it describes only white people. At the same time, they identify with American values and have a strong sense of belonging to American society. The chapter identifies two key narratives concerning the predicament of Dominicans in the United States. The first sees Dominicans as an ethnic group that follows the path of previous immigrant groups in making it in

American society. The second describes Dominicans as a discriminated minority group. Dominicans draw from both narratives in making sense of their life experiences.

Chapter 7 investigates the relationship between transnationalism and incorporation in the construction of the boundaries of the Dominican identity in the United States. It shows that first- and second-generation Dominicans construct their ethnic identities using a transnational framework. The presence of Dominican references and symbols is very strong in the discourses of identity of both generations. The transnational identity frame also informs the construction of community organizations. Yet, when it comes to actual practices, transnationalism is shown to be mostly a first-generation phenomenon. The chapter shows that the main investment of both generations is in forging a place for Dominicans in American society. It also proves that transnational involvement and incorporation are simultaneous and complementary processes.

Chapter 8 addresses the construction of panethnic identities. In Providence, there are numerous Latino groups, and none of them are numerically, politically, or economically dominant. This situation facilitates the emergence of panethnic identities and collective action. This chapter analyzes the ways in which Dominicans participate in creating a Latino community in Providence. It pays particular attention to the creation of panethnic organizations and to political mobilization. It shows that the incorporation of Dominicans into the political life of Rhode Island is done under the banner of Latino empowerment. The assertion of panethnicity in the political realm is very important for incorporation because racialization leads to the need for affirmation of group identity. At the same time, chapter 8 argues that to address the socioeconomic problems that affect the Latino community, Latino politics need to move beyond the assertion of identities and build coalitions that will be effective in promoting policies that benefit working families.

Finally, the concluding chapter discusses the theoretical implications of the findings, arguing that they support the claims of the stratified ethnoracial incorporation approach. The conclusions also discuss the possibilities for change in the patterns of class stratification and racialization in American society. As scholars working within the new assimilation framework argue, the boundaries of class and racial exclusion have been blurred in the past and can become blurred again in the future (Alba 2005; Perlmann and Waldinger 1997). Yet, the argument of this book is that the equalization of the socioeconomic conditions of the children of immigrants and the mainstream and the attenuation of the strength of ethnoracial identities will not come as a result of the mere passing of generations. The future of immigrant generations depends on the continuity or change of the current class and racial stratification system. Whether and how the pattern of stratified ethnoracial incorporation described in this book changes depends on the political organization and action of the groups in the lower ends of the class and racial stratification and on the overall political trends in American society.

PART II

Class, Race, and Mobility

CHAPTER 3

In a Land of Opportunities?

Dominicans come to the United States in search of economic opportunities denied them in the Dominican Republic. Dominican immigrants share the mainstream vision of America as a land of opportunity. This chapter examines whether the Dominican experience of socioeconomic incorporation corresponds to this vision of American society. To assess the opportunities available for immigrants, I compare the positions of first- and second-generation Dominicans in the Providence and American socioeconomic structures. First-generation immigrants are hindered by their lack of knowledge of English, their low levels of job skills, their inability to make their educational credentials count, and in many cases, by their undocumented status. The second generation, on the other hand, is American by birth, has English as its first language, and is socialized in the American school system. Hence it is with the second generation that we can begin to see the real pattern of incorporation of Dominicans into American society.

SOCIOECONOMIC INCORPORATION

The first Dominicans to arrive in Providence came to a manufacturing city and found jobs in factories. Rhode Island and Providence have a long tradition of immigration driven by manufacturing jobs. Blackstone Valley, in which Providence lies, was the cradle of the American industrial revolution. In the second half of the nineteenth century and early twentieth century,

Italian, Irish, Portuguese, and French Canadian immigrants filled the ranks of a booming industrial working class (Sterne 2003). Even as late as the 1960s, Colombian workers were recruited to work in the textile industry, which by that point was experiencing labor shortages. This was in fact the beginning of Latino migration to the Providence area.

In the 1970s and 1980s, Dominican immigrants could expect to get a low-level manufacturing job and rise to a skilled or supervisory position within the same company. Roberto's trajectory provides an example of that process. Roberto is a first-generation immigrant who came to Providence in the early 1970s, when he was in his twenties. He remembers that when he first arrived employers would give him bonuses if he brought his friends to work in the same enterprise. Roberto started work in an assembly line in 1974 and, when I interviewed him in 1999, was working as a skilled machinist at the same company. Roberto was indeed satisfied with his work experience in Providence.

Manufacturing employment, however, has declined and changed over time. The internal ladder that benefited Roberto has progressively disappeared. Ana's story is a case in point. Ana is also a first-generation Dominican who arrived in Providence in the 1970s. She worked for many years in a factory until it closed in the early 1990s. In that factory Ana earned a good wage and fringe benefits. After the factory closed, she could get jobs only through temporary employment agencies—jobs that came with lower salaries, no benefits, and no job security. Ana moved into self-employment, opening a catering business she ran from her home. She was successful in this endeavor, but bitter in recalling how the good jobs disappeared. Others with similar experiences of losing good manufacturing jobs also moved to the service sector for lower salaries and worse working conditions than they had previously enjoyed. It is in this context of a declining manufacturing economy and a growing service sector that first- and second-generation Dominicans now enter the Providence labor market.

To examine the incorporation of Dominicans, I look first at four indicators of socioeconomic status (SES): employment, education, poverty, and income. After that I analyze their labor market position. In each of these analyses, I compare Dominicans to Puerto Ricans, other first- and second-generation Latinos, blacks, and whites.[1] Each of these groups provides an interesting contrast to Dominicans. Puerto Ricans are a Spanish-speaking Caribbean group with a similar history of initial employment in manufacturing and a similar experience of racialization. There are, however, two important differences between these groups. First, the migration history of Puerto Ricans to the

United States is longer than that of Dominicans. Second, Puerto Ricans are U.S. citizens and Dominicans are not. The Dominican experience is in that sense closer to that of other immigrants from Latin America. Hence it is important to compare the incorporation of Dominicans to that of other Latinos. Comparing Dominicans to blacks provides a measure of the effect of racialization on different minority groups. Finally, white Americans constitute the mainstream of U.S. society; they are the yardstick against which the socioeconomic position of immigrant groups is measured. When assimilation scholars talk about the children of immigrants becoming indistinguishable from the mainstream, what they mean is that the second generation is expected to reach the economic and educational levels of white Americans. This is intuitively recognized by Dominican and other immigrants for whom the word *American,* without any modifier, is used to refer to white Americans.

Table 3.1 presents socioeconomic information for each of these groups.[2] First-generation Dominicans occupy a very fragile position. Their educational, occupational, and income levels are among the lowest shown in the table. First-generation Dominicans and first-generation Latinos have the highest percentage of those not graduating from high school. First-generation Dominicans have very low median household incomes and a high poverty rate. They also have high levels of unemployment. In Providence, only Puerto Ricans have a similarly fragile socioeconomic position.

Despite growing up in poverty, with parents who have little education and often do not speak English, the Dominican second generation shows impressive progress—a much better rate of labor market participation, a lower rate of unemployment, and higher levels of education than the first generation. The improvement, however, is not consistent. Second-generation Dominicans have the highest rate of poverty and the lowest median household income.

One possible explanation for these results could be that the Dominican second generation is young. In fact, 80 percent of the second-generation population included in the table are between twenty-four and thirty-five. Among the total population of Providence, however, only 36 percent is within the same age range. A young age structure may explain the high rate of poverty and low median household income among the Dominican second generation, because it takes time for people to reach the peak of their occupational and earning careers. This, however, is not the case. The socioeconomic indicators for the segment of the second generation who are between twenty-four and thirty-five are better than those for the second generation as a whole.[3] Within this group,

Table 3.1 Socioeconomic Indicators in Providence, Ages Twenty-Four to Sixty-Four

	Dominican, 1st Gen	Dominican, 2nd Gen	Latino/a, 1st Gen	Latino/a, 2nd Gen	Puerto Rican	Black	White
Employed	48.8	65.8	60.0	62.3	41.4	63.2	74.9
Unemployed	8.0	2.9	6.5	6.0	6.6	5.9	3.3
Not in labor force	43.2	31.3	33.5	31.7	51.9	30.9	21.8
Less than high school	55.3	31.7	56.1	28.9	48.4	26.2	16.5
High school	23.7	20.1	25.7	29.6	27.7	30.9	26.0
Some college or associate's degree	14.8	33.5	11.8	28.9	18.8	26.2	25.9
Bachelor's degree or more	6.2	14.7	6.4	12.6	5.1	16.7	31.6
Below poverty line	35.6	43.6	20.8	27.8	41.03	24.2	9.2
Median income ($1,000)	28.3	27.0	36.6	30.0	19.3	32.9	52.9

Source: Author's compilation based on the 5 percent Public Use Microdata Sample (PUMS) (U.S. Bureau of the Census 2000).
Note: Numbers in percentages except income.

the poverty rate drops considerably, from 43.6 to 34.5 percent, and the median household income rises, from $27,000 to $46,800, second only to whites within this age group. Within this segment of the population, improvement between the generations across all the indicators is consistent. Yet a 34.5 percent rate of poverty is still very high and 20.4 percent did not finish high school.

A second element to consider is the labor market incorporation of Dominicans. This information is presented in table 3.2. Second-generation Dominicans experience a shift in their occupational incorporation in respect to the first generation. Whereas the first generation is concentrated in manufacturing, the second generation finds employment in the service sector: 50 percent of the second generation works in sales and office or service occupations as opposed to 26.9 percent of the first generation. Only 17 percent of the second generation works in manufacturing, as opposed to 46.4 percent of the first generation. These numbers show that employment in manufacturing is not an important option for the second generation.

The picture of the occupational incorporation of the Dominican second generation in Providence is similar to that found in New York (Kasinitz et al. 2008). The Dominican second generation—as well as the Latino—is mainly concentrated in sales and office and service occupations, and secondarily in management and professional occupations. In these we see an undeniable improvement of the situation of the second generation over the first generation. Also, as in New York City, a higher percentage of second-generation Dominicans and Latinos work in managerial and professional occupations than non-Latino blacks and Puerto Ricans (Kasinitz et al. 2008). Yet, the percentage of the second generation in these occupations is lower than that of whites.

These facts can be read from different perspectives. As always, numbers do not in fact speak for themselves. It is our interpretation that tells the stories that construct our understanding of social phenomena. The first question to emerge is whether these results are good news. From the perspective of assimilation theory, one can emphasize the undeniable fact that the second generation is doing considerably better than the first. Even in a place like Providence, where there is no ethnic enclave to speak of and where the first generation does not have human or economic capital, the Dominican second generation improves its position in relation to the immigrant generation. This is certainly good news. The boundaries of mobility are blurred.

This optimistic picture, however, needs to be qualified. The improvement is real but limited and uneven. The tables show that though the majority of

Table 3.2   Selected Occupations and Industries in Providence, Ages Twenty-Four to Sixty-Four

	Dominican, 1st Gen	Dominican, 2nd Gen	Latino/a, 1st Gen	Latino/a, 2nd Gen	Puerto Rican	Black	White
Management, professional, and related	10.1	27.5	8.7	32.2	14.3	24.5	38.2
Services	15.1	9.9	11.7	8.0	18.8	31.0	12.5
Sales and office	11.8	40.1	13.1	36.8	17.3	20.3	26.2
Construction, extraction, and maintenance	7.7	0.0	7.3	4.4	8.0	4.8	8.1
Production, transportation, and material moving	54.9	22.4	57.6	18.6	37.9	19.2	14.7
Manufacturing	46.4	17.0	51.0	22.0	33.7	14.0	16.5
Education, health, and social services	14.6	45.4	10.5	22.4	20.5	45.4	31.2

Source: Author's compilation based on the 5 percent Public Use Microdata Sample (PUMS) (U.S. Bureau of the Census 2000).
Note: All numbers in percentages.

the Dominican second generation joins the services working class, a significant proportion remains in poverty and do not finish high school. This pattern— partial mobility with internal stratification—is what I call stratified incorporation. It is necessary to point out, though, that internal stratification, unlike segmented assimilation, does not mean relegation into marginality—although some among the second generation indeed suffer this fate. Instead, internal stratification means that the majority of the second generation join the services working class and that some of them live their lives a paycheck away from poverty and, in some cases, as working poor.

To be sure, incorporation to a stratified society means by necessity that the group will experience a measure of internal stratification. As Kasinitz and his colleagues aptly put it, "in saying that the second generation is not downwardly mobile, we are not suggesting that they have universally bright economic futures. It is a common mistake to equate assimilation with upward mobility" (2008, 203).

Still, the relevant question is whether the pattern of stratification of the second generation and beyond corresponds to the pattern of stratification of the American mainstream. Much research on immigrant incorporation compares the relative standing of immigrant groups to native minorities. This is indeed the approach taken in *Inheriting the City* (Kasinitz et al. 2008). The authors have showed that second-generation Dominicans and West Indians are doing better than native-born Puerto Ricans and blacks. They attributed the second-generation advantage to immigrant self-selection, to access to institutions that emerged in the wake of the civil rights movement to allow for the mobility of minorities (such as unions or black studies programs), and to the ability of the second generation to develop creative strategies, an ability that is the result of the fact that the second generation spans two cultural worlds.[4]

Perhaps the paradigmatic debate on the relative position of immigrant versus native minorities and whites concerns the case of West Indian immigrants (Vickerman 1999). The sociologist Milton Vickerman pointed to two waves of research on West Indian socioeconomic incorporation. The first suggested that West Indians were doing much better than African Americans. This literature argued that the individualistic and materialistic cultural attitudes of West Indian immigrants, expressed in their orientation toward small businesses, made them more apt than African Americans to adapt to American society. This literature presented the case as proving that race and racism are not barriers to mobility (Glazer and Moynihan 1970; Sowell 1981). Yet

Vickerman points out that the percentage of self-employed West Indians is rather low. They are indeed mobility-oriented, but primarily through the public sector or personal services.

A second wave of research pointed out that for all their economic success, West Indians and African Americans have much more in common socioeconomically than they are similar to whites (Bryce-Laporte and Mortimer 1983; Model 1991). Milton Vickerman proposed a third view, one that parallels the stratified ethnoracial incorporation argument proposed in this book. "That West Indians, overall," he said, "exhibit somewhat better social indicators than African Americans is significant and probably amounts to real differences in quality of life. However, to say that the fates of both groups diverge only partially implies that these fates join at some point. The connection is that both African Americans and West Indians continue to experience invidious discrimination" (1999, 80–81).

The debate on West Indian immigrants is instructive for the analysis here. I could put the emphasis on trying to explain the differences between Dominicans and Puerto Ricans and Dominicans and blacks. In that case, one would probably point to self-selection among immigrants, to ethnic businesses, and to access to schooling. This analysis would certainly be appropriate because the groups vary in their centers of gravity—to use the expression coined by Kasinitz and his colleagues (2008) to reflect the socioeconomic differences they found between second generations in New York City.

The question, however, is what stratification dynamic is at work in American society. Is American society one in which different ethnic groups assimilate at different paces? Or does racialization guide the process of socioeconomic incorporation of immigrant groups? I think that the second statement is a more accurate description of the stratification process in America. I therefore follow Vickerman (1999) in emphasizing the commonalties between the socioeconomic incorporation of second-generation Dominicans and other immigrant and native minorities and their shared experience of racialization. What the data presented in the two tables discussed so far indicate is that Dominicans in Rhode Island are part of a system of ethnoracial stratification where minorities—immigrant and native alike, with the possible exception of a segment of the Asian American population, which is not included in the tables—have a lower socioeconomic center of gravity than the white population. The overall pattern of stratification of second-generation Dominicans is closer to that of other second-generation Latinos and blacks than to that of whites. In other words, the differences between the centers of gravity of whites and minority groups as a whole are larger than the differences between those of ethnoracial minorities.

Yet the pervasiveness of ethnoracial stratification does not mean that the various ethnoracial groups are homogeneous communities. As argued, a segment of all minority groups—immigrant and native alike—is experiencing mobility into the middle class and even to the upper class. The stratified ethnoracial incorporation approach emphasizes both aspects of the Dominican experience: the presence of an ethnoracial system of stratification and the presence of internal class stratification within the immigrant community.

Race and class both affect the experience of incorporation of Dominicans—and other minority immigrants. The interactive effect of these two social facts is expressed in different patterns of stratification for whites and Dominicans. Certainly, not all whites are in the middle class and many of them are poor. But the proportion of the middle and working classes among whites and minorities is different. Whites have a larger proportion of people in middle-class occupations and enjoying a middle-class lifestyle, whereas Dominicans—and other minorities—have proportionally larger number of people in working-class occupations and among the marginalized sectors.

To summarize the analysis so far, three elements characterize Dominicans in Rhode Island. First, the second generation has improved its position in the American socioeconomic structure over the first generation. This conclusion is supported by both the socioeconomic and occupational data. Second, there is a split in the occupational incorporation of the second generation between those who join management and administrative jobs and those who join the services working class. Third, second-generation Dominicans are part of an overall structure of ethnoracial stratification. Their pattern is similar to that of other minorities and different from that among whites.

A COMPARATIVE DETOUR

Is the pattern of socioeconomic incorporation of Dominicans in Providence an isolated case or is it similar to that of Dominicans in other cities? To assess the specificities and commonalties of the Providence Dominican experience we compare it to that of Dominicans in New York City, in Lawrence, Massachusetts, and nationwide. Each comparison has its own rationale. New York is the center of the Dominican presence in the United States and the main port of entry for Dominican immigrants. It has, in fact, the second largest Dominican population in the world after Santo Domingo, the capital of the Dominican Republic. This comparison indicates whether the socio-economic incorporation of Dominicans in small secondary cities is similar to or different from that in the main gateway.

Studies of Dominicans in New York City indicate that first-generation Dominicans are employed in the declining sectors of the economy and experience both low wages and high rates of unemployment and poverty (Hernández 2002). At the same time, the entrepreneurial sector is growing. Moreover, an important proportion of the Dominican youth who finish high school go on to higher education (Aparicio 2006; Guarnizo 1994; Hernández 2002; Hernández and Rivera-Batiz 2003; Ricourt 2002).

As to the second generation, Kasinitz and his colleagues found that Dominicans are doing slightly better than Puerto Ricans and African Americans, that they are better educated than their parents, and that those who pursue higher education have no disadvantage vis-à-vis native whites. Yet the authors of *Inheriting the City* also showed that Dominicans have less of a second-generation advantage than the other groups studied (Kasinitz et al. 2008).[5] They assert that "it is not clear whether Dominicans, caught between remaining in one of the poorest immigrant communities and assimilating into the poorest of the native communities, enjoy much of a second generation advantage" (364). This overall picture of second-generation mobility, internal class differentiation, and ethnoracial stratification corresponds to the pattern of stratified ethnoracial incorporation.

Providence and Lawrence are similar. Both are medium-sized to small cities in the same region of the country with a shining manufacturing past that has been in constant decline for several decades. Lawrence has the largest Dominican population in Massachusetts, per the 2000 Census, almost 23,000—just over 34 percent of the Dominican population of the state and 15.7 percent of the city.[6] Dominicans are the largest Latino group and have a larger weight within the Latino population than in Providence. There are some 6,901 second-generation Dominicans in Lawrence, 30 percent of the Dominican population. The population of interest in this analysis, however, is much smaller. Only 722 second-generation Dominicans are twenty-four years old or older. Given the commonalties between Lawrence and Providence, we expect the socioeconomic incorporation of Dominicans in these two places to follow a similar pattern. Finally, the comparison with the nationwide data controls for possible regional differences. We look at three cities in states where close to 70 percent of the U.S. Dominican population is concentrated, but those cities are all in the same region. The nationwide data indicate whether the pattern of Dominican socioeconomic incorporation is similar across the country.

Following the earlier analysis, table 3.3 presents the socioeconomic data for first- and second-generation Dominicans in New York City, in Lawrence, and in the United States as a whole, comparing them to the white American population in each place. The picture that emerges is similar to that for Dominicans in Providence. The second generation is doing better in almost all the socioeconomic indicators than the first generation: higher rates of labor market participation, higher rates of high school completion, higher percentages of people with a college degree, lower rates of poverty, and higher median household incomes. There are some local variations in this picture. In both New York City and Lawrence, for example, first-generation Dominicans have lower rates of unemployment. In Lawrence, like in Providence, the second generation has a higher rate of poverty. Nationwide, however, the second generation has lower unemployment and poverty rates than the first generation.

The table also shows both the progress made by the second generation in terms of educational achievement and the limits of this progress. On the one hand, the percentage of the second generation who did not finish high school is less than half that of the first generation. In Providence the percentage is higher than in the other two cities, but even in Providence second-generation Dominicans have much better educational indicators than the first generation. The table also shows an impressive growth in the percentage of those who have a bachelor's degree or higher. On the other hand, the percentage without a high school diploma is still very high, and much higher than the rate for the white population.

As was the case in Providence, in the two cities as well as nationwide, the socioeconomic indicators of white Americans are much better than those of the Dominican second generation. Across the board, white Americans have higher rates of labor market participation, lower school dropout rates, higher percentages of people with college degrees, lower rates of poverty, and higher median household incomes than second-generation Dominicans. With any indicator, the picture is the same, and the differences are not small. The percentage of employed white Americans is consistently between eight and ten points higher than the rate of employed second-generation Dominicans. The dropout rate of white Americans ranges between eight and thirteen percentage points lower. It is evident that the ethnoracial system of stratification we

Table 3.3 Socioeconomic Indicators in New York City, Lawrence, Mass., and the United States, Ages Twenty-Four to Sixty-Four

	Employed	Unemployed	Not in Labor Force	Less than High School	High School	Some College or Associate's Degree	Bachelor's Degree or More	Below Poverty Line	Median Income ($1,000)
First generation									
New York City	49.7	8.1	42.2	52.9	20.0	18.9	8.2	28.9	33.1
Lawrence, Mass.	56.6	5.5	37.8	54.6	23.3	15.6	6.4	23.2	32.1
United States	53.9	7.1	38.9	48.7	21.5	19.8	10.0	25.1	35.8
Second generation									
New York City	62.2	9.3	28.4	22.4	23.0	36.7	18.0	21.8	41.5
Lawrence, Mass.	68.8	10.0	21.2	20.5	26.0	51.2	2.2	28.9	29.2
United States	67.3	6.9	25.8	18.2	21.3	38.7	21.8	18.9	47.8
White									
New York City	72.8	3.2	24.0	9.7	20.4	20.4	49.5	9.8	67.0
Lawrence, Mass.	76.4	2.2	21.4	9.8	27.4	25.0	37.8	6.5	71.2
United States	76.3	2.5	21.2	10.3	28.8	31.1	29.8	7.2	58.0

Source: Author's compilation based on the 5 percent Public Use Microdata Sample (PUMS) (U.S. Bureau of the Census 2000).
Note: Numbers in percentages except income.

found in Providence matches the overall predicament of second-generation Dominicans in the United States.[7]

Table 3.4 looks at the occupational position of Dominicans. Three main trends characterize their labor market incorporation. First is the well-established decline in manufacturing employment. In New York City and nationwide, the percentage of first-generation Dominicans working in education, health, and social services is larger than that in manufacturing. In Lawrence, as in Providence, manufacturing is still the main sector of employment for the first generation. For the second generation, however, manufacturing is not an employment niche. In Lawrence the percentage of the second generation in manufacturing jobs is still high, but the proportion in service occupations is nonetheless larger. Nationwide, the percentage of second-generation Dominicans in manufacturing is lower than the percentage of whites in this sector.

The second significant trend is the concentration of the second generation in sales and office occupations. As in Providence, this is the main employment niche for second-generation Dominicans in New York, Lawrence, and in the country as a whole. Nationwide, the concentration of second-generation Dominicans in these occupational niches is 15 percent higher than that of whites. The third trend is a doubling of the percentage of the second generation in managerial and professional occupations in relation to the first generation. In New York City and Lawrence, as in Providence, the figure for the second generation is close to 30 percent. Nationwide, the proportion is slightly above 30 percent. We see again the same bifurcation we observed earlier in Providence between those in managerial and professional positions and those in sales and services.

These numbers also show the underrepresentation of second-generation Dominicans in managerial and professional occupations. In New York City and Lawrence, the proportion of whites in these fields is a considerable 23 and 18 percentage points higher than that of Dominicans. Nationwide, as in Providence, the gap is narrower but still significant—10.7 percentage points in Providence and 5.9 percentage points nationwide.

Given the consistent picture of internal stratification within the second generation, it is important to assess the size of the segment in middle-class occupations. Table 3.5 illustrates a breakdown of Dominicans who are either self-employed or in managerial and professional occupations, that is, who have middle-class jobs. The table shows again the significant progress of the second generation over the first. In New York City, the proportion of Dominicans

Table 3.4   Selected Occupations and Industries in New York City, Lawrence, Mass., and the United States, Ages Twenty-Four to Sixty-Four

	New York City			Lawrence, Mass.			United States		
	1st Gen	2nd Gen	White	1st Gen	2nd Gen	White	1st Gen	2nd Gen	White
Management, professional, and related occupations	13.3	28.8	52.0	13.1	27.8	45.7	15.0	33.2	39.1
Services	29.4	19.8	10.4	22.0	8.4	9.9	26.5	16.1	10.9
Sales and office	21.4	34.2	24.8	14.6	33.9	24.1	21.6	34.4	25.8
Construction, extraction, and maintenance	7.5	6.4	6.0	6.8	8.1	7.3	7.9	5.7	10.1
Production, transportation, and material moving	25.5	8.2	6.0	41.9	21.8	17.4	26.6	8.9	13.5
Manufacturing	14.5	4.3	4.6	35.3	18.6	19.4	18.3	7.9	14.8
Education, health, and social services	28.5	34.8	28.8	26.0	22.8	24.0	27.3	31.4	26.2

Source: Author's compilation based on the 5 percent Public Use Microdata Sample (PUMS) (U.S. Bureau of the Census 2000).
Note: All numbers are percentages.

Table 3.5 Middle-Class Occupations of Dominicans, Ages Twenty-Four to Sixty-Four

	Self-Employed			Management, Professional, and Related Occupations	Middle-Class Occupations**
	Unincorporated Business	Incorporated Business	Managers and Professionals*		
First generation					
Providence	2.8	3.1	1.2	10.1	14.8
New York City	6.2	2.6	0.9	14.2	22.1
Lawrence, Mass.	3.5	1.5	1.2	13.1	16.9
United States	5.5	2.6	1.4	15.0	21.7
Second generation					
Providence	11.1	0.0	0.0	27.5	38.6
New York City	2.1	2.3	1.7	28.8	31.5
Lawrence, Mass.	14.2	0.0	10.4	27.8	31.6
United States	2.7	1.6	1.6	33.2	35.9

Source: Author's compilation based on the 5 percent Public Use Microdata Sample (PUMS) (U.S. Bureau of the Census 2000).
* As a percentage of those members of the group in the labor force.
** Managerial or professional occupations plus self-employed, less those who overlap these two categories (third column of the table).

in middle-class occupations was 22.1 percent in the first generation and 31.5 percent in the second. In Providence, the numbers were even more impressive—14.8 in the first generation and 38.6 in the second. Nationwide, about 35 percent of second-generation Dominicans are in middle-class jobs. This is impressive. At the same time, it also reminds us that 65 percent are either part of the working class or of the more marginalized sectors of American society.

Providence shows the sharpest social contrasts. It has the largest percentage of Dominicans in middle-class occupations, but at the same time the highest rate of poverty and the lowest median income. In New York, the main place of settlement of Dominicans outside of the Dominican Republic, the second generation is doing less well in terms of middle-class occupations but has lower rates of poverty and higher incomes. Overall, the data indicate more similarities than differences in the pattern of socioeconomic incorporation of Dominicans in the three cities. So whatever the specificities of life in Providence and the reasons that led Dominicans to leave the gateway city for a small secondary city, the same trends characterize the socioeconomic incorporation of Dominicans in Providence, New York City, and Lawrence.

The analysis of the nationwide data by and large fits the patterns in New York City, Lawrence, and Providence. There is, however, one important caveat. The national indicators are slightly higher than those in the three cities we examined. The national rate of poverty of second-generation Dominicans is lower, the median income is higher, and the percentage of high school graduates is higher. In areas outside of these three northeast cities, then, Dominicans seem to be doing better. A look at Dominicans in New Jersey and Florida clarifies this observation.[8] The socioeconomic profile of Dominicans in the state of New Jersey as a whole is slightly better than the nationwide socioeconomic profile. But the position of Dominicans relative to whites in New Jersey is similar to that in the country as a whole. The socioeconomic profile of whites in New Jersey is also higher than elsewhere in the country. New Jersey, that is, simply seems to have higher socioeconomic indicators for all ethnoracial groups.

The one exception to the overall pattern is second-generation Dominicans in Florida, where the rates of poverty and the occupational distribution of second generation Dominicans are very similar to that of white Floridians. This is the result of a particular migration stream, because Florida is the destination of choice of middle-class—and lighter skin—Dominican immigrants (Hoffman-Guzman 2004). Florida is also a frequent destination for Dominicans who do well enough in Providence or New York to be able to move to a climate closer to what they are used to. It is therefore not surprising that Dominicans in Florida do considerably better than those in other parts of the country. The data suggests a process of geographic class differentiation within the Dominican population in the United States, with Florida the destination of choice for the better off and the Northeast home to the majority of the working class.

This analysis suggests that the three propositions that describe the socioeconomic incorporation of second-generation Dominicans in Providence—improvement over the first generation, internal differentiation between a managerial and professional class and a service working class, and incorporation into an ethnoracial system of socioeconomic stratification—also describe the socioeconomic position of their counterparts in New York City, in Lawrence, and nationwide, with the exception of Florida.

GENDERED PATHS

So far we have looked at trends for Dominicans as a whole. Recent scholarship, however, indicates important differences in the socioeconomic position of men and women. In her ethnography of a public school in New York City, Nancy Lopez showed that second-generation girls do better than boys in terms of educational achievement. Similarly, the sociologists Cynthia Feliciano and Rubén Rumbaut analyzed the California segment of the Children of Immigrants Longitudinal Study and found that second-generation women have better educational achievements than second-generation men (2005). They also find that second-generation women have higher occupational aspirations than their male counterparts. Therefore it is necessary to look whether this pattern of gender segmentation in trajectories of incorporation is also found in Providence.

The next three tables reproduce the analysis conducted earlier but compare the socioeconomic position of second-generation men and women. Table 3.6 shows that second-generation Dominican women in Providence are clearly doing better than second-generation men in all socioeconomic indicators but one. Women have higher rates of labor force participation, higher rates of high school completion, a higher percentage of college degrees, and a lower poverty rate. In spite of these, however, they have a much lower median household income than men.

Table 3.6   Socioeconomic Indicators for Second-Generation
              Dominicans in Providence, Ages Twenty-Four to Sixty-Four

	Men	Women
Employed	57.9	74.4
Unemployed	0.0	6.1
Not in labor force	42.1	19.6
Less than high school	38.6	24.2
High school	21.4	18.7
Some college or associate's degree	36.2	30.5
Bachelor's degree or more	3.8	26.5
Below poverty line	50.9	42.2
Median income ($1,000)	46.8	23.0

Source: Author's compilation based on the 5 percent Public Use Microdata Sample (PUMS) (U.S. Bureau of the Census 2000).
Note: Numbers as percentages except income.

Table 3.7 shows that second-generation women do better professionally than men. Nearly 50 percent of second-generation women are in management and professional occupations, a rate 14 percent higher than that of men. Interestingly, the table indicates that the transition to the service working class is much more pronounced among women than among men. The proportion of second-generation Dominican men in manufacturing is much higher than that of women. For men, manufacturing appears to still be an employment option, whereas very few women work in the sector. The opposite is true in sales and office occupations. Finally, table 3.8 shows that the proportion of women working in middle-class occupations is 17 percent higher than that of men. Women also have higher rates of self employment.

Tables 3.6 and 3.7 indicate that the paths of incorporation are indeed gendered and that the trends of stratified incorporation identified in this chapter are much more pronounced for women than for men. Women seem to make use of the opportunities offered by the American educational system and labor market much more than men. This is certainly good news in terms of challenging the established patterns of gender stratification. Yet the very low median household income of women suggests that they also experience a

Table 3.7   Selected Occupations and Industries for Second-Generation Dominicans in Providence, Ages Twenty-Four to Sixty-Four

	Men	Women
Management and professional	19.7	34.0
Services	16.0	4.9
Sales and office	31.6	47.2
Construction, extraction, and maintenance	0.0	0.0
Production, transportation, and material moving	32.7	13.9
Manufacturing	28.6	7.4
Education, health, and social services	23.8	63.3

Source: Author's compilation based on the 5 percent Public Use Microdata Sample (PUMS) (U.S. Bureau of the Census 2000).
Note: Numbers as percentages.

much stronger polarization than men. The differentiation between those who are succeeding and those who are staying behind seems more pronounced among women than among men. This is in part the result of the higher achievement among second-generation women, but also suggests that women who are not doing as well are in a difficult position. Still, women clearly show more upward mobility than men.

We are at the early stages of the incorporation of the second generation and need to see whether this pattern of incorporation consolidates over time. It is important to point out, though, that the findings here coincide with those presented by Nancy López (2003) and Cynthia Feliciano and Rubén Rumbaut (2005). It remains the task of future work to see how these trends in gender stratification affect gender subjectivities and gender relations. What is important to emphasize is that the trends described here represent a potential chink in the structural armor of gender inequality.

RACE, CLASS, AND MOBILITY

The assumption of the various forms of assimilation theory is that over time immigrants learn the ropes of American society and enter educational and labor market institutions that open for them avenues for upward mobility. Scholars working within this framework interpret the very real improvements of the second generation as an indication that new immigrants are follow-

Table 3.8   Middle-Class Occupations for Second-Generation
             Dominicans in Providence, Ages Twenty-Four to Sixty-Four

	Men	Women
Self-employed, not-incorporated	9.7	12.3
Self-employed, incorporated	0.0	0.0
Self-employed, managers and professionals	0.0	0.0
Management, professional, and related occupations	19.7	34.0
Middle-class	29.4	46.3

Source: Author's compilation based on the 5 percent Public Use Microdata Sample (PUMS) (U.S. Bureau of the Census 2000).
Note: Numbers as percentages.

ing the same path of incorporation as southern and eastern European immigrants during the first half of the twentieth century (Bean and Stevens 2003; Perlmann 2005). The vision of American society that underlines this assumption is one in which the boundaries of accessing the middle class are, in Richard Alba's words, blurred (2005). The data reviewed indicate that this is in part the case, but also that the possibilities of mobility are limited and that immigrants become part of a racialized class system.

In raising the question of the future of the third generation the authors of *Inheriting the City* argued that "there are many reasons to be concerned what the future will hold for the young people we are studying. Household incomes are becoming more unequal, unionized manufacturing and other blue-collar jobs are dwindling, and labor market insecurity is on the rise" (Kasinitz et al. 2008, 203–04). They suggested the possibility of a segmented assimilation downward mobility scenario of sorts but played out in the third generation. Will the Dominican third-generation socioeconomic position improve in respect to the second generation? Or will the pattern of stratified ethnoracial incorporation continue across generations?

It is impossible to infer from the data presented here the likely trajectory of future generations. First, the analysis is based on cross-sectional data. This information does not tell us anything about trends over time. Second, the comparison is between generational groups as wholes. We do not have information about individual mobility. We do not know if the parents of those in the second generation who are doing well are doing well themselves or are working class. To establish a baseline for predicting the likelihood of mobility among Dominicans, we would need to construct transition tables comparing the income, occupation, or education of parents and children over time.[9] Unfortunately, there is no nationally representative database of Dominicans that would make this kind of study possible. The Dominican second generation is still very young and is not present in the large longitudinal databases used for studies of mobility. In addition, the immigrant parents have atypical socioeconomic and occupational trajectories. Even though they may have a low socioeconomic status, they are highly motivated and self-selected. For these reasons, the pattern of transition between the first and the second generation may not predict the pattern of transition between the second and the third generations.

What we can do is examine the mobility patterns of other groups to try to grasp the dynamics of intergenerational change and continuity in American society. Understanding the general patterns of mobility would allow us to hypothesize about the future of Dominican generations. Fortunately, an existing body of research provides clues as to the contemporaneous mobility trends. I first examine the work of Frank Bean and Gillian Stevens on the mobility of Mexican American generations (2003). After that, I look at studies of intergenerational mobility in the United States by the economists Bhashkar Mazumder and Tom Hertz (Hertz 2005; Mazumder 2005). These data suggest that minorities and the poor face significant structural barriers to mobility.

Bean and Stevens asserted that Mexican Americans are following in the footsteps of early twentieth-century immigrants, albeit at a slower pace (2003). The empirical basis for their argument is a multigenerational analysis of the differentials in educational attainment and earnings between Mexican Americans and whites. These authors compared the educational attainment and earnings of first, second, and third (and beyond) generation Mexican Americans with American-born whites at the end of the 1990s.[10] They found that the educational gains of second-generation Mexican Americans improved significantly over the first generation, but without reaching the same level of educational attainment as white Americans.

Their findings also show a big reduction of earnings differentials between Mexican Americans and whites between the first and the second generation. The reduction is particularly strong among the groups with higher levels of education. These results suggest that a continuous intergenerational increase in the education levels of Mexican Americans and a reduction of the education gap between Mexican Americans and whites would reduce the earning gap between the groups. Bean and Stevens, however, found no further improvement in educational attainment between the second and third generations (2003). Their data show slight improvements in some of the educational indicators of the third generation and slight declines in others. Overall, the educational profile of the third generation looks very similar to that of the second generation (2003). In fact, they also showed that the earning differentials between whites and third-generation Mexican Americans are similar to those between whites and second-generation Mexican Americans. They found a large improvement in socioeconomic status between the first and the second generation but almost no change between the second and third. It seems then that second-generation Mexican Americans occupy a position in the American social structure similar to that of the Dominican second generation. Bean and Stevens data, in fact, support the stratified ethnoracial stratification approach proposed in this book.

Recent research on intergenerational income mobility in the United States also supports this approach. The body of literature on income correlations between parents and children points to a pervasive intergenerational continuity. The economist Bhashkar Mazumder, for example, found that 60 percent of the differences in parent's incomes are transmitted to the children's generation (2005).[11] Furthermore, this is an average measure that masks different rates of mobility across the income distribution. Mazumder argued that there is more mobility in the middle of the income distribution than at the bottom or the top. He showed that 38 percent of children born to parents in the bottom quartile will end up in that quartile and only 32 percent of all children born at the bottom quartile will have incomes above the median. On the other hand, 43 percent of those born in the top quartile will stay in that quartile and only 34 percent of children born in the top quartile of the income distribution will experience downward mobility to incomes below the median.

Interestingly, Mazumder's findings would actually fit the Bean and Stevens hypothesis of a four or five generation convergence between the children of immigrants and the white mainstream (Bean and Stevens 2003). But Mazumder's data refers to the population as a whole and hides profound racial differences in rates of mobility. The economist Tom Hertz, on the other hand, showed that the intergenerational continuity at the bottom of the income distribution is much higher for blacks than for whites (Hertz 2005). Hertz found that for the entire population the rate of persistence in the bottom decile is 31.5 percent. Yet this number obscures the fact that among the white population only 16.9 percent of those born in the lower decile remain there. This is actually a quite high proportion. Among the black population, however, the proportion is an over-whelming 41.5 percent. Hertz repeated the exercise looking at quartiles rather than deciles. According to these results, across the whole population, 46.6 percent of those born in the lower quartile remain there, but again, the number conceals important differences between blacks and whites.[12] Among the white population, 32.3 percent of those born in the lowest quartile remain there, versus 62.9 percent among the back population. It seems that in spite of all the debates on the declining significance of race, race is still an important predictor of a person's position in the socioeconomic structure.

Finally, Hertz looked at the people born at the bottom of the income distribution who make it to the top (2005). For the population as a whole, the rate of mobility between the bottom and the top quartile is 9.3 percent—quite a low rate for a society that thinks itself as classless. Yet again, this rate hides racial differences in mobility. Among the white population, 14.2 percent of those born in the lower quartile make it to the top quartile. The corresponding proportion for the black population is 3.6 percent. These results are telling. Class and race appear as structural barriers to mobility. Minorities born to low-income families are likely to experience a high rate of intergenerational transmission of low socioeconomic status. Although Hertz's study focuses on African Americans only, his findings also explain the lack of mobility between second- and third-generation Mexican Americans apparent in Bean and Stevens's results. For poor minorities, American society is much less mobile than is commonly imagined.

The Dominican history of incorporation is different from that of both African Americans and Mexican Americans, but at the same time the groups share a number of experiences. Both Dominicans and African Americans are racialized as blacks, and both Dominicans and Mexican Americans are considered mostly low-skilled workers and categorized as Latinos. Furthermore, the parallels in the low mobility rates of African Americans and third-generation Mexican Americans found in the works reviewed point to a general pattern of low mobility for minorities in American society. Based on the data presented in this section, we can hypothesize that the pattern of stratified ethnoracial incorporation—a pattern characterized by partial upward mobility and a majority insertion in the services working class—will continue into the third generation.

Of course, the peril in any prediction is that we assume the continuation of the present conditions. The Yankee City study illustrates this point clearly. Warner and Srole predicted, in the mid-1940s, that it will take several generations for Italians to assimilate to the American mainstream and that the assimilation of the Jews was possible but there was no applicable temporal horizon (1945). A generation later, Italians and Jews were well on their way into the American mainstream. As Joel Perlmann and Roger Waldinger aptly argued, the upward mobility of the children and grandchildren of European immigrants was the result of structural changes in American society, changes that Warner and Srole could not or failed to predict (1997). The assimilation of European immigrants was also the product of a major shift in racial boundaries that allowed white ethnics to become part of the racial mainstream (Perlmann and Waldinger 1997).

The future socioeconomic position of Dominicans and other minority groups depends on the evolution of the socioeconomic structure, the dynamics of racialization and discrimination, and on their political action. The recent history of African Americans is a case in point. In the 1940s, Warner and Srole correctly predicted that only a radical change in the pattern of American race relations would open the doors of mobility for African Americans and black immigrants. Indeed, it was necessary to have the massive popular mobilization of African Americans—and other minorities—in the civil rights movement to partially push open the doors of mobility and belonging for minorities. Since then, there has indeed been upward mobility for minorities. We have witnessed the formation of a black and minority middle class. At the same time, we are living today with the results of the incomplete success of the civil rights movement—the achievement of political and civil rights, to the detriment of an agenda of economic equality (Wilson 1978). In these conditions, the structural economic change brought by the fast decline of manufacturing in the 1970s and 1980s, coupled with persistent residential segregation, pushed important segments of the African American population into marginality (Massey and Denton 1993; Wilson 1996).

CITY OF OPPORTUNITIES?

Is, then, Providence a city of opportunities for Dominicans? Is the United States a society of opportunities as immigrants hope and as Americans believe? If we look only at the impressive improvements of the Dominican second generation over the first generation, the answer should be positive. If we go beyond the broad outlines of the intergenerational comparison and pay attention to the internal stratification within the second generation, the answer would have to be more nuanced. For those who can access middle-class jobs, the answer is yes. But for the large concentration of people in the new services working class, and for those in poverty, the land of opportunities may prove to be a mirage. The United States is indeed a society of opportunities but not of equal opportunities for everybody. The stratified ethnoracial incorporation approach best describes the ways in which the Dominican second generation is entering the American socioeconomic structure.

The answer to the land of opportunities question, however, transcends the experience of the second generation. It depends also on what we think would happen in the transition between the second and further generations. It is at this point where the debate on the racial position of immigrants becomes central. Is race going to be a stern barrier to the incorporation of future Dominican generations into the mainstream as it has been for African Americans? Or are the ethnoracial boundaries of the mainstream going to be extended to encompass contemporary immigrants as they were extended to incorporate European immigrants during the first half of the twentieth century? Scholars associated with the assimilation approach emphasize the socially constructed character of race and the fact that racial boundaries can, at least in theory, become blurred (Alba 2005; Perlmann and Waldinger 1997). The evidence presented in this book suggests that racialization remains a pervasive element of stratification in American society. There is no doubt of upward mobility within immigrant communities as there is among African Americans. Yet the pattern of stratification of minority immigrants and African Americans is different from that of whites. Furthermore, studies on middle-class minorities suggest that class mobility mediates but does not eliminate the effects of racialization (Hochschild 1995; Lacy 2004; Pattillo 2005).

From this perspective, it becomes apparent that the future pattern of socioeconomic stratification among Dominicans—as well as among other immigrant generations—depends not on gradual improvement over several generations but on the change or continuity of ethnoracial class stratification. This depends, on the one hand, on the structural evolution of the American economy, a process that is beyond the control of particular individuals. On the other hand, the future pattern of racial and class stratification depends also on the political trends that will dominate social life in the next decades. The political participation of Dominicans and other immigrant groups and the type of alliances they build can affect how broad economic changes and racialization affect their economic opportunities and their everyday life. I return to this topic in the conclusions to this book.

CHAPTER 4

Entering the Mainstream?

The path of incorporation leads through the institutions of mainstream society. One of the key institutions for mobility is the education system. Education is central to high-paying jobs in the American economy. Education provides skills, certifications, and social networks that channel people into different sets of occupations and positions in the class structure. The previous chapter showed that there is a marked improvement in the education profile of the second generation over their parents—a clear sign of success and mobility. At the same time, important segments of the second generation are being left behind. One-third of the second generation in Providence does not finish high school, and when we add those who do not go on to college we are talking about more than half of the second generation. The importance of the encounter with the education system came up with a sense urgency in my conversations with Dominicans who grew up in the United States.

In this chapter I present the stories of five young Dominicans and examine how stratified ethnoracial incorporation is experienced in everyday encounters with the school system and other mainstream institutions. The stories are based on the in-depth interviews I conducted. I do not claim that these stories are representative of the Dominican experience as a whole. Furthermore, the analysis is not based on events I observed but on my interpretation of the memories these five people have of their formative years. I have chosen to narrate and analyze stories that allow me to examine how the encounter with mainstream institutions affects the socioeconomic incorporation trajectories of the children of Dominican immigrants in Providence. I have chosen the stories of people that have done well or at least moderately well because they illuminate the mechanisms for social mobility and also their limitations.

RACE, CLASS, AND THE SCHOOL EXPERIENCE

In her ethnography of a New York public school, Nancy López wrote about the everyday experiences of Dominican and other Caribbean working-class kids (2003). She described a school where teachers and school authorities worry more about maintaining discipline than actual learning. For minority working-class students, the school experience is characterized more by repression than by encouragement and support. López added that gender intersects with class in explaining the trajectories of minority students. She pointed out that girls are doing better than boys in the New York educational system,[1] which, as we saw in the previous chapter, is also the case in Providence.

The authors of *Inheriting the City* also found that students in low-performing schools "described large anonymous schools who expected little from their black and Hispanic students" (Kasinitz et al. 2008, 157). They found that second-generation Dominicans, especially men, experienced the most difficulties in schools among the New York second generations. These descriptions remind us of the economists Samuel Bowles and Herbert Gintis in their classic work *Schooling in Capitalist America* (1976). Bowles and Gintis argued that the key process in schools is not the teaching of cognitive skills but the socialization into the behaviors and beliefs expected from people in different classes. For these authors, working-class schools were more about teaching the discipline of the workplace rather than providing students with the knowledge necessary to achieve upward mobility.

Ricardo Stanton-Salazar went to great lengths to analyze the specific mechanisms through which schools reproduce class inequality (1997). He emphasized the roles of social networks in steering people into different class positions and of institutional agents, defined as individuals who can provide or deny access to important resources or information. In the school context, the concept of institutional agents refers to teachers, counselors, and school administrators who can pass on relevant knowledge, provide role models and emotional support, and generate contacts with mainstream institutions and people. These agents serve as gatekeepers opening or closing avenues of mobility.

One key difference between the schooling experience of middle-class and working-class children is the type of access to institutional agents. Stanton-Salazar likened the social networks of middle-class children to "social freeways that allow people to move about the complex mainstream landscape quickly and efficiently. In many ways, they function as pathways of privilege and power" (1997, 4). Working-class children, on the other hand, do not have access to the same type of networks. The public schools that serve working class and minority children do not provide the same kind of support or bridges to opportunities as middle-class schools. For working-class and minority youth, the encounters with school institutional agents takes place "within the context of differential power relations and within social contexts that are culturally different from, if not alienating to, cultural outsiders" (4). The lack of networks outside of the working class milieu in which many children of immigrants grow up affect what they know about mobility opportunities and the aspirations they develop. The result is that working-class youth are more likely to be discouraged from pursuing an education and therefore are more likely to end up in working-class positions.[2]

LATINOS IN THE PROVIDENCE PUBLIC SCHOOL SYSTEM

To provide a context for the analysis of the school experiences of young Dominicans, I briefly describe the position of Latinos in Providence's high schools.[3] The Providence School Department reports that in the 2007–2008 academic year Latinos made up 59 percent of the students enrolled in the system but only 8.5 percent of the teachers and 10 percent of the administrators.[4] In other words, in spite of the fact that Latino students are the absolute majority in the Providence public schools, they are severely underrepresented among the teachers and administrators. Table 4.1 presents information provided by the Rhode Island Department of Elementary and Secondary Education (RIDE) on the proportion of Latino students in Providence's high schools, their graduation rates, and the state's education department classification of the schools they attend.[5] The table shows that the graduation rate of Latinos is similar to the rate of the rest of the students. The graduation rate of Latinos who attend schools with high graduation rates is high, and of those who attend schools with low rates are low. The table also shows that in the 2006–2007 school year, most of the schools in which Latinos were a majority were classified by RIDE as showing inadequate progress in achieving their yearly goals.[6]

Table 4.1   Latinos/as in Providence Public High Schools, 2005 to 2006

School	Enrollment	Percent Latinos/as	Graduation Rate	Latina Rate	Latino Rate	2006 School Performance
Central	1647	61.6	64	65	62	Insufficient progress
Classical	1088	30.4	97	95	97	High performing and commended
Cooley/HSTA	407	54.8	73	75	86	Moderately performing with caution
E-Cubed	364	51.2	84	88	76	Insufficient progress
Feinstein High School	366	61.2	66	75	62	Insufficient progress
Hope Arts	370	54.6	85	90	N/A	Insufficient progress
Hope Leadership	363	68.1	80	84	73	Moderately performing
Hope Technology	382	52.6	72	75	65	Insufficient progress
Mt. Pleasant	1321	54.6	60	68	47	Insufficient progress
PAIS	425	79.5	69	85	53	Insufficient progress
Textron Chamber of Commerce Academy	225	60.0	95	100	91	High performing and commended
Times 2 Academy	123	50.4	N/A	100	100	High performing and commended

Source: Rhode Island Department of Elementary and Secondary Education (Available at: http://www.ride.ri.gov/applications/statistics.aspx).

In most cases there are important gender differences that confirm López's claim that Latino girls are doing better than boys. There are two exceptions, however. One is Classical High School, ranked as the best public high school in Providence. Although Latinos are the majority in the system, they are underrepresented at this school. Their graduation rate is almost 100 percent but the graduation rate of boys is higher than girls. From the information provided by the Rhode Island School Department, we can tentatively conclude that the type of school Dominicans and Latinos attend determines their educational achievement. When Latinos attend good schools, their graduation rate is high for both boys and girls.

It is important to add that the parents of Latino and Dominican youngsters have high aspirations for their children and show interest in their schooling. The results of the Latino National Survey for Providence show that 92.3 percent of Dominicans and 97.7 percent of Latinos would like to see their children graduate from college or receive a graduate or advanced professional degree. Similarly, 88.9 percent of Dominican parents and 91.5 percent of Latino parents have met with their children's teachers. Furthermore, 96.2 percent of Dominicans and 91.3 percent of Latinos reported that their meetings with school officials have been either somewhat good or very good. These results suggest that there is no lack of parents' encouragement of educational success or interest in their children school experience. Nevertheless, when parents do not know the workings of the educational system, when they do not speak the same language as the teachers and administrators, and when they have to work long hours to make ends meet, their ability to guide and control the youngsters is limited and the onus falls on the schools.

THE HURDLES OF EVERYDAY INCORPORATION
The use of personal stories in studying the works of society draws from C. Wright Mills's understanding of the sociological imagination as the link between history, social structure, and individual biography. This analytical approach illustrates how broad social processes impinge on individual lives and illuminates the forms of agency with which people confront their circumstances (Auyero 2003; Mills 1959). In the following stories, I examine the social mechanisms that produce both mobility and class stratification in the United States and how young Dominicans cope with them.

The first story is Alejandra's.[7] She is in her thirties and came to the United States at the age of eleven. In the Dominican Republic, her father was a skilled worker and her mother stayed at home. Their economic situation there was not bad but they nevertheless decided to emigrate to Providence in search of more opportunities and a better life. Like many Dominican immigrants, they told themselves that they would come to the United States to work for a few years, save money, and return to the Dominican Republic. Like most with such plans, they ended up staying for good. In Providence, they worked in manufacturing until their retirement. Although they were factory workers with little schooling, from a young age they instilled in Alejandra the value of education.

In her native city, Alejandra was a star student and very well connected socially. When she arrived in Providence, she attended a middle school that at that time did not have a bilingual education program. Without knowing English, she could not perform in school as well as she had done in the Dominican Republic. As a result, the former confident and outgoing student began to doubt herself and became socially reclusive. Her situation improved somehow when she moved on to high school, which offered a bilingual program that allowed her to learn the different class topics as she improved her knowledge of English. She also encountered a few Latino teachers who encouraged her to take the necessary classes to be admitted to college. Nevertheless, she ended up in a vocational program and finished high school with a diploma as a hair stylist.

She remembered that she "entered the vocational track knowing that it was not my vocation, and I never abandoned the dream of going to college."[8] That dream was the result of her parents' encouragement and of her relationship with two aunts in the Dominican Republic, who had gone to the university and who were role models for her. How then did the girl who was an academic star in her native country and who dreamed about going to college end up in the vocational track in high school? The answer had to do with her encounter with institutional agents in the school: "My Hispanic professors kept telling me 'you can do it, you can do it' . . . but the guidance counselors, who are the ones who look at your history and make the final decision, were the ones who told me that I should go to a vocational track. . . . So that is what I ended up doing."

Nevertheless, Alejandra ended up going to college. A lucky encounter with someone who could relate to her was decisive. Alejandra recalled it this way:

> It was the last year of high school and most of my friends were planning to take the SAT and to apply to college. Then my counselors told me "no, you can't,

because you are in the vocational school" . . . and then I met a Dominican who was a translator in the vocational school. She saw me one day very depressed and asked me "what is going on?" And I started to talk with her and I told her that I was depressed because my dream was to go to the university. . . . And she told me "it is not too late, start applying."

A program at the University of Rhode Island, she learned, gave minority students and students from disadvantaged backgrounds the opportunity to attend college. Alejandra applied even though most of her courses were from the vocational track. She did not qualify. She attended a special year-long program at the University of Rhode Island to make up for the missing credits, and ultimately managed to fulfill her dream of going to college. "I was admitted to the university," she recalled, "then I went back to be the person I was. That is, an activist involved in many organizations."

Alejandra's story raises the question of the expectations that teachers and counselors have of their students, and the message immigrant students get about what they should legitimately aspire to. In the guidance counselor's advice that sent Alejandra to the vocational track, one can intuit the presence of stereotypes and prejudices concerning the ability and potential of working-class immigrant students. Her story resonates with López's description of a New York City high school and illustrates Stanton-Salazar's point concerning the power and cultural differentials between minority working-class youth and the school institutional agents. Alejandra's story suggests, however, that schools are heterogeneous organizations. The random encounter with an individual within the school who knew about specific mainstream opportunities and the willingness to provide emotional support and guidance made the difference in Alejandra's educational trajectory. This again emphasizes the importance of the presence of institutional agents who can and will encourage and guide minority and working-class students.

The second story is Luisa's. Luisa is twenty years old and the fourth of six siblings. She grew up mostly with her mother, her father having left for Santo Domingo when she was a child. The six children grew up in what was most of the time a single-parent household. Luisa's mother recalled very difficult years. She worked in different jobs for a living, from manufacturing to house cleaning to secretarial work. She says that short of selling drugs or her body she has done every imaginable job. She remembered times she did not have enough money to put food on the table, times the heating in their apartment was cut in the middle of the Rhode Island winter because she could not afford to pay the gas bill. She said that during all those years she told her children about the value of staying together and working hard. Today Luisa's mother works as an executive secretary for a nonprofit agency and, after raising six children, is studying for a degree in human services.

Luisa graduated from a public high school in Providence and her story echoes Alejandra's in many ways.[9] Luisa's story is about using adversity as a force to move forward and of generating resources where none are to be found. Luisa graduated from high school despite rather than thanks to the school system. She recalled, "I had teachers that told me, 'you're never gonna be anything.' I had a teacher tell me that, because my sister had gotten pregnant while she was at high school, 'you're gonna be just like her; I betcha you're gonna get pregnant by the time you leave.'. . . It was on me to show them, we'll see about that, and I didn't."

We can intuit racism in this teacher's response, but Luisa added that the person who told her this was an African American teacher, showing how class prejudices can be internalized by people belonging to all groups: "So like there's all kinds of teachers in school. There are teachers that will do anything. They'll take you to their house just to help you accomplish your goals. There's teachers that join like every kind of program they can just to help you, but then there's teachers that'll be like, I'm just here for the money, I gotta get paid, I'm leaving, you know."

The key to Luisa's graduating was her ability to create a group of supportive peers. She and several friends helped establish a special program at school where they would have special workshops and take field trips. The program was run by a man who worked for a local nonprofit. He had a program for boys at the school that dealt with issues of manhood. Luisa remembered asking a friend how the program works: "She explained exactly what it does. They go to workshops where they teach them how to become stronger men and how to deal with society and things like that, and I'm like, that sounds interesting."

They inquired more and found out that the reason the program was for boys only was that the person running it was not sure whether he could connect with girls in the same way he connected with boys. But Luisa and her friends organized, petitioned, and eventually succeeded in having a similar program for girls. The two programs were eventually joined into one. Luisa recalled that although the program was open to all students, only minority students attended. Luisa admits that a big draw of the program was that those who attended had permission to leave class—though they had to make up the work they missed. Still, other important things went on in the program:

> If we wanted to swear and throw things because we was mad, we could do it in front of him, and he'll understand us because he was, he's also a minority. He's a black guy, and our school didn't have money to take us on trips whenever we needed to go somewhere, he would make sure he would get some money for his program to take us somewhere. The only reason why we ever went to trips in school and stuff like that was because of him, but only his program went.

In Luisa's case—as in the case of Alejandra—we see a negative encounter with many institutional agents at school. Luisa explained that in her first years in high school she had what she describes as an attitude, which she explains as meaning that "if you wasn't telling me nothing I wanted to hear, you couldn't tell me nothing." Luisa recalled that on graduation the person who ran the special program told her that when he first met her, he thought that she was not going to finish because of the way she related to teachers. But she said that although she was not listening to people the way they expected, she would still go ahead and do her work. Luisa's story shows again that schools are not homogeneous organizations. Several teachers conveyed discouraging messages to her and others offered their support. In this context, she was able to generate the institutional support that allowed her to complete high school successfully. Luisa's story also emphasizes the importance of cultural recognition and of spaces for self-expression. In the special program she helped create, she and her friends could express themselves in ways that the school would probably see as improper or threatening.

Both Luisa's and Alejandra's stories suggest that when students and school personnel can relate across class and ethnoracial boundaries, the encounter between immigrant working-class students and the school institutional agents can be positive and effective. Their stories also show, however, that in many instances the school institutional agents cannot transcend the boundaries of culture, class, and race and end up discouraging students from pursuing higher education.

The third story is about Carlos. Born in Providence in the early 1970s, Carlos's father left the family, his mother and five children, when Carlos was seven. It was very hard for Carlos's mother to control the five children because she had to work all the time, leaving the children at home alone without any planned activity. The neighborhood had no resources for teenagers, he explained: "There's really not enough to do in this community. I mean if you look around, community centers, there's not that many. There's no park really. I mean here we have a basketball court, but we used to have an amusement park, which somewhat helped."

Carlos first went to a high school with a large number of immigrants and children of immigrants in its student body—the same high school that Alejandra went to. He does not have good memories of his time there. He reminisced about his teachers in high school:

> They didn't pay any mind. . . . The one teacher I do remember . . . is actually a bad thought. I don't see any teacher that stuck out besides that English teacher, and it wasn't in a good way it's just that he used to come in, write some words on the board, tell us to look them up, look up the definition, write them in a sentence due on Friday. The rest of the week you came in, he read his newspapers, drank his coffee, fell asleep and that was the work for the whole week. So he really wasn't teaching us anything.

As a youngster, he recalled, he repeatedly got into trouble: "I was the type of person that used to get into fights. I was, I was a trouble maker, I was running around the streets." When he was sixteen, to keep him out of trouble, his family sent him to the Dominican Republic to live with his father. Carlos has fond memories of that time. He remembers learning a lot about the Dominican Republic and improving his Spanish, but at the end he came back to Providence. Because his father had left him when he was only seven, he did not feel close to him and wanted to return to his mother and siblings. On returning from the Dominican Republic, he was accepted into a high school that he describes as being "just for bad kids." It was a small school, though, with a low teacher to student ratio that allowed the teachers to pay attention to the students. There he found a more supportive environment: "I think all my teachers were great . . . [they] actually try and see what's going on at home, how's everything going, and doing your school work. . . . Instead of worrying about what a child is eating, or what he's wearing, or why he's chewing gum, they worried about is he doing his work, is he reading the book, is he doing the assignment, is he understanding the assignment. Stop worrying about everything they're wearing."

Carlos's memories of the first high school he attended correspond to Stanton-Salazar's description of the encounter between working-class students and

school institutional agents. Like those of the other students interviewed, however, his story shows that the educational system is a heterogeneous field. Indeed,
at the smaller school he had a completely different experience. What appealed
to Carlos there was that the teachers were interested in whether the students
were doing and understanding their work. Carlos's story also points to the
importance of cultural self-expression. After returning from the Dominican
Republic, he joined a youth group that came together to organize activities
for young people and to develop a pride in their Dominican identity. In that
organization, he channeled his energies into community activities that kept
him busy and found the encouragement and emotional support that helped
him stay out of trouble.

After he graduated from high school, Carlos decided to enroll in the army.
Explaining this decision, he remembered that he did not like the kind of
activities that some of his friends were involved in so decided to take another
direction. He remembers himself in those days: "I was in a bad stroke; I was
actually not such a good kid so it was pretty much downhill, so I decided to
join the army." He credits the army with disciplining him and giving him a
different perspective on things. He explained that after seeing how people live
in other countries he had a better appreciation for the circumstances of his
own life.

Today Carlos works as a supervisor for a contractor in the telecommunica-
tions field, having gotten his training in the army. He supervises a crew of
about fifty mostly immigrant workers. Carlos became a skilled member of the
services working class, but hopes one day to own his own business. In Carlos's
case, the attention of his teachers and the small size of the school together with
the support of the youth group—which acted as an institutional agent outside
of the school—allowed him to finish high school. The army gave him both
skills and an organization in which he was valued. These institutional agents,
then, provided him mobility to make his way into the skilled segments of the
services working class.

The fourth story is Miguel's. Miguel is in his mid-twenties and grew up
with his mother and stepfather. His father left the family early and later died
in a car accident. His mother remarried, but Miguel never got along with his
stepfather. Miguel does not have good memories of his early school years.
After his first year in middle school, in which he "got in trouble too much,
so they told me," he was sent to an alternative school for youth at risk where
he had to stay back a year. Sending problematic kids to special schools is not

necessarily something that will help them graduate, but in this particular case it worked for Miguel:

Teachers . . . we call[ed] them [by their] first names . . . and the classes, they were, they were different, you know, there were no desks. Everything was put like in a square or in a circle facing each other so the aesthetics of the building was really different well than any of the classrooms. They'd switched up themes. You had like African American history for one quarter, next quarter was Native American history, the history of mechanics. So something to try to make classes real interesting. Instead of books they had packets. A lot of field trips. So we had like real education . . . real world education.

Miguel found that in the alternative middle-school teachers were not focused on disciplining students but were instead trying to stimulate their interests. Going to that school also offered him a perspective on his own situation:

I thought I had problems, you know, I just got in trouble; I had an attitude, you know what I'm saying. You know, I had a share of my own stuff at home, you know, but compared to, you know, drug addiction. . . . I mean I was low, but there were a lot of people who were going much lower than I was, that about every time they look up they see dirt, you know what I'm saying, they're that low, and it's not their fault it's just where they found themselves; what they were born into you know.

After two years (the length of the program) in the alternative school, Miguel was able to continue his education in the mainstream public education system. He remembers that at that point he did not pay much attention to school. He wanted a fancy car and to get girls. He also wanted an apartment and to leave his parents' home. He started thinking that the way to do that was to drop out of school, get a job, and get a GED. At sixteen, he was working, providing for himself, and going home only to sleep. "I was real nearsighted. I could understand when a kid says, 'I want money, I want a car,' you know what I'm saying. He just wants to be a man. Same thing for a lot of the females, you know. But I think it is a little bit different for the males, is like that whole you got to be a man, what you see on television, the bonus, the guy with the bling bling."

Here, and in Carlos's story, we see the elements of gender socialization that López emphasizes. Both Miguel and Carlos had experienced little control in their households. Carlos credited his mother with having done a wonderful job when he was growing up, but admitted that her long hours at work made it very difficult for her to control or help the five children. Miguel never got along with his stepfather and this troubled relationship pushed him away from home. Like Luisa, they both had an attitude but whereas Luisa's attitude was mixed with determination to succeed in school, Carlos and Miguel had things other than education on their minds during their teenage years.

Miguel's story also shows the importance of self-assertion and of being able to make sense of the everyday experience of racialization and class exclusion. Two people reached him and got him thinking in a different way, two who do not usually appear in the narratives of second-generation Dominicans—Louis Farrakhan and Malcolm X. Miguel is a dark-skin Dominican and growing up was often at the receiving end of racist insults. As a result, he—like Luisa—developed an identity as a black Dominican. In this, as we will see in the second part of the book, he is not typical of the processes of identity formation among the second generation. Miguel encountered Farrakhan by chance, flipping through public access channels, and through him became acquainted with Malcolm X.

> And I just woke up. That's where I'd like to say I woke up. At junior year of high school. 'Cause I finished reading the autobiography of Malcolm X. Before that, I was gonna see like, Louis Farrakhan every Tuesday and Thursday on television, right, on public access, and I just flipped through the channels on 10:30, Tuesdays and Thursdays, and he'd say some crazy things, I mean obviously, Louis Farrakhan is Louis Farrakhan, nation of Islam right? . . . [Farrakhan] just mentioned some things in terms of I could say black plight, how things repeat themselves, the cycle. You know, the system is made for people to fail, and I started thinking about that. . . . I read Malcolm. I got mad. I was like, alright; I see what he's talking about.

Miguel remembered that once he began reading the biography of Malcolm X, he could not put it down. The ideas of Malcolm X helped him make sense of his experience of poverty and his encounters with racism. They gave him an interpretative framework to channel his anger in constructive directions. He embraced, as his philosophy of life, the idea that the best revenge is to live comfortably.

In high school, Miguel went to a magnet program that prepares students to go into teaching. There he worked hard, and for that was liked by his teachers, but he wasn't a particularly good student. Then, however, he got a break. His principal told him to apply to be a counselor in a summer program aimed at preparing minority middle school students for high school. He would be working with people who were going through experiences similar to his. Miguel wrote an application that he describes as grammatically messed up, but his older sister saw the proposal and wrote it over. Miguel was accepted into the program, although he had no idea what was expected from him or what he was going to do there. In that program he was exposed to a different world.

> I remember talking to a bunch of these other Brown students and high school students that went to Wheeler, Moses Brown, Classical, and they were talking some craziness, you know what I'm saying, like conversations I never heard before, you know. . . . They'd have a party or something like that, and yo, their houses were nice. . . . I thought I was middle class growing up; bullshit, bullshit, man. I realized then I was poor. . . . I just happened to have a color TV, you know what I'm saying. A little bigger room, a little bigger yard, cement yard, whatever, driveway, but I remember seeing these folks, man, and how they talk; their values; my car's a piece of shit; a brand new Saab. . . . And I was like, damn, and they didn't know I, 'cause I didn't have money for the bus 'cause they didn't pay us 'til the end of the program. I'd run; I'd run from my house up there. I stayed in shape.

In the same way that attending the alternative middle school showed him that there were people who were doing much worse than he, participating in that program brought him in contact with people who were doing much better than he. That experience opened a new horizon for him. Still, he was not doing well in school, decided to quit, and bought a one-way ticket to the Dominican Republic, where he stayed with his grandmother. He was not able to get a job there and that prompted his grandmother to confront him. He explained to her that he was overwhelmed by the double pressure of school and home. His grandmother challenged him to return to Providence, get an education, and prove those who had dismissed him wrong. With the help of his sister, he got a ticket back to Providence and eventually finished high school.

Miguel took a meandering path through higher education. He was accepted at one of the colleges in the state but did not feel prepared, so after his freshman year took a year off to work for a program for middle-school students at risk. During that year, he read as much as he could to prepare himself for college: "I came from being really nearsighted to being farsighted so I had a good way of adjusting my eyes. I knew I wanted to go to college, but I wanted to go to the right college. . . . That year, I read every book I could get my hands on. Basically stayed at the library, took a writing class so I could work on my grammar and stuff like that."

After that year, he decided to attend a historic black college in the south because he was attracted to the idea of being in a setting where young black men are the norm rather than a minority. He was happy there but had to leave for financial reasons. He considered joining the ROTC but decided against that because, unlike Carlos, "I didn't believe in the system that much, not even to sacrifice for school. No army for me." Eventually, he managed to finish college in Massachusetts and to earn a bachelor's degree.

Miguel's story shows again the importance that effective contacts with institutional agents can have in the lives of youngsters. The support he received in the alternative school helped him stay at school and the access to the summer program showed him a different set of opportunities. He is still undecided as to what he wants to do, but is thinking about getting a master's degree in education. He says he still wants the fancy car and the big house, as he did when he was sixteen years old, but he now knows better what to do in order to achieve his goals.

Two themes recur in these four narratives. The first is that schools appear as alienating environments, places not set to help minority working-class students progress in life. The four interviews reveal negative and discouraging encounters with teachers and counselors, confirming Stanton-Salazar's argument. The stories, however, also present a nuanced picture of the education system as field where some institutional agents are able to offer support and guidance and in that way can make a great difference in the trajectories of the students. But the contact with those agents is not as easy as one would expect. On the contrary, the institutional agents who can make a difference are few and far between and the contact with them is often more the result of chance— as in Alejandra's case—or the active initiative of the student—as in Luisa's case—rather than institutional design.

The second recurrent theme is the importance of cultural recognition and self-affirmation. We encounter this in Alejandra's account of her relation with her Hispanic teachers and in Luisa's ability to relate to the person who ran the special program she helped to create and in her emphasis on the ability to express herself in her own way in the group she created. In Carlos's narrative, the theme of cultural affirmation appears in his joining of a Dominican youth group, and in Miguel's case was triggered by his casual encounter with Farrakhan's television appearances and his reading the biography of Malcolm X. These diverse forms of self-affirmation strengthened these four individuals and allowed them to overcome the negative views about themselves that they encountered in their school experiences.

Carlos thinks that connecting with the forms of self-expression of youngsters can help address the problem of kids dropping out of school. He explained:

> I mean, you got these teenagers now that's so much into music and dancing and all that, but you don't see any type of performing arts or anything around here, and that's what they're really into right now. A lot of people don't get teenagers. They think, "oh the music they listen to is this, this, this." But you gotta figure when we grew up it was the same thing, all that music we listened to, your parents thought it was some crazy noise, and it's the same thing, and now we're going through that. You know this rap stuff, we only hear the bad words, we don't actually even try to understand the story behind it, and in reality a lot of it is just letting out their frustrations and them expressing what they see in the streets; it's normal you know. I don't see enough programs for kids; there really isn't. . . . You know there is no place to go. But if you had some place where they can go and play a drum or go and listen to music, dance, even after-school programs, if they had something to do it would solve a lot of problems that we have here.

Unfortunately, in a context of constant cuts of city and state budgets and increasing emphasis on tests, there are not many education policymakers willing to explore Carlos's ideas.

CHANCE AND OPPORTUNITIES

An interesting point about the stories of Luisa, Carlos, and Miguel is that if we had met them during their teenage years we would have seen in them youngsters who had developed values contrary to the American mainstream idea of progress through study and hard work. Both Carlos and Miguel quit school at some point during their education. Luisa said that at sixteen she had a negative attitude and was not willing to listen to her teachers, who perceived her as someone who would not graduate from high school. Furthermore, although all four have done well, each spoke of friends who did not follow the same road. Carlos went into the army because he wanted to separate himself from the path that some of his friends were taking, a path that he saw as leading to trouble. Luisa's middle-school friends had promised to graduate together but as the years went by abandoned the idea. One of the last times I talked with Miguel, he was, at the request of his family, hosting a cousin who had been in jail for dealing drugs. He hoped to help his cousin start again on a legitimate path. Miguel was happy to do so, but worried that his cousin might get him into trouble. Miguel explained that he can understand why people enter the drug trade. They want the things that he wanted as a youngster, the things that a consumer culture pressures people to have, but they do not have access to legitimate means to get them.

These four people—Alejandra, Luisa, Carlos, and Miguel—are remarkable individuals, but they needed all the breaks they either got or created for themselves to finish high school. Their stories show how the lives of minority working-class youth are precarious and how the difference between making it into the mainstream—even in its lower ranks—or being marginalized depends on chance encounters with institutional agents. They show that the worlds of the working class and the "underclass" are not separated but intertwined. Improving the living conditions and mobility opportunities of the former would also reduce the ranks of the latter.

Claudia's story further illustrates this point. Claudia was twenty-eight when I interviewed her and was born and grew up in the Providence area. Her mother is Dominican and her father South American. She grew up with her mother, who did all sorts of work, from manufacturing jobs to hairdressing, whatever was available. Claudia also grew up working. Her mother was very strict, would not let her go out, and said she needed to come home immediately after school. At home, Claudia would work putting jewelry a contractor would bring to them into boxes, a form of putting out work in the jewelry industry.

In spite of her mother's tight control, at eighteen she got pregnant, left school, and was married. She describes her husband as an American, that is, white. Her daughters have very light skin and she has dark. When she goes to parent-teachers meetings, people don't quite believe that she is their mother. She described her husband as very controlling. He would not let her go out and did not want anything that had to do with Latinos in their home. "I could not cook Latino food, I could not speak Spanish, I could not play music. I don't know why he married me. . . . I am Latina." After three years, they separated.

Claudia was then twenty-one, with a baby in tow and pregnant again. She was frightened and did not know what to do. Her mother suggested that she go on welfare. Claudia did not like the idea but applied for it: "My mom said 'go on welfare, don't worry about it, you have a child,' I did not want to be on welfare for the rest of my life. I wanted to be like my uncle—he owns his own business."

At this point Claudia's story shows again the importance of encounters with institutional agents in creating opportunities. At the welfare office, by chance, she met an organizer for a local nonprofit that advocates for low-income families. As a result of that encounter, Claudia became a community activist and organizer. She got a GED and currently works as a secretary in an office, and she also volunteers several hours a week doing outreach for the organization she joined. When she volunteers she takes her girls with her so that they can learn about involvement in the community. Because she has appeared in many public forums as an advocate for the poor, people recognize Claudia. She has also been an advocate against domestic violence, something she learned to fight in her own life.

The organization she joined also registered her to vote and inspired her interest in politics. Part of her volunteer work now is to organize people to go to the state house when issues that affect poor families are being discussed. "I always felt there always been an issue with low-income families trying to struggle to get ahead. And they aren't being heard, they were scared some of them. Some Latinos they wouldn't go . . . to [not] bother them [elected officials], and I tell them 'you can go bother them, that is what they are there for, knock on their door.'" She also started voting regularly. Claudia hopes to be able to go to law school, in part to make her mother proud, and one day she hopes to run for office.

Claudia was a teenage mother, a school dropout, and a female head of household—some of the elements often considered the "social pathologies" of the "underclass." Yet a lucky break, a chance encounter with an organization that provided her with a meaningful alternative, changed her life. Claudia's story underscores the relevance of networks and the importance of not giving up on people. In saying this I do not mean to imply that these issues are not a problem. Teenage motherhood is a serious issue. Dominican parents are very worried about this and try to educate and control their children so they don't become teenage parents. Dominicans I interviewed—like the public in general—would like to see the rates of teenage pregnancy decline. Claudia's story suggests, however, that stigmatization is not a good way to address the predicament of teenage mothers. Claudia was afraid, not knowing where to turn or how to go on welfare, yet once an opportunity presented itself she was able to find a direction for her life. She is a single mother and perhaps she has less income and education than she might have had, had she not been a teenage mother. The point, though, is that with guidance and support—in this as in many cases, the result of a chance encounter—she became an independent provider for her family and a person deeply and constructively active in the community.

HIGHWAYS AND POTHOLES

In this chapter I focus on people who have done moderately well rather than on those on the margins of society to better describe the hard structural barriers that second-generation Dominicans encounter in their attempt to enter the mainstream of American life. I want to emphasize the difficult hurdles those who enter the mainstream face rather than those of marginality. The class origin of these five youngsters affected their school experiences. Alejandra's parents, Carlos's and Claudia's mothers, and Miguel's stepfather were factory workers. Luisa's mother worked odd jobs raising her kids. Miguel's mother worked as a secretary. Yet, all five managed to improve their class position.

To be sure, not all have done equally well. Alejandra went on to college, got a master's degree, and is working in a managerial position in the public sector. Luisa is studying toward an associate's degree in human services and when she finishes will be a skilled employee in the service sector. This is also the case for Claudia, whose mother was a factory worker. Luisa, Carlos, and Claudia are within the better off segments of the service working class. They acquired skills to help them find jobs with some control over their work, relatively decent pay, and perhaps even benefits. Alejandra did better in securing a managerial job in the public sector. Miguel will most likely become a teacher or an education professional.

The stories of these five shed light on the mechanisms that create the bifurcation of class trajectories characteristic of stratified ethnoracial incorporation. Extending Stanton-Salazar's image of social highways to describe the social networks of middle-class kids, those of working-class children of immigrants resemble a secondary road full of potholes and detours. It is still possible to travel through them, as these five stories show, but it is much more difficult, dangerous, and discouraging than the highway. This is not a chance pattern but the result of institutional arrangements that, in turn, are the result of societal choices expressed through the political system.

Parts of the existing institutional settings that the second generation encounters are the consequences of the political mobilization of minorities. The authors of *Inheriting the City* pointed out how the second generation in New York benefits from institutions originally developed during the civil rights movement to help African Americans. The children of immigrants have benefited from programs to promote diversity in the universities, both in admissions and in the curriculum, as well as from access to unions and the presence of ethnic-based professional associations (Kasinitz et al. 2008). Alejandra found such a program at the University of Rhode Island. Luisa could build a program that catered to the needs of minorities in her high school. The civil rights movement created an institutional climate in which the demands of immigrant groups are seen as legitimate claims. As a result, when immigrants started to arrive in large numbers, the political system of the state was responsive to some of their demands, in terms of creating programs to address their needs. Yet, institutionally there is still a long way to go. The stories narrated in this chapter, for example, show that teachers and administrators of all ethnic and racial groups can make a difference, certainly in the lives of Dominican youngsters. They also show, however, that the kind of relationship that can make a difference is easier with teachers and administrators who share a common cultural background and experience in American society. It is important to remember in this context the low proportion of Latino teachers and administrators in the public school system.

Ultimately, the experiences of Alejandra, Luisa, Carlos, Miguel, and Claudia reflect social and political decisions about the place of urban education in the national and state priorities. The civil rights movement opened many avenues for mobility and claim making, but, as William Julius Wilson argued, it compromised on the topic of equality of economic opportunities (1978). Changing this situation is not only a matter of designing appropriate policies of school reform but also a matter of fundamental political choices about the collection and use of public funds. The design of good policies and their proper implementation is of course necessary, but policy always follows politics, it cannot substitute it.

A cursory visit to the public schools of wealthy suburbs or small towns shows that there are excellent public schools in this country. This is well known by every family that moves to a different school district so that their children can attend better schools. The know-how of building first-rate public schools is there for everyone to see. Why is it so difficult, then, to do it in poor cities where the children of immigrants and minorities are concentrated? Similarly, easing the difficult hurdles of entering the mainstream is related to decisions concerning the compensation that people can obtain for their work. If working-class parents can afford an acceptable standard of living and access to health insurance with an eight-hour day, they will have more time and more energy to control and help their children.

CHAPTER 5

Upward Mobility?

In addressing two questions, this chapter deepens the analysis of the ways in which class and race shape the Dominican experience of incorporation. The first question concerns the patterns of intergenerational class mobility among second-generation Dominicans. The second focuses on Dominican views of American society, whether and how different class strata vary in their understanding of the Dominican experience in the United States. The two questions illuminate the ways in which structural ethnoracial incorporation affect the opportunities and views of Dominicans in Providence.

HOW MANY CLASSES?

Most Americans—with the exception of the very rich and the very poor—think of themselves as being part of a vast middle class defined by access to mass consumption. This popular understanding hides the fact that the middle class so defined encompasses different levels of socioeconomic status, diverse lifestyles, and indeed, different degrees of access to mass consumption. Therefore, before starting the analysis of intergenerational class mobility, it is necessary to make a short theoretical detour to present a model of the class structure of American society. This book adopts an occupations-based definition: class is seen as a position in a system of social relations organized around the production and distribution of goods and services.[1] It is the position a person occupies in the system of production and distribution of goods that determines income, social status, and opportunities opened to the next generation (Breen 2005; Erikson and Goldthorpe 1992; Wright 2005b). Furthermore, it is structural changes in the organization of production that lead to widespread upward mobility—such as that experienced by the children or grandchildren of European immigrants after World War II (Perlmann and Waldinger 1997)—or pervasive downward mobility—such as that experienced by parts of the African American community as a result of the deindustrialization of the Northeast and Midwest in the 1970s and 1980s (Wilson 1996).

An occupations-based definition of class, however, does not in itself indicate how many and what classes there are. Scholars agree that the system of class positions can be divided different ways depending on the question one wishes to answer (Wright 2005a). For this analysis, I adopt a modified version of the class classification model developed by the British sociologist John Goldthorpe and his collaborators (Erikson and Goldthorpe 1992; Goldthorpe and McKnight 2004; Goldthorpe, Lewellyn, and Payne 1987). This model is constructed around the forms of regulating labor characteristic of different sets of occupations. Goldthorpe and McKnight distinguished two main types of employment relationship: service relationships and labor contracts. They defined service relationships as "a contractual exchange of a relative long term and diffuse kind in which compensations for service to the employing organization comprises a salary and various perquisites and also important prospective elements—salary increments, expectations of continuity of employment (or at least of employability) and promotion and career opportunities" (2004, 5). Labor contracts are defined as "an approximation to a simple if recurrent spot contract for the purchase of a quantity of labor on a piece- or time-rate basis" (Goldthorpe and McKnight 2004, 5).[2] Different forms of employment relationship are related to very different working and living experiences (Breen 2005).[3] Each form determines different levels of authority and autonomy at work and also different levels of remunerations and benefits. On the one hand are people who command resources, power, and a certain degree of autonomy in their work. On the other are people who experience daily work as a form of subordination.

Using the type of employment relationship as a classificatory principle, Goldthorpe developed a model based on seven classes.[4] The upper stratum, which he calls the salariat, includes two classes. Class I—Goldthorpe uses Roman numerals to designate classes—includes higher-grade professionals, administrators, and managers, who experience the most developed form of service relationship. Class II includes lower-grade professionals and administrators, supervisors of nonmanual employees, and higher-grade technicians. Class II employment is also through service relationships, but in this group the latter may include forms of monitoring and/or lesser levels of compensation or prospective elements. The lowest stratum of Goldthorpe's model is the blue-collar working class. Two classes constitute this stratum: Class VI includes skilled manual workers in all branches of industry and class VII includes all manual workers in industry in semiskilled and unskilled grades. Employment in this group is generally regulated by labor contracts that establish the specific duties that the worker is expected to fulfill and the level of remuneration that the worker will receive.

Between the salariat and the blue-collar working class is an intermediate stratum of three classes. These classes work in conditions that combine, in different degrees, service relationships and labor contracts.

Class III includes employees in routine nonmanual positions: clerical, sales, and personal-service jobs. In a more detailed class scheme, Goldthorpe differentiates between high grade and low grade routine nonmanual occupations (classes IIIa and IIIb). The difference is that people in class IIIa enjoy more autonomy at work and higher remunerations. Those in IIIb have working conditions closer to those of the blue collar working class—in other words, more routine and easily monitored jobs and lower salaries.

Second-generation Dominicans are concentrated in class III. As shown in chapter 3, about half of second-generation Dominicans in Providence work in service and sales and office occupations. In New York City, the proportion is 54 percent, and nationwide it is 50.5 percent. This does not mean that the majority of the second generation is part of the middle class. On the contrary, some of the jobs with lowest pay are in the service sector, where unions are focusing much of their organizing efforts. Class III service sector workers constitute in fact the new working class in postindustrial societies (such as the United States). From this perspective, class IIIa is the new skilled working class and class IIIb is the new unskilled working class. Some of the people in the services working class, mostly those in class IIIa, indeed have incomes and consumption capacities that allow them to think of themselves as part of the large and amorphous American middle class. Others would be considered part of the lower middle class. Those in class IIIb would often be considered part of the working poor.

Class IV includes small proprietors and the self-employed, the proverbial petite bourgeoisie. This group enjoys autonomy at work, given the self-employment, and in that sense its work experience is closer to the salariat. But small business owners and self-employed people often experience high instability in terms of income and employment and do not typically have the prospective elements involved in the service relationship. Class V includes supervisors of manual workers and lower-grade technicians. Employment among this group is regulated by labor contracts, but class V workers have a certain degree of flexibility and authority in the workplace and incomes higher than blue-collar workers.

Mobility between these classes does not necessarily indicate upward mobility. It is clear that moving from the blue-collar working class (classes VI and VII) or from the services working class (classes IIIa and IIIb) to the salariat constitutes upward mobility in terms of working conditions, remuneration, and possibilities of a career. But it is not clear whether moving, for example, from class VI—skilled blue-collar workers—to class IIIb—routine nonmanual occupations—should be considered upward, lateral, or downward mobility.

INTERGENERATIONAL CLASS MOBILITY

Equipped with a model of class stratification, we can now revisit the trajectories of the young Dominicans whose stories were told in the previous chapter. Carlos's mother was a factory worker—class VII (unskilled manual workers)— and Carlos is a supervisor in a cable company—class V (lower-grade technicians and supervisors of manual workers). Alejandra's parents were factory workers—class VII—and she is in public administration, making her part of class II (the lower salariat). When Luisa was growing up, her mother did all sorts of jobs that put her in classes VII and IIIb, although by the time I interviewed her she was an executive secretary for a nonprofit, making her part of class IIIa. Luisa also was on her way to a professional associate's degree, which will put her in class IIIa as well. Claudia's mother was a factory worker— class VII—and Claudia was an organizer for a nonprofit organization—class IIIa. All these cases show a measure of upward mobility, but for Carlos, Luisa, and Claudia it was mobility from unskilled manufacturing or services to the new skilled services working class.

The survey of first- and second-generation Dominicans provides a further opportunity to explore the patterns of intergenerational class mobility in Providence. The survey included several questions about the current occupation of the respondents.[5] It also asked about the composition of the respondents' households when they were sixteen years old and about the employment of each of the household members at that point in time. This information makes it possible to construct mobility tables comparing the class of origin— the class of the respondent's household at age sixteen—and the current class of the respondent. To do so, I codified, using Goldthorpe's class scheme, the occupational information of the respondent and of the adult members of the household at sixteen years of age.[6]

The following analysis assumes that respondents remember from when they were sixteen years old what their parents' jobs were—as opposed to their parents' income, which they probably did not know. The analysis also assumes that the occupation of the parents—or whoever respondents happened to be living with—at the time is relevant to understanding the conditions under which a person encounters the institutions that facilitate or hinder mobility. This is indeed what the life histories presented in chapter 4 show.[7]

Given the small sample size, I use a reduced class model that divides the respondents and their households of origin into three classes.[8] The first includes the lower salariat and the petite bourgeoisie (classes II and IV). This is the same scheme I used in chapter 3 to estimate the size of the middle-class occupational stratum among Dominicans in Providence and nationwide.[9] These two classes have in common a measure of autonomy and authority in their work. In the sample, Dominicans who are part of the salariat work in jobs that locate them in class II, the lower level. Occupations in this class include teachers, registered nurses, social workers, program directors at non-profit organizations or the state, lower-level managers in the private or public sector, and human services professionals.

Goldthorpe considered class IV an intermediate ranking. But in the United States in general and in the immigrant experience in particular, to be able to own a business—even if it is a small business—is a mark of upward mobility. Ownership of small businesses has been made the cornerstone of the success of some immigrant groups (Light and Gold 2000; Portes and Bach 1985; Zhou 1992). For these reasons, I included the petite bourgeoisie at the upper level of the class stratification model used here. It is important to remember, though, that these two classes are not at the top of the American class structure. People in class II are part of the lower levels of managerial and professional positions, which means that they are subject to supervision and that their income is not very high, and people in class IV are part of the most economically unstable ranks of entrepreneurial activities.

The second class is composed of people in routine nonmanual occupations—class III, the services working class. This includes a wide variety of jobs with different qualifications and working conditions, ranging from cashiers and sales persons to certified nurse assistants. In a more detailed analysis, I divide this group into high- and low-grade routine nonmanual activities (Goldthorpe's classes IIIa and IIIb). The third class in the analysis is the blue-collar working class. This includes classes V, VI, and VII. The working conditions of these groups are of course different, ranging from supervisors in class V to unskilled workers in class VII. Ideally class V should be analyzed separately, but there were not enough cases in the sample to do so.[10] In addition to these three classes, the analysis includes students and people who are not working.[11]

The sample is divided into two generations. The second includes all respondents who were born in the United States or arrived at age five or younger. The latter are usually considered part of the 1.5 generation, that is, those who are born abroad but spend their formative years in the country of reception. It would have been better to analyze this group separately, but the low number of cases makes this impossible. The reason to choose five years of age as the dividing line between the first and second generation is that people who arrive at that age or less go through every stage of the American educational system. Their formal education and the making of their worldviews takes place fully in the United States.

Table 5.1 presents the class stratification of the sample by generation. A comparison of the survey results with the census data presented in chapter 3 shows that the proportion of the first generation in the blue-collar working class in the survey is lower than in the Dominican population in Providence. On the other hand, the proportion in the salariat and petite bourgeoisie is higher than in the survey. In the survey, 11.5 percent of the Dominican first generation work in manufacturing occupations and 29.5 percent work in lower salariat or are self-employed. The census data presented in chapter 3 show that 46.4 percent of the first generation work in manufacturing and only 14.8 percent are in middle-class occupations.

On the other hand, table 5.2 shows that the occupational distribution of the second-generation respondents who are twenty-four or older is similar to that found in the census data (presented in tables 3.2 and 3.5): 34.1 percent in the survey and 38.6 percent in the census work in class II occupations or in self-employment; 45.2 percent in the survey and 50 percent in the census are part of the services working class. Table 5.2 disaggregates the occupational

Table 5.1   Class Position

Class	Generation		Total
	First	Second*	
Lower salariat, petite bourgeoisie	18	18	35
	(29.5)	(15.0)	(19.4)
Services working class	24	51	76
	(39.3)	(42.5)	(41.7)
Manufacturing working class	7	4	11
	(11.5)	(3.3)	(6.1)
Students	6	34	40
	(9.8)	(28.3)	(22.2)
Unemployed, welfare	3	5	8
	(4.9)	(4.2)	(4.4)
Not working	3	8	11
	(4.9)	(6.7)	(6.1)
Total	61	120	180
	(100.0)	(100.0)	(100.0)

Source: Author's compilation based on survey of first- and second-generation Dominicans.
Note: Percentages in parentheses.
* Includes people who arrived in the United States at age five or younger.

data by gender, showing a larger proportion of men than women in the salariat and the reverse in the services working class. Chapter 3 shows the opposite. In Providence, the percentage of women in managerial occupations is larger than that of men. Yet in the survey women constitute a larger proportion among the students. Because access to higher education is the path of access to salariat occupations, the larger presence of women among the students brings the survey closer to the Providence gender occupational structure.

Table 5.3 throws light on the patterns of mobility of the second generation.[12] The table shows the class of origin and current class of second-generation Dominicans who are twenty-four years old or older.[13] Overall, the data show three main intergenerational movements. The first is a moderate upward mobility trend from working-class positions to the lower salariat. The second is a smaller downward trend from the petite bourgeoisie to the service working class. The third is a large movement from the manufacturing to the service working class.

Table 5.2 Class Position, Second Generation

Class	All Second Generation*		Twenty-four and Older		
	Women	Men	Women	Men	Total
Lower salariat, petite bourgeoisie	8 (10.4)	10 (23.2)	6 (24.0)	9 (47.4)	15 (34.1)
Services working class	36 (48.6)	15 (34.8)	12 (48.0)	8 (42.1)	20 (45.5)
Manufacturing working class	1 (1.3)	3 (6.9)	0 (0.0)	2 (10.5)	2 (4.5)
Students	24 (31.2)	10 (23.2)	3 (12.0)	0 (0.0)	3 (6.8)
Unemployed, welfare	3 (3.9)	2 (4.6)	1 (4.0)	0 (0.0)	1 (2.3)
Not in labor force	5 (6.5)	3 (6.9)	3 (12.0)	0 (0.0)	3 (6.8)
Total	77 (100.0)	43 (100.0)	25 (100.0)	19 (100.0)	44 (100.0)

Source: Author's compilation based on survey of first- and second-generation Dominicans.
Note: Percentages in parenthesis.
* Includes those who arrived in the United States at age five or younger.

Looking at the class of origin of the second generation in the sample, we can see that the modal class of origin is the manufacturing working class (38.1 percent). Yet, there is an important proportion, however, 33.3 percent, whose parents are in the lower salariat and the petite bourgeoisie. Of the fourteen people in this group, half of the parents' households are in the lower salariat and half are in the petite bourgeoisie. The second generation in this sample, then, has a higher class origin than the Providence second generation. As shown in chapter 3, in Providence only 14.8 percent of the first generation is in managerial, administrative, or professional positions or in self-employment.

The lower salariat and petite bourgeoisie encompass 35.7 percent of the second generation (this proportion rises to 41 percent if we consider only those who are working). Half of these have an origin in lower classes. Indeed, one-third of the people with a manufacturing working-class origin, such as Alejandra in the previous chapter, move up into the lower salariat. On the other hand, one-third of those with a lower salariat or petite bourgeoisie origin move downward into

Table 5.3 Class of Respondent by Class of Household of Origin

	Class of Respondent					
	Lower Salariat, Petite Bourgeoisie	Services Working Class	Manufacturing Working Class	Students	Not Working	Total
Class of origin						
Lower salariat, petite bourgeoisie	7 (50.0)	5 (35.7)	0 (0.0)	2 (14.3)	0 (0.0)	14 (33.3)
Services working class	1 (20.0)	2 (40.0)	0 (0.0)	0 (0.0)	2 (40.0)	5 (11.9)
Manufacturing working class	5 (31.3)	8 (50.0)	1 (6.3)	1 (6.3)	1 (6.3)	16 (38.1)
Not working	2 (28.6)	4 (57.1)	1 (14.3)	0 (0.0)	0 (0.0)	7 (16.7)
Total	15 (35.7)	19 (45.2)	2 (4.8)	3 (7.1)	3 (7.1)	42 (100.0)

Source: Author's compilation based on survey of first- and second-generation Dominicans.
Note: Percentages in parentheses.

Table 5.4   Class of Origin of Services Working Class

	Low Routine Nonmanual Occupations	High Routine Nonmanual Occupations	Total
Lower salariat, petite bourgeoisie	2 (20.0)	3 (33.3)	5 (26.3)
Services working class	2 (20.0)	0 (0.0)	2 (10.5)
Manufacturing working class	3 (30.0)	5 (55.6)	8 (42.1)
Not working	3 (30.0)	1 (11.1)	4 (21.1)
Total	10 (100.0)	9 (100.0)	19 (100.0)

Source: Author's compilation based on survey of first- and second-generation Dominicans.
Note: Percentages in parentheses.

the services working class. Upward mobility in the sample is larger than downward, but both trends are present. The largest group in the second-generation sample—as in the census data presented in chapter 3—is the services working class. This group comprises 45.2 percent of the sample (a proportion that is somehow smaller than the percentage of second generation service workers found in the census). The table shows that the most common form of intergenerational transition is from the manufacturing to the service working class. One-half of the people with a manufacturing working-class origin are in that group. This is what we saw with Luisa, Carlos, and Claudia in chapter 4.

Because class III is the modal group in the sample, as well as in the Dominican population generally, we ought to look at it in more detail. Table 5.4 presents a decomposition of this group into higher and lower routine nonmanual occupations (Goldthorpe's classes IIIa and IIIb) as well as their classes of origin. It is interesting to note that the class of origin for those in class IIIa is for the most part the manufacturing working class, but for those in class IIIb is quite evenly spread out among all classes, including the lower salariat and the petite bourgeoisie. A closer look at those who experienced downward mobility shows that their class origin is in the petite bourgeoisie (Goldthorpe's class IV). In other words, the parents of those who experienced downward mobility were self-

Table 5.5   Class Origin of Second-Generation Students

	Community College	Four-Year College	Total
Lower salariat,	2	7	9
petite bourgeoisie	(40.0)	(31.8)	(33.3)
Services working class	1	5	6
	(20.0)	(22.7)	(22.2)
Manufacturing	1	9	10
working class	(20.0)	(40.9)	(37.0)
Not working	1	1	2
	(20.0)	(4.5)	(7.4)
Total	5	22	27
	(100.0)	(100.0)	(100.0)

Source: Author's compilation based on survey of first- and second-generation Dominicans.
Note: Percentages in parentheses.

employed or small business owners. It seems that the difficulty in reproducing the social position is in this class, rather than in the lower salariat.

Given the importance of accessing higher education for social mobility, students are another group of interest. Table 5.5 shows the class origin of second-generation students by the type of college they are attending. Twenty-two are in four-year institutions, five are in community colleges, and six are finishing high school.[14] Among those in four-year colleges, fewer than 30 percent are children of parents in the salariat or petite bourgeoisie class. That is, at least in this sample, most students in four-year colleges have a working-class origin, whether in manufacturing (40.9 percent) or services (22.7 percent). These numbers suggest a process of upward mobility, because studying in a four-year college is an avenue to the professions. The data from the survey indicate that in spite of the difficulties described in chapter 4, many working-class youth are making it to college—the cases of Alejandra or Miguel, described in chapter 3, illustrate this trend.

This analysis suggests a great deal of fluidity in class positions between the first and second generations. Even though the point of incorporation of the first generation is at the bottom of the class structure, upward mobility in the second generation is significant. This mobility comes through entering mainstream institutions and occupations, not through an ethnic enclave. At the same time, the findings indicate that most of the Dominican second generation finds itself in the ranks of the services working class. These results fit the analysis of the Dominican position in the Providence occupational structure conducted in chapter 2. This overall picture also fits the findings of Bean and Stevens concerning the transition between the Mexican American first and second generations (2003) as well as those of Kasinitz and his colleagues concerning second generations in New York City (2008).

CLASS POSITION AND VIEWS OF AMERICAN SOCIETY

What is the relationship between the class position of first- and second-generation Dominicans and their perspectives on American society? The survey and the qualitative interviews allow us to examine the views of Dominicans on three aspects of life in America: language preferences, perceptions of discrimination, and views concerning opportunities for minorities in the United States. Assimilation theory expects incorporation into the American mainstream to be accompanied by acculturation and a favorable outlook on American life. Proponents of segmented assimilation, on the other hand, argue that selective acculturation—that is, adopting certain elements of American culture while keeping an attachment to the parents' culture and identity—may be the most effective way to make it in America. Yet selective acculturation should also lead to a positive view of life in American society. The available evidence, however, shows that among immigrants and minorities, the middle class has a more critical view of American society than the poor (Hochschild 1995; Kasinitz et al. 2008; Wilson 2001). The analysis that follows shows that this is also the case among first- and second-generation Dominicans.

Language Preferences

Language has become a contentious issue in immigration debates. Nativists argue that the position of English as the common language of the United States is in danger and they mobilize to promote the adoption of English-only legislation. The analysis of the everyday experience of immigrants, however, reveals a more sober reality. Table 5.6 presents the survey data on language preference by generation and class. Because of the small number of cases in the survey, for this analysis—and for the analyses conducted in the second part of the book— I combine those respondents in the manufacturing and in the services working class. The survey question was "what language do you prefer to speak most of the time?" A majority of the first generation—half of the sample—prefers to

Table 5.6   Language Preference

	Second Generation			First Generation		
	English	Spanish	Both	English	Spanish	Both
Lower salariat	12	2	4	1	10	7
and petite	(66.7)	(11.1)	(22.2)	(5.6)	(55.6)	(38.9)
bourgeoisie						
Working class	19	6	29	5	12	14
(service and	(35.2)	(11.1)	(53.7)	(16.1)	(38.7)	(45.2)
manufacturing)						
Students	17	2	15	1	1	4
	(50.0)	(5.9)	(44.1)	(16.7)	(16.7)	(66.7)
Not working	4	3	6	0	6	0
	(30.8)	(23.1)	(46.2)	(10.0)	(100.0)	(10.0)
Total	52	13	54	7	29	25
	(43.7)	(10.9)	(45.4)	(11.1)	(47.5)	(39.7)

Source: Author's compilation based on survey of first- and second-generation Dominicans.
Note: Percentages in parentheses.

speak in Spanish most of the time, but a large group—almost 40 percent—expresses a preference to speak in both languages. The pattern of answers for the second generation is bimodal. Close to half of the respondents prefer to speak English most of the time and a similar percentage prefers to speak both languages. Only a tiny minority prefer to speak Spanish. The Latino National Survey also illustrates the generational language differences. Respondents were asked if they preferred to conduct the interview in English or in Spanish. The absolute majority of the first generation, 79.8 percent, chose to answer in Spanish, whereas ten of the eleven second-generation Dominicans included in the survey, or 90.9 percent, chose to answer in English.

The qualitative interviews show that, in spite of their strong preference for bilingualism, second-generation Dominicans are more fluent in English than in Spanish.

An example is the interview with Claudia—whose story we encountered in the previous chapter—and her sister Maria (I interviewed them together). The conversation began in English. At some point in the conversation, the question of the language of the interview came up and the sisters told me that they started talking to me in English because they thought that it was more comfortable for me. When I told them that my first language is Spanish, they said that in that case it would be better to continue the interview in Spanish. From that point on, the interview continued in both languages, but the pattern of the conversation was that whenever the sisters had difficulty in finding words in Spanish—and this happened often—they turned to English and the conversation continued in English until we exhausted the particular topic of conversation and the interview switched back to Spanish. At no point during the interview did they switch to Spanish because they had difficulties finding an expression or a word in English. This was the general pattern of my interviews and conversations with second-generation Dominicans.

The interviews with Carlos and Miguel were conducted in English with brief Spanish interludes. The interview with Alejandra was in Spanish. She was born in the Dominican Republic and came to the United States at age eleven and is indeed much more fluent in Spanish than the second-generation people I interviewed. The interview with Luisa is very interesting in this context. I interviewed her together with her mother, and although both understand and speak Spanish and English, their language preferences were different. The interview was conducted in the two languages at the same time. I talked with Luisa in English, but with her mother, a first-generation Dominican, in Spanish. Similarly, the interview with State Representative Grace Diaz, who came to the United States as an adult, was conducted in Spanish. On the other hand, State Senator Juán Pichardo, who arrived in the United States at age nine, opted to conduct the interview in English. This pattern of language choices shows clearly that whenever second-generation people need to express themselves fluently and clearly, their language of choice is English.

Spanish remains an important language in the lives of second-generation Dominicans but as a marker of identity rather than as instrument of communication. When asked how she identifies, Claudia answered, "I am a Latin woman, I'm a Dominican woman, I speak Spanish." I then asked her what makes her Latina. She replied that it was her ability to speak Spanish. Having some knowledge of how to speak Spanish is a core element of identity. Second-generation Dominicans are attached to the Spanish language because it is something that defines who they are in a society that labels them as ethno-racial others. Nevertheless, their language of choice for everyday expression is English.

This emotional attachment to Spanish and the emphasis on English as the language for communication also appears in the responses of both generations of Dominicans to the Latino National Survey. Asked how important is for them that their family maintains the ability to speak Spanish, 90 percent of the first-generation and nine out of the eleven second-generation respondents answered that this was very important. At the same time, 96.7 percent of the first-generation and, again, nine out of eleven second-generation respondents answered that it is very important for everyone in the United States to learn English.[15]

The combination of a preference for English as a vehicle of communication and an emotional attachment to Spanish as an element of identity is evidence of selective acculturation. This pattern, as segmented assimilation predicts, is more developed among those who are more incorporated into the American mainstream. Table 5.6 shows that, within the second generation, those who have a higher class position are more acculturated in terms of language preference. Two-thirds of those in the lower salariat and petite bourgeoisie ranks prefer to speak English most of the time, whereas only one-third of those in working-class positions do. Among the students, a group in the process of incorporating into the American mainstream, a majority—half—also prefer to speak in English most of the time.

When asked about the language they want to use in raising their children, almost 90 percent preferred both languages. This preference cuts across classes and generations.[16] This is the kind of answer that fuels the fears of contemporary nativists. But, as shown, there is a very important generational difference in the use of Spanish in everyday life. First-generation households are Spanish-speaking. First-generation parents speak to their children in Spanish effortlessly. Second-generation parents need to make a conscious decision to speak in Spanish to their children, and are not always able to do so. This means that, in spite of the expressed preferences of second-generation respondents, the third generation will grow up in English-speaking households. This reality does not bode well for the aspiration to pass on the knowledge of Spanish beyond the second generation.

Experiences of Discrimination

The next topic I investigate is the relationship between generation, class position, and perceptions of discrimination. Table 5.7 shows that a majority of both first and second generations report experiences of discrimination, though the proportion is larger among the first generation. Asked to describe those experiences, most respondents referred to a variety of everyday encounters at work or in public places. Some pointed to well-known situations, such

Table 5.7 Experiences of Discrimination

	Lower Salariat and Petite Bourgeoisie	Working Class (Service and Manufacturing)	Students	Not Working	Total
Second generation					
Experienced discrimination due to race-ethnicity	13 (72.2)	29 (53.7)	23 (67.6)	5 (38.5)	70 (58.8)
Believe Dominicans are discriminated against in the United States	16 (88.9)	41 (75.9)	29 (85.3)	9 (75.0)	95 (80.5)
Dominicans are as discriminated against as African Americans	9 (50.0)	34 (63.0)	19 (55.9)	6 (46.2)	68 (57.1)
First generation					
Experienced discrimination due to race-ethnicity	16 (88.9)	20 (64.5)	3 (50.0)	3 (50.0)	43 (70.5)
Believe Dominicans are discriminated against in the United States	17 (94.4)	23 (76.7)	6 (100.0)	5 (83.3)	51 (85.0)
Dominicans are as discriminated against as African Americans	6 (33.0)	16 (51.6)	4 (66.7)	4 (66.7)	30 (49.2)

Source: Author's compilation based on survey of first- and second-generation Dominicans.
Note: Percentages in parentheses.

as being followed in stores or stopped by policemen in the highway for no apparent reason. Others reported bad service or being stared at in restaurants, or complained about being harassed for speaking in Spanish in public places. A few mentioned experiences that affected their position in the social structure. Respondents reported instances in which they felt passed over for employment hiring or job promotions because of their ethnicity. Asked what groups discriminated against them, a large majority of all classes and of both generations identified white Americans.

Table 5.7 shows that among both the first and the second generations, it is the lower salariat and the petite bourgeoisie—that is, those who are better off—who are more likely to report experiences of discrimination. These results suggest that the more people incorporate into the mainstream, the more they encounter racialization. Carlos's story illustrates this point. After high school, Carlos decided to join the army to stay out of trouble. After finishing his service, he moved to a city nearby Providence where there are not many Dominicans or Latinos. There he was constantly stopped by the police when he drove home: "I used to drive home every day, and I used to get stopped everyday by the same policeman, and what am I doing, where am I going, and everyday was the same answer, I'm going home, I live here, and every day I got pulled over for no reason. The only reason I could think of is being Hispanic going into a white neighborhood."

Carlos said that he was certain that the reason he was stopped was discrimination. He was certain because he has a white-looking Guatemalan friend and whenever they went places and did things together they would get different treatment. It was only when Carlos moved to a white neighborhood, that is, when he tried to live amidst the American mainstream, that he encountered discrimination. Carlos eventually got veteran plates for his car and the policeman left him alone.

A majority of the respondents believe that Dominicans as a group are discriminated against in the United States. A large majority of all class groups and generations believe that it is white Americans who discriminate against Dominicans. As with individual experiences, most who believe this are in the lower salariat and petite bourgeoisie. Table 5.7 also shows the percentage of Dominicans who relate the Dominican experience of discrimination to that of African Americans. Respondents were presented with the statement: "Dominicans are as discriminated against as African Americans."[17] The intent was to examine whether the encounter with American racialization leads to an identification of the

Dominican predicament with that of African Americans. A majority of the second generation and half of the first generation indeed see a parallel between the Dominican and the African American experiences. But in this case, the class distribution of answers is different from the one seen so far. People in working-class positions are more likely to agree with the statement than people in the lower salariat and petite bourgeoisie. Those who are more incorporated into American society are more likely to believe that Dominicans are discriminated against in the United States but less inclined to make a parallel between the Dominican experience and that of African Americans. This suggests that identification with the African American experience depends more on the recognition of occupying a common low position in the American class structure than on perceptions of individual experiences of discrimination.

Students are the exception to this pattern because they tend to identify the experience of Dominicans with that of African Americans. This is not surprising, given that students are often exposed to different forms of ethnic and racial activism in campuses and to courses on African American and Latino studies. Juana provides an example of the changes in her way of thinking produced by access to higher education. She came to the United States when she was twelve years old. Thanks to the support and encouragement of Latino teachers in her high school, she was accepted at an elite private college. Attending college socialized Juana into a new way of thinking about race. She considers it more liberal than the ideas with which she grew up.

She explained that the education she received "makes me think about race in a totally different way. I wouldn't want to classify the way I think about race as the way all Dominicans here in the United States think about race. But I think that my education has made me more open-minded about other races, and the existence of other races."

The results of the survey clearly indicate that Dominicans experience their encounter with mainstream society as one in which they are discriminated against. Of course, feeling discriminated against on a personal level, or believing that the group as a whole is discriminated against, is not in itself proof of discrimination. In fact, when asked about the frequency of instances of discrimination, only 31 percent of those who reported having experienced discrimination said that they were discriminated against often and regularly, whereas 69 percent reported only rare occasions of discrimination.[18] The low percentage reporting having been individually discriminated against may put into question the widely shared sense that Dominicans suffer discrimination.

On the other hand, individuals may often not be aware that they are being discriminated against. An experience recalled by State Senator Juán Pichardo illustrates this point.

In 2005, Pichardo was working to introduce legislation to prevent predatory lending in the housing market. He was having a very hard time convincing other legislators of the need to pass the law. He felt, as he put it, "in many ways undermined, at some point even discriminated against." He explained it this way:

> The reason I say so is because I was aware of it. As you may know, I am also part of the military and my current position in the military is as a military equal opportunity advisor. So I went to their training and in fact prior to that training I didn't feel that I received any discriminatory actions. But when you see it, and when you are aware of it, you know that is happening to you and you have to take it in to make sure that certain things pass and live with some of them.

It was the training that he received as equal opportunity advisor in the National Guard that made Pichardo aware of instances of discrimination that he did not perceive before. Like many other Dominicans, he chooses to adapt to the situation and move on to attain his goals. Indeed, the law he was working on eventually passed as the Rhode Island Home Loan Act. But the fact that you can succeed in spite of discrimination does not eliminate its toll. What the Pichardo experience implies is that the widespread sense that Dominicans are discriminated against reported in the survey may be more rooted in individual experiences than the low frequency of reported instances of discrimination suggests.

Opportunities for Minorities

Table 5.8 presents the responses to statements concerning economic opportunities in America.[19] Most first- and second-generation Dominicans think that in the United States there is discrimination against minorities in economic opportunities and that minorities have to work twice as hard as whites to get as far. If the descriptions of experiences of discrimination often made reference to daily personal encounters, the agreement with these statements points to a critical view of the structure of opportunities in American society. Following the same pattern of answers to the previous questions on individual experiences of discrimination, the upper-class stratum in the sample—the salariat and the petite bourgeoisie—has the largest percentage of agreement

Table 5.8 Views on Economic Opportunity

	Lower Salariat and Petite Bourgeoisie	Working Class (Service and Manufacturing)	Students	Not Working	Total
Second generation					
In the United States there is discrimination against minorities in economic opportunities	18 (100.0)	48 (88.9)	30 (88.2)	10 (76.9)	106 (89.1)
Minorities in America have to work twice as hard to get to the same place	15 (83.3)	45 (83.3)	21 (61.8)	11 (84.6)	92 (77.3)
In America there are no barriers to the success of black people	1 (5.6)	11 (20.4)	15 (44.1)	0 (0.0)	27 (22.7)
Dominican Americans can do as well as white Americans	12 (66.7)	41 (75.9)	20 (58.8)	8 (61.5)	81 (68.1)
First generation					
In the United States there is discrimination against minorities in economic opportunities	16 (88.9)	26 (83.9)	3 (50.0)	5 (83.3)	50 (82.0)
Minorities in America have to work twice as hard to get to the same place	17 (94.4)	27 (87.1)	3 (50.0)	5 (83.3)	52 (85.2)
In America there are no barriers to the success of black people	3 (16.7)	8 (25.8)	2 (33.3)	2 (33.3)	15 (24.6)
Dominican Americans can do as well as white Americans	13 (72.2)	21 (67.7)	5 (83.3)	4 (66.7)	43 (70.5)

Source: Author's compilation based on survey of first- and second-generation Dominicans.
Note: Percentages in parentheses.

with these statements. Nevertheless, agreement is high across all classes. A very low percentage of the sample agrees with the statement that in America there are no barriers to the advancement of black people. The percentage of second-generation respondents who agree is lower than that of first-generation respondents, and those in higher class positions are the least likely to agree.

On the other hand, the table shows that in spite of the critical view of the American social structure suggested by the previous answers, the majority of first- and second-generation Dominicans have a positive outlook about their future. Above two-thirds of the respondents agree that Dominicans can do as well as white Americans. Interestingly, it is those in working-class positions, those who are struggling, who are most optimistic. This positive outlook is expressed also in the answers to the Latino National Survey, where 88.9 percent of the first generation and seven out of the eleven second-generation respondents agree that poor people in the United States can get ahead if they work hard. Similarly, 90 percent of the first generation and eight out of eleven second-generation respondents agree that Latinos can get ahead in the United States if they work hard. These results indicate that an optimistic view is an important component of the Dominican understanding of their experience of incorporation. This view is particularly prevalent among the working class. Whether the optimistic view is realistic is a different matter.

The analysis so far presents a consistent picture: those in the upper ranks of the Dominican class stratification are more critical of the place of Dominicans in American society than those in the working class. These findings coincide with those of political scientist Jennifer Hochschild (1995) concerning African American attitudes toward the American dream. Hochschild found that better-off blacks are critical of the tenets of the American dream and that their lower-class counterparts, in spite of their predicament, still believe in it. She argued that the critical consciousness of middle-class African Americans derives, on the one hand, from the closed opportunities they see in front of them despite their achievements and, on the other hand, from the solidarity they feel with those segments of the black community being left behind. For the poor, the belief in opportunity is a way to deal with their predicament given the absence of viable alternatives. Hochschild argued that as a result, the belief of the poor in the American dream is not very deep and often does not serve as guidance for behavior.

The findings reported here also coincide with those of the New York City second-generation study (Kasinitz et al. 2008). That study also found that middle-class blacks and the Hispanic second generation are more likely to report experiencing discrimination. The reason for this pattern is that incidents of discrimination are more likely in integrated settings and that the middle class are more likely to be part of those settings. The authors therefore concluded that the "more integrated one's life, the more likely one is to experience discrimination in a number of spheres" (Kasinitz et al. 2008, 327). On the other hand, they argued, those who experience the brunt of structural racism and live in segregated settings are less likely—except for their encounters with the police and, I would add, with the justice system—to experience everyday discrimination. This explanation fits well the findings presented in this chapter.

NARRATIVES OF INCORPORATION

The qualitative interviews add an important nuance to the analysis of how Dominicans understand their experience of incorporation. They show that Dominicans use two contradictory narratives to explain their place in American society. First- and second-generation individuals speak of themselves as both a new immigrant group on its way to making it in America and as minorities discriminated against by white Americans. The interviews suggest that Dominicans are not divided between those who embrace one discourse or the other for understanding the Dominican experience in the United States. Instead, the same individuals use the different frameworks to explain different aspects of the Dominican experience.

This is shown, for example, by Carlos in his story about being regularly stopped by police on his way home. He recognized it as an act of discrimination but added that discrimination should not stop people from achieving what they want: "I think it's yourself because if you put your mind to it, I think you should be able to accomplish anything whether the discrimination is there or not. If you want it bad enough, you should be able to get it. So does it make it harder, yes, but does it keep me from doing it, I don't think it actually keeps you from getting what you want; it's more obstacles that you have to overcome." Luisa expressed the same mind-set when she argued that "everyone comes into a situation where either they come into a racist situation, they bump into one of them, I think you're going to go through in life at least once, and I've bumped into some, but it doesn't bother me. I brush it off." Carlos and Luisa recognized the pervasiveness of racial discrimination in America's everyday life but maintain the belief that there are opportunities in America if one works hard enough.

Alejandra highlighted another aspect of this dual understanding of the position of Dominicans in American society. Asked if Dominicans are discriminated against, she answered emphatically and positively. She went on to differentiate between two types of discrimination: "Obviously, there is direct discrimination, cases in which a person of race x does not like a person of race y. But there is also indirect discrimination, which is the belief that a certain group of people, in this case Latinos, are not capable of doing certain things." The process of political organization and mobilization of Latinos in the state, a process which she was part of, however, has changed the way in which mainstream Americans view Latinos: "They look now at Latinos as a political force that contributes and I believe that it can still improve a lot." Alejandra suggested that it is the collective action of the group, rather than the individual determination to succeed, that can help overcome discrimination.

This tension between the two narratives concerning the predicament of Dominicans in the United States is best articulated by Miguel. Miguel, as described in chapter 4, was influenced by Malcolm X and Louis Farrakhan's critique of "the system." Their words provided him an explanation for his plight: growing up in poverty was not his personal failure but a result of racism in America. Miguel's critique of American society, however, did not lead him to reject the discourse of immigrants making it in American society. Instead, he argued that understanding the structural barriers that limit people is necessary to pushing them away and opening opportunities for all. His assertion expresses beautifully the ethnic ethos of making it in America:

> That's how immigrants are. I remember the Italians, the Irish, the Jews, motivated, you know. . . . If you look at Broad Street, you look at Washington Heights, it's already happening. It's a business. Bodegas, selling cars. Even the hustlers on the street; they're smart; they're not like before. . . . We wouldn't be in the United States if it wasn't for that motivation. . . . Our parents saw it, we saw it, they came here, sure, we work in a factory, we're mopping floors, but we're thinking about something bigger though, we're thinking about having a house, we're thinking about a business. I love all the small businesses. I feel so happy when I walk on Broad Street. I love Washington Heights. . . . I think instead of having one bodega, we'll have a chain of bodegas. Instead of having a rickety bus line, we'll have fleets of buses. We'll have our own Bonanza, we'll have our own Greyhound, but we have to understand the grand scheme of things; we don't have that yet. We're still too new, but I'm telling you,

ten/fifteen years from now, I'm telling you, it's going to be some serious stuff. I'm trying to get there personally. I like seeing my people make money; I like seeing them make money.

The words of Carlos, Luisa, Alejandra, and Miguel synthesize the two narratives that inform the Dominican understanding of their predicament in the United States. These contradictory and coexisting views reflect the contradictory experiences of Dominicans—and other racial-ethnic minority immigrants. On the one hand, Dominicans are racialized and experience discrimination in their everyday encounters with the American mainstream and its institutions. On the other hand, many second-generation Dominicans experience upward mobility—or know people who have experienced it—and have access to consumption levels that signify middle-class status in American society. Because in Providence there is poverty but not social isolation, the presence of successful first- and second-generation Dominicans in the neighborhood or the public sphere gives empirical plausibility to the optimistic outlook. The visibility of numerous ethnic businesses and of people who have had success in professional or managerial careers indicates the possibility of economic success. Within the same families and the same communities, some people experience upward mobility while others stay in the ranks of the services working class. This complex experience, characteristic of what I call racialized stratified incorporation, is what produces the dual frame of interpretation.

COMPLEXITIES OF INCORPORATION

The analysis conducted in this chapter shows fluidity in class mobility between the first and the second generation and a measure of intergenerational upward mobility for those whose parents are part of the manufacturing working class. Among those who are in lower salariat positions or studying in four-year colleges, the proportion of people with working-class origins is significant. At the same time, as chapter 3 shows, the main intergenerational transition is from the manufacturing to the service working class.

Overall, the findings so far do not correspond to the predictions of either assimilation or segmented assimilation theory. The former emphasizes the convergence of the children of immigrants and the white American mainstream. These three chapters of part II show that the majority of the second generation becomes part of the lower ranks of a racialized class structure. Segmented assimilation theory would predict that, given their low levels of human capital and the absence of an ethnic enclave, Dominicans will experi-ence marginalization. Yet the majority of the second generation is doing bet-ter than the first and important segments experience upward mobility into the middle class.

The evidence presented illustrates the arguments of the stratified racialized incorporation argument proposed in this book. Dominicans become part of a racialized class system that allows for some intergenerational mobility and the formation of a Dominican middle class. At the same time, their pattern of class stratification is closer to that of African Americans and other minorities than to that of whites. The analytical approach developed here emphasizes the cen-trality of the dynamics of class and racial stratification in shaping the incorpo-ration of Dominican immigrants and their children. The receiving society is more than a context for the incorporation of immigrants; it is a powerful struc-tural frame that molds the trajectories of immigrant generations.

The second part of this chapter shows that Dominicans believe that they are discriminated against and that there are barriers to the mobility of racial minori-ties in the United States. Those who have a higher class position and are more incorporated into American society have a more critical view of life in the United States. Yet a majority of Dominicans of all classes and generations are optimistic about their future in the United States and see themselves as part of an ethnic group that is settling in much as previous immigrant groups did. These contradictory views are the result of the complex position and experience of Dominicans in the United States, an experience that includes at the same time mobility and marginalization, economic improvement and racialization. This nuances and contradictions also characterize the process of ethnoracial, panethnic, and transnational identity formation analyzed in the third part of this book.

PART III

Incorporation and Identity Formation

CHAPTER 6

American Identities

The identities of Dominican immigrants and their children tell us how they see their place in American society and what solidarities they forge in the process of incorporation. Moreover, as the new migration reopens old debates on national identity, cultural diversity, pluralism, and transnationalism, the study of immigrants' identities also brings to the forefront the terms in which American society thinks and speaks about itself (Foner 2005; Glazer 1993; Hattam 2004; Higham 1955; Huntington 2004).[1] The investigation of these identities is then, on the one hand, an investigation of their incorporation in American society and how they make sense of their place in it. On the other hand, it is an investigation of the patterns of categorization in American society.

In his 1964 book *Assimilation in American Life,* the sociologist Milton Gordon set identification with the mainstream as the end point of the assimilation process. His theoretical framework corresponds to the historical experience of European immigrants. These were initially seen as nonwhite, but over time were included within the boundaries of whiteness. At that point, European-based ethnicities became a matter of personal choice (Alba 1985, 1990; Waters 1990). On the other hand, research on the identity formation of minority immigrants and their children shows that their identities are shaped by the process of racial classification in the United States (Halter 1993; Waters 1999).

Building on these findings, the stratified ethnoracial incorporation approach argues that incorporation into a racialized society leads to the emergence of ethnoracial identities and groups. Yet the form, boundaries, and content of those identities and groups need to be investigated empirically. This chapter looks at the self-identification labels Dominican use and the ways in which Dominicans articulate their different identities, the meanings that they attach to them, and the relationship between identification and everyday practices. It shows that Dominican identities are formed at the intersection of the processes of acculturation and racialization.

IDENTITIES

Identity—much like class—is one of those concepts that have diverse and sometimes contradictory meanings (Brubaker 2000). Therefore, before venturing into the analysis of the ways in which Dominicans think and speak about themselves, it is necessary to specify what we mean by identity. As social psychologists Richard Ashmore, Kay Deaux, and Tracy McLaughlin-Volpe have argued, the basic block of identity is self-categorization (2004). People identify with certain labels that they then use for self-definition and self-description. These labels function as cognitive schema through which people understand themselves and those who surround them. The meanings of those identity labels are articulated in narratives about self and group. Moreover, identities are expressed in behavior that is related to the meaning a person attributes to the identity categories (Ashmore, Deaux, and McLaughlin-Volpe 2004). I find this way of thinking about identity very useful because it allows us to draw links between self-identification labels, identity narratives, and the individual and collective practices based on those labels and narratives.

Individual identities, however, are neither homogeneous nor uniform. People fill different social roles, and each of these roles potentially constitutes a potential source for identity formation. People also belong to several of the social categories used to classify individuals—such as ethnicity, race, class, gender, and sexuality—and each of these categories can be a base for identification (Deaux and Martin 2003; Sellers et al. 1998; Stryker, Serpe, and Hunt 2005). Furthermore, these categories are not discrete social positions, but overlap, creating complex intersections of identity (McCall 2005). Also, the ways of being of people—that is, their everyday relationships and practices—always transcend their ways of belonging—that is, the boundaries of the identities that they adopt (Glick-Schiller 2004; Levitt and Schiller 2004).

Individual identities are multiple and fragmented. Yet, this does not mean that they are forever shifting or constantly negotiated. At any time, the individual self has a certain structure and stability. Certain components of the multiple individual identities held by people can acquire a more important place in the definition of self because they are recognized by those with whom the person interacts. Also, people develop emotional attachments to certain components of their multiple identities and those occupy a more central position in their self-definition.[2] As a result, certain identities are more regularly invoked, and people invest time and energy in individual and collective projects related to those identities (Stryker and Serpe 1994).[3]

Those central elements of the multiple self-identities are by no means fixed or unchangeable. Those elements vary with the life cycle, with the different social positions people occupy, and with shifts in the social valuations of different identities. But the process of change in the central components of identity is often the result of major life transformations and it is sometimes accompanied by individual crisis. Migration is one of those events because the categories and narratives people used in the country of origin will not necessary be socially relevant in the country of reception. Migrants are subjected to new forms of external categorization and demands of identification from the receiving society. As a result, they need to create new definitions of self and new languages to talk about who they are individually and as a group.

In this chapter I am concerned with the formation of categorical collective identities—that is, those identities that link individuals to groups formed around broad categories of social classification. I focus on ethnoracial collective identities, as opposed to political or religious identities, which can also be very central in the lives of individuals but are not a matter of analysis here. The anthropologist Richard Jenkins identified two key characteristics of processes of formation of categorical collective identities (1997). First, collective identities are formed through related processes of external categorization and internal identification. Groups of people are seen and defined by society in particular ways. People can accept those labels, try to reject them, or challenge their meaning. This interaction between the way societies look at groups of people and the ways people deal with the external gaze is one of the sources of formation of collective identities.

The second element is that collective identity boundaries always encompass elements of similarity and diversity. Group identity always involves a claim of similarity with other members of the group. These similarities are constructed around cultural elements that define the group's boundaries and the meaning of belonging to the group. The flow of everyday experience, however, is always more complex than established group boundaries. As a result, within the boundaries of any group there is always a diversity of interpretations of the cultural meanings that define the group. In other words, there is always a potential for contestation over the content and boundaries of collective identities (Jenkins 1994, 1996, 1997).

Identities are constructed through social interaction in particular historical contexts. As such, they are subject to constant change. Yet, at any time they display what appears to be a remarkable sturdiness. People invest a great deal of emotional energy in maintaining the boundaries of the group and the meanings attached to their identity. Understanding the process through which categories of identity emerge and develop, and the way people use and understand them, allows us to address both their socially and historically constructed character and the fact that people often experience them as essential and perennial (Sokefeld 2001).

IDENTITY LABELS

Equipped with this understanding, we can take on the task of investigating identity formation among Dominican immigrants and their children. The survey included five questions aimed at capturing their identity choices. The first asked the respondents about their identity in open terms. The second was an open-ended question about ethnic identity. The third was an open-ended question about racial identity. The fourth was a closed question about racial identification that resembled the census race question but offers only three options: black, white, and other (the three answers, in fact, that Dominicans gave to the census racial question). The fifth was a closed question asking how the respondent believed that mainstream Americans perceived her or his race.[4]

Table 6.1 presents the answers to the five survey questions by generation. It shows that Dominicans use many labels to refer to themselves and that they answer differently to identity questions posed in a different way.[5] Depending on the situation—in this case, depending on how the question is asked—Dominicans make different self-identification choices. Only thirteen people, 7.3 percent of the sample, answered the five questions in a similar way. At the same time, the repertoire of answers to each question is limited, and most of them are concentrated in a few identity categories. The panethnic category Hispanic was the modal answer to all the questions for both generations.[6] The range of people who chose this answer ranges from a quarter to almost half of

Table 6.1   Identities of First- and Second-Generation Dominicans

	Second Generation					First Generation				
	General Identity	Ethnic Identity	Racial Identity (open)	Racial Identity (closed)	How Others See Self Racially	General Identity	Ethnic Identity	Racial Identity (open)	Racial Identity (closed)	How Others See Self Racially
Hispanic	35 (29.2)	42 (35.0)	42 (35.0)	55 (45.8)	35 (29.2)	16 (26.2)	30 (49.2)	25 (41.0)	29 (47.5)	24 (39.3)
Latino	12 (10.0)	14 (11.7)	8 (6.7)	8 (6.7)	9 (7.5)	9 (14.8)	8 (13.1)	8 (13.1)	7 (11.5)	6 (9.8)
Spanish	6 (5.0)	2 (1.7)	7 (5.8)	3 (2.5)	5 (4.2)	2 (3.3)	0 (0.0)	2 (3.3)	1 (1.6)	1 (1.6)
Hyphenated panethnic/ Dominican	0 (0.0)	9 (7.5)	8 (6.7)	5 (4.2)	2 (1.7)	1 (1.6)	4 (6.6)	1 (1.6)	2 (3.3)	2 (1.1)
Panethnic total*	53 (44.2)	65 (55.9)	65 (55.9)	71 (59.2)	51 (42.6)	28 (45.9)	42 (68.9)	36 (59.0)	39 (63.9)	33 (51.8)
Dominican	19 (15.8)	33 (27.5)	34 (28.3)	25 (20.8)	8 (6.7)	13 (21.3)	13 (21.3)	18 (29.5)	12 (19.7)	0 (0.0)
Dominican American	6 (5.0)	7 (5.8)	6 (5.0)	4 (3.3)	3 (2.5)	0 (0.0)	1 (1.6)	1 (1.6)	0 (0.0)	0 (0.0)
Dominican total**	25 (20.8)	40 (33.3)	40 (33.3)	29 (24.1)	11 (8.9)	13 (21.3)	14 (22.9)	19 (31.1)	12 (19.7)	

(Table continues on p. 122.)

Table 6.1 (Continued)

	Second Generation					First Generation				
	General Identity	Ethnic Identity	Racial Identity (open)	Racial Identity (closed)	How Others See Self Racially	General Identity	Ethnic Identity	Racial Identity (open)	Racial Identity (closed)	How Others See Self Racially
American	3 (2.5)	3 (2.5)	4 (3.3)	2 (1.7)	0 (0.0)	0 (0.0)	0 (0.0)	1 (1.6)	0 (0.0)	0 (0.0)
White	0 (0.0)	1 (0.8)	2 (1.7)	5 (4.2)	12 (10.0)	0 (0.0)	0 (0.0)	0 (0.0)	1 (1.6)	2 (3.3)
Black	1 (0.8)	1 (0.8)	4 (3.3)	9 (7.5)	32 (26.7)	0 (0.0)	0 (0.0)	0 (0.0)	4 (6.6)	22 (36.1)
Mixed race	1 (0.8)	0 (0.0)	3 (2.5)	3 (2.5)	4 (3.3)	0 (0.0)	0 (0.0)	2 (3.3)	3 (4.9)	2 (3.3)
Other nonracial	32 (26.7)	4 (3.3)	0 (0.0)	0 (0.0)	1 (0.8)	19 (31.1)	3 (4.9)	1 (1.6)	0 (0.0)	3 (4.9)
No answer	5 (4.1)	4 (3.3)	2 (1.7)	1 (0.8)	8 (6.7)	1 (1.6)	2 (3.2)	2 (3.3)	2 (3.3)	1 (1.6)
Total	120 (100)	120 (100)	120 (100)	120 (100)	120 (100)	61 (100)	61 (100)	61 (100)	61 (100)	61 (100)

Source: Author's compilation based on survey of first- and second-generation Dominicans.

Note: Percentages in parentheses.

*row presents sum of panethnic answers; **row presents sum of Dominican answers.

the respondents. This answer is invoked mostly in the ethnicity and the two racial identity questions, but the panethnic answers in their different forms constitute the majority of the answers given to all the identity questions.

The second-largest response to the questions on ethnic and racial identity is Dominican. This is true for both first- and second-generation respondents. Interestingly, the percentage of second-generation respondents who answer Dominican is larger than the percentage of first-generation respondents. In two instances, however, Dominican is not the second-most-frequent answer. The first is the general open-ended identity question. Hispanic was still the modal answer, but after that came nonracial or ethnic answers, a category that includes many different responses, such as hard worker, mother, educated, middle class, and more. When asked for their identity in general terms, many chose to identify in terms related to their work, their family roles, or their socioeconomic status. The second instance is the question concerning how respondents think mainstream Americans see them in terms of race. Hispanic was again the modal answer for both generations. In this case, though, again for both generations, black was a close second.

These answers suggest two important points. First, they show the presence of a structure of identity options. A number of answers repeat themselves, particularly the panethnic response. As shown in table 6.2, there is an important degree of overlap in the answers to pairs of specific questions: 55 percent of the second generation and 54.1 of the first generation give the same answer to the open-ended and closed racial identification questions; 48.3 of the second generation and 50.8 of the first generation respond similarly to the ethnic and closed racial identification questions; and 43.3 percent of the second generation and 49.2 percent of the first give similar answers to the ethnic and open-ended racial identification question. In all these cases, the answer that repeats itself the most is Hispanic. The percentage of people who give overlapping Hispanic answers to these questions is slightly higher than 50 percent of those who give that answer to either of the questions. A very large segment of the sample, 59.1 percent, responded Hispanic to either the ethnic identity or one of the racial identity questions, and 45.9 percent used Dominican in one of these three questions. An astounding majority, 85.6 percent, used one of these two labels to answer one of these three questions.

The second point that emerges from this analysis is that first- and second-generation Dominicans understand panethnicity as both an ethnic and a racial identity. Moreover, they believe they are seen by Americans as a differentiated

Table 6.2   Answers to Identity Questions

	Second Generation			First Generation		
	Open and Closed Racial Identities Similar	Ethnic and Closed Racial Identities Similar	Ethnic and Open Racial Identities Similar	Open and Closed Racial Identities Similar	Ethnic and Closed Racial Identities Similar	Ethnic and Open Racial Identities Similar
Hispanic	35	34	28	20	23	20
Percent who answered Hispanic to both questions	(55.5)	(53.9)	(50.0)	(58.8)	(63.8)	(57.1)
Percent total respondents	(19.3)	(18.8)	(15.5)	(11.0)	(12.7)	(11.0)
Dominican	16	13	17	7	6	8
Percent who answered Dominican to both questions	(37.2)	(28.8)	(34.0)	(30.4)	(31.6)	(34.7)
Percent total respondents	(8.8)	(7.2)	(9.4)	(3.9)	(3.3)	(4.4)
Total	66	58	52	33	31	30
	(55.0)	(48.3)	(43.3)	(54.1)	(50.8)	(49.2)

Source: Author's compilation based on survey of first- and second-generation Dominicans.
Note: Percentages in parentheses.

Hispanic or Latino racial group. In a previous work, I argued that the label Hispanic allows Dominicans to reproduce their own racial classification system in which they see themselves as mixed-race people (Itzigsohn, Giorguli, and Vazquez 2005). The results of the current survey, with the preponderance of Hispanic answers for ethnic and racial identity question, suggest the same thing. Dominicans use the panethnic label to establish their position within the American classification system as nonwhite and nonblack. As the stratified ethnoracial incorporation approach asserts, incorporation into a society organized around ethnic and racial categorizations results in the formation of new ethnic and racial identities.

The answers to the Latino National Survey support these two points. This survey asked respondents about their race and offered a menu of options that included the census racial categories. A large majority, 69.2 percent of the first generation and ten out of the eleven second-generation respondents identified as some other race. An additional 12.1 percent of the first generation refused to answer. The large majority of respondent who chose other or refused to respond were asked to specify their answers. The results are similar to those of the survey I conducted, 35.2 percent of the first generation responded Hispanic, 25.3 percent Latino, and 9.9 percent Dominican. Among the handful of Providence second-generation respondents, seven responded Hispanic and three responded Latino. First- and second-generation Dominicans responded Hispanic or Latino to questions concerning their racial identity. Asked specifically if Hispanics or Latinos make up a distinctive racial group, 36.7 percent of the first generation responded positively, and an additional 7.8 percent answered maybe. Nine out of the eleven second-generation respondents answered that Hispanics constitute a distinctive racial group in America.

A final point concerns the comparison of the answers to the closed racial identity question with those to the census racial question. Because the structure of the questions is similar, it is worthwhile to compare them. The answers to the census racial question for Providence, New York, Lawrence, and the United States are presented in table 6.3. There are variations in the proportions that identify with each group between the places, but the overall distribution of the answers is similar across the table. Other is the main racial choice for Dominicans in the census as it is in our survey—in the survey, the request to specify the response other yielded mainly panethnic answers. The proportion of people who answer black in the survey is slightly lower than that in the census, but the percentages are very close.

Table 6.3   Selected Responses to Racial Identity Question
             in 2000 Census

	White	Black	Other	Two or More Races
Second generation				
Providence	21.2	9.7	61.0	7.5
New York City	19.4	8.4	63.3	7.8
Lawrence	20.1	1.1	68.3	9.2
United States	24.1	8.3	59.0	9.2
First generation				
Providence	16.8	10.6	62.9	9.5
New York City	18.7	8.3	62.3	9.7
Lawrence	16.7	7.4	67.9	6.5
United States	21.7	8.2	57.5	9.2

Source: Author's compilation based on the 5 percent Public Use Microdata Sample (PUMS)
(U.S. Bureau of the Census 2000).
Note: All numbers are percentages.

The main difference between the survey and the census is in the proportion
who self-identify as white. In the Providence census answers, this proportion
is 21.2 percent for the second generation and 16.8 percent for the first. In the
survey, the proportion who self-identify as white is lower than that identifying as black. This difference may be related to who is asking the question. The
census represents mainstream society's demand for identification. In that situation, many Dominicans—probably those with lighter skins—knowing that
whiteness is the dominant category in the American system of racial classification, decide to claim it for themselves. However, when asked by Dominican
interviewers in an academic survey, very few do so.

IDENTITY STORIES

Dominicans self-identify using panethnic belonging and national origin. This
does not imply any form of essentialism or primordialism because these identities are constructed and interpreted through the process of incorporation.
This section looks more in depth at the understanding that Dominicans have
of these different labels. I rely on the qualitative interviews and my own interactions with Dominicans in Providence in my analysis. First, I look at how
they articulate the two main forms of self-identification: panethnicity and

national origin. Second, I address the meanings and narratives attached to those labels. What themes are evoked by each of these labels? What do those stories tell us about the relationship between identity choices and incorporation into American society? Finally, I examine the relationship between ways of being and ways of belonging in the experience of Dominicans in Providence.

National Origin and Panethnicity

The relationship between the national-ethnic identity—Dominican—and the panethnic one—Latino—is not an either-or one but one of complementarities. Although the survey suggests that the panethnic identity is the most used identity choice, the qualitative interviews indicate that national origin self-identification is the main anchor. I address the reasons for the diverse results between different methodologies later on. At this point, I examine the relationship between national origin and panethnicity in the identity narratives. There are two main patterns of articulating these identities. In the first, national origin serves as the main anchor of identity and panethnicity is used as a political statement in the public realm. We can see this in Alberto's explanation of his choices.

Alberto is a second-generation Dominican in his thirties. His story reflects—as do those in chapter 4—the importance of the encounter with institutional agents. In the Dominican Republic, his father was a small business owner and after migration his parents became factory workers. Manufacturing jobs allowed them to save money to send Alberto to a private Catholic school, where he did quite well. Alberto credits his school success to one of his teachers' taking an interest in him and encouraging him to continue his studies. After high school, he went to the University of Rhode Island, where he received a BA degree. He has worked for a community nonprofit agency since graduation. He is also an activist for immigrant rights, having first become an activist as a teenager in the youth group of the church he attended. Answering my question concerning his identity, he asserted: "Depends on who I am talking to, who the audience is. If my audience are government officials, I am Latino. If I am talking to a friend, I am Dominican. If I am talking to my neighbor who happens to be Caucasian, I tell him I was born in New York City and that I am also a citizen. So it depends on who I am relating to."

Alberto identifies differently in different situations and in interactions with different people. At the same time, we see a structure in his answers. He has specific answers to different situations that demand self-identification. In his personal life, with the people he is close to and cares for, he is Dominican. This is his main identification. But he is Latino when dealing with government officials. Alberto explained his identification as Latino this way: "I am trying to be in solidarity with other people, Ecuadorians or Puerto Ricans. So they see us as a group, and we are one. We are in the same boat. We are what the Irish, what the Italians were, what the Polish were. We are fighting to get the same rights that other people have."

In his words we can also see the combination of minority and ethnic narratives I described in chapter 5. He insists on defining himself as a citizen in front of his white neighbors—and it is important to note that he emphasizes his citizenship, not his being American. Alberto explained this choice: "You have people who blame immigrants, who scapegoat immigrants for being the problem. In that sense, you have to teach them a lesson and say: You know what? I am born from immigrants and I was born here. I have a job, and I contribute to society here as well so don't even start."

Alberto is cognizant of the negative images of immigrants in certain mainstream discourses, and he adopts an "in your face" attitude toward white people when he perceives that they embrace the negative views of immigrants. In those cases, in spite of being born in the United States, he emphasizes his immigrant origin and the contribution of immigrants to American society. On the other hand, he explicitly compares Dominicans and the European immigrant groups of a century ago.

A variation in this pattern of combination of identity labels is explained by Alejandra. Alejandra is one of the five young Dominicans whose stories I described in chapter 4. I discuss the identity choices of the five—Alejandra, Luisa, Miguel, Carlos, and Claudia—in this chapter. When asked about her identity, Alejandra replied that she considered herself "as a woman, first of all, Dominican and strong. A strong Dominican woman. Those are the three words I generally use to describe myself."

In Alejandra, we see the intersection of national origin and gender identities. For her, gender and national origin are tied together. Her identity choices reflect a positioning vis-à-vis American society as Dominican but also a positioning vis-à-vis American society and the Dominican community as a strong woman. As our conversation continued, Alejandra told me that she also identifies as Latina, but she established a clear difference between being Latina and being Dominican: "For me, being Dominican is a feeling, it is something concrete, something that I can sense. When I say that I am Latina, I am simply letting the other person know that I am of Latin American descent, and that I am a woman, but I don't feel anything when I say it."

The difference between Alejandra and Alberto is that Alejandra emphasized her emotional attachment to the Dominican identity much more strongly than Alberto did. This difference probably derives from the fact that Alberto was born in the United States and Alejandra in the Dominican Republic. Still, the lack of a strong emotional attachment to the panethnic identity does not preclude her from being a very active person in Latino community organizations. In fact, both are Latino activists. For Alejandra, as for Alberto, the panethnic identity is invoked in dealing with the mainstream institutions and in public life. She explained, "being Latina is like a profession that I share with many brothers from other Latin American countries . . . my Dominican identity is not necessarily in conflict with being Latina. The fact that I am 100 percent Dominican and very proud of that does not mean that I can't appear publicly as Latinoamericana. One is part of the other. Being Dominican is part of being Latina, so that when I appear in public as Latina I am still Dominican."

The second pattern of combination of national origin-ethnic and panethnic identities is one in which both are used interchangeably to talk about self and group. We see this pattern in Luis's narrative. Luis is a second-generation Dominican in his mid-twenties. When asked about his identification, he said, "I could not define my identity when I was younger, but now I identify, I do my own research. I look at my identity, and I know that I am Hispanic."

Luis's parents are small-business owners and he has three siblings, two brothers and a sister. When they first arrived in the United States, Luis's parents went to New York. Luis's father worked for a while as a janitor at one of the city's universities and his mother worked in retail stores. A few years later, they moved to Providence, where they owned several businesses that had different degrees of success.

When Luis was going from middle school to high school, his parents moved to a nearby town where the schools are better than in Providence. But because minority enrollment in the school Luis attended was increasing, the relation between some teachers and Latino students was not always smooth. Luis remembered that some of his teachers would make disparaging comments about minority students. He explained that he simply ignored the remarks because he knew that the claims were factually wrong. His understanding of the position of Dominicans in American society corresponds to the ethnic narrative described in chapter 5. Luis is the only one of those I interviewed who defined himself as Republican and said that he voted for George W. Bush. At the same time, he recognized that Dominicans are discriminated against.

Luis finished high school without much trouble and went on to get a degree in business management. The last time I talked to him, he was working at a social services nonprofit as a case manager for youth in trouble. Luis's siblings also went to college, but none had a professional job. One of his brothers is trying his luck with a small business, the other works as a sales representative, and his sister is an employee for a federal government agency.

Luis exemplifies the pattern of mixing of national-ethnic and panethnic identity labels. He identifies as Hispanic, but when I asked him to explain what he meant by that he began referring to himself as Dominican. When I pointed out this switch, he replied, "Oh, it's so different, let's stick with Dominican. . . . I guess we have different dialects and different meanings." As he continued elaborating on the differences between Dominicans and other Latino groups, I asked him whether in the face of those differences we can talk about Hispanics at all. His answer was an emphatic yes because of the common origin and he continued using national and panethnic labels interchangeably during the interview. For Luis, being Dominican is the core of his self-definition, but he sees continuity between being Dominican and being Hispanic, and used the latter term to refer also to Dominicans.

We encounter the same pattern in Claudia's answers—Claudia, like Alejandra, is one of the five stories told in chapter 4. Asked what her identity is, Claudia answered with Dominican: "Because my mother and all my family are Dominican and they struggle and get ahead and have their businesses. For me, to be Dominican is pride. . . . I don't know how to express it in words."

Claudia, like Luis, was born in the United States and is proud of being Dominican, which for her is tied to her family and their efforts to do well in the United States.

Paradoxically, she said that her mother insists in telling her that she is American because she was born in this country. Claudia, on the other hand, is adamant in identifying as Dominican because she wants to make her mother proud. Claudia also identifies as Latina. Asked to elaborate what she means by being Latina, she answered this way: "I'm a Latin woman, I'm a Dominican woman, I speak Spanish." As in Alejandra's case, gender and national origin identities are tied to each other, and as in Luis's case, national origin and panethnic identities are invoked interchangeably. Claudia, however, adds language—

specifically, speaking Spanish—as a definitional element of what being Latina means.[7] I have found this pattern of invoking both national origin and panethnicity interchangeably widespread among both first and second generations. In fact, almost half of the second generation in the survey, 49.2 percent, agrees that "Dominicans and Latinos are one and the same." A high proportion of first generation respondents, 45.9 percent, also agree.

The qualitative interviews and my own interaction with Dominicans suggest that the basic block of identification is national origin—Dominican identity—and that panethnicity, although important, does not generate the same level of emotional attachment. This seems to contradict the survey results in which Hispanic was the modal identity choice. In American everyday life, however, people learn to fill forms that often offer Hispanic or Latino—and not Dominican—as a choice. As a result, it is not surprising that, in survey-based identity questions, a large proportion choose this answer. In qualitative interviews, people have an opportunity to express better the complexities of their identity choices.[8]

Meanings and Boundaries

The second question concerns the meanings and narratives attached to national origin and panethnic identities. When asking what it means to be Dominican, a few keywords emerge. The first and most common is pride in origin. Dominican identification also elicits references to knowledge and sharing of Dominican culture. These references usually include tastes in food and music, knowledge of the history of the Dominican Republic, speaking or at least knowing Spanish, and being a people who know how to enjoy life and are welcoming to others. Another theme is attachment to family. This is sometimes articulated as having united families who care for each other and sometimes as strong families who enforce values of respect for the elderly and proper behavior.[9]

The people I interviewed sometimes mentioned negative stereotypes attached to Dominicans, but did not internalize those negative images. Alejandra put it this way: "It is an identity that although sometimes is seen by other groups in the United States as inferior. . . . Why? Well, there is always a stereotype of Dominicans, they don't know how to speak, they don't have a formal education, they are good for parties but not very good for intellectual endeavors. That is what I mean. But I have found many, many, many characteristics and traits that make me feel proud wherever I go."

Panethnic identification also elicits references to pride in origin. When asked what it means to be Latino, Luis answered: "It's pride in being Hispanic. Pride in knowing where you come from!" Panethnicity also evokes racial meanings. Alejandra responded to the question of how she believes mainstream Americans see her: "I would say African American until I speak. And from my accent they can deduce that I am Hispanic. . . . although that has been changing, because now people who are not Latinos . . . they know how to better distinguish the features."

Doris, a nineteen-year-old second-generation Dominican who self-identifies as Hispanic and Spanish spoke about what those labels mean for her. "It means to me, it means my color. . . . I don't know, and knowing Spanish, I'm Spanish. You know, if you say you're Spanish, 'oh, she looks Spanish'. . . . that's something that comes up: 'If she's a little dark, she's Spanish. If she is a little darker, she's black.'"

Doris was born in New York but when she was a young girl her mother moved to Providence in search of a quieter place. Doris explained that her mother was afraid of what Doris might end up doing if they stayed in New York City, but said that she really misses New York and visits her relatives there as much as she can. Doris went to school in a town near Providence, where she was one of a small group of Latinos. Latino students, Doris said, were discriminated against in that they were not allowed to speak in Spanish. For her last few years of high school, her family moved to Central Falls and she attended the public high school there. She has fond memories of that high school, which included students from all over Latin America who were free to express their identity as Latinos as they liked. Her family has a modest income and Doris decided that she wanted not to attend a four-year college but instead to get a degree that would allow her to get into a job—and make money—quickly. For that reason, she opted for an associate professional degree at the Community College of Rhode Island, where she is a member of a Latino student organization. In Doris's account, as in Claudia's, being a minority and speaking Spanish defined being Hispanic, a label that separates Dominicans from both whites and blacks.[10]

A minority rejects this understanding of the panethnic label. Miguel, whose story is also told in chapter 4, strongly identified as Dominican, but did not feel comfortable with the Latino label. He asserted, "If anything, I'd say, I don't know, like Afro Latino, I'd buy that. Like African Americans, I'm like, yes, Afro Latino, yes, I'll take that. Dominicans are mixed. Okay. But just to say Latino, I can't do that."

Miguel is part of a group of Dominicans who emphasize the African roots of Dominican-ness—roots that are undervalued in the official discourse of nation in the Dominican Republic. This group is small in numbers but has an important presence in the cultural production of Dominicans in the United States (Torres-Saillant and Hernández 1998).

Miguel's self-identification as Afro Latino led him to attend for a year a historic black college in the south. There he felt that he had found his place among other black young men who, like him, were working hard to improve their position in society. He could not finish his studies there because he did not have the financial means to do so, but he has good memories of the institution and the experience. Although he identifies as Afro Latino and seeks the company of other black men, he nonetheless strongly identifies as Dominican. He does independent research and writes about the Dominican migration experience and has bought land to build a house in his father's town in the Dominican Republic.

We see a different form of identification in Hector's self-definition. Hector is in his twenties, was born in the Dominican Republic, and came to the United States at the age of eight. He chooses to identify as American: "My parents were immigrants, and I am proud of that, but I have adopted American culture. I know a lot about Dominican culture, but I feel better here."

Hector grew up in a project in a working-class household, did well in school, and now attends the University of Rhode Island, where he is studying for a BA. He is a light-skin Dominican who speaks English without an accent. He is acculturated and feels comfortable within American culture. The key to his identity choice as American, however, lies in his belief that mainstream Americans do not see him as an ethnoracial other. Referring to how other people see him, he said, "sometimes Hispanic, but most people see me as American. Sometimes they are surprised that I speak Spanish. . . . It has to do with the way I look and with the way I speak English."

Most people I interviewed, however, argued that they cannot identify as American because they believe they are not seen as such. For example, Maria, Claudia's half-sister, said that although she was born here she never defines herself as American: "I never say I'm American just because people are not going to believe you are American when you have this whole Spanish look." When asked what Americans look like, she responds without hesitation, "blond hair, blue eyes."

Maria and Claudia are daughters of the same mother but different fathers from different Latin American countries. Maria's father is a factory worker and her mother worked in factories and also did all sorts of odd jobs. Maria, unlike Claudia, finished high school and went on to study at one of the city colleges. She dreams of having her own business and being a famous fashion designer. At the same time, she works as a manager in a store where she has worked since high school and volunteers in a nonprofit agency that helps low-income people. Maria defines herself as Latina because she values both her mother's and her father's origins. She is nevertheless quite attached to her Dominican heritage. She travels often to the Dominican Republic, listen to Dominican music, and hopes one day to pass the Dominican heritage to her children.

Doris has a similar understanding of who can take on American identification. She mentioned that there were American students who were members of the Latino student organization at her college. I asked what she meant by American. Her answer was "white people . . . you know, Americans, white Americans . . . I don't know . . . people who speak only English."

For Doris, being an unhyphenated American is tied to whiteness and to being a monolingual English speaker. I discussed in chapter 5 the symbolic importance of Spanish in defining Dominican and Latino identity. More than an instrument of communication, knowing Spanish becomes an element of self-definition. Maria agrees. She asserts that it is not that easy to become an unhyphenated American. To do that a person needs to forget where he or she came from, abandon his or her community, speak proper English without an accent, and not speak Spanish. Maria said that some people are able to abide by these conditions but others cannot or are not willing to do so.

Rubén Rumbaut suggested that the choice of national origin or panethnic identities indicates an unassimilatory position vis-à-vis American society (1997). I disagree. Becoming part of a society that identifies people along ethno-racial lines, Dominicans cannot choose to be simply American. In their eyes, this label is strongly associated with racial connotations, specifically, whiteness. As a result, they develop a strong ethnic identification. At the same time, they see themselves as part of American society, identify with its values, and are proud of being part of it. Maria, for example, explained that she sees being American as a privilege: "You have rights, you can vote, you can do things that you can't do in other countries, freedom of speech. It's like the law actually helps you. . . . I have a dream and I can fulfill it. You know what I mean? So being an American is like I can do all that."

Carlos, whose story is told in chapter 4, identifies as Dominican despite being born in the United States and having served in the U.S. Army for four years. "In my blood, I'm Dominican. Yes, I was born here. If you want to write down on paper, I'm American as far as [that goes], but Dominican runs in my blood."

For Carlos, being Dominican means that he is "proud to be a Latino." Like Luis and Claudia, he uses national origin and panethnic identity interchangeably. Yet he also sees himself as American. "Being American is being proud of the freedom we have. That's the big part. Being able that when you want something, you can walk out the door and it's not impossible to get it. It's just being able to do things that a lot of people just can't. . . . Here, everybody complains, but we have it so easy compared to other countries so I'm glad we have it that way, and I'm proud of that."

These themes repeat themselves in the interviews. Being American is consistently associated with the themes of rights, freedom, and opportunity. Kasinitz and his colleagues also found that second-generation New Yorkers use the term American two ways. On the one hand, they describe how they "do things the American way in contrast to how their parents do things in more ethnic and less American ways" (2008, 337). On the other, they "describe the white middle-class people they see mostly on TV but hardly ever in real life" (338).

There are two differences and one important similarity between the Providence and the New York findings. The similarity is that in both places the second generation uses the word American to refer to white people. The first difference is that I did not find any effort among the second generation to differentiate themselves from their parents through a self-description as American. I did find, though, that the second generation greatly appreciates the opportunities they find in America and are proud of being part of the American society. The second difference is that, given the different demographic composition of the population of the two cities, second-generation Dominicans in Providence do not see the white middle class mostly on television but instead in their daily lives.

In chapter 5, I showed how Dominicans use two different and seemingly contradictory discourses to explain their position in American society. On the one hand, they embrace a minority discourse that criticizes racialization and emphasizes being discriminated against. On the other, they appropriate an ethnic discourse that compares the trajectory of Dominicans with that of previous immigrant groups such as the Italians or the Irish. In this chapter, we see again a combination of two contradictory discourses. For Dominicans, the boundaries of the label American excludes them because it has a racialized meaning and refers only to whites and monolingual English speakers. At the same time, they adopt the mainstream narrative that sees American society as the embodiment of liberty and opportunity, and they feel a strong sense of belonging and pride in being American.

Ways of Being and Ways of Belonging

A final topic is the relation between the Dominican ways of belonging and ways of being, that is, between the boundaries of identity and the boundaries of everyday social life. Dominicans keep a strong symbolic attachment to their national-ethnic identity, but do the relationships and networks they build in everyday life correspond to the boundaries of group belonging? Residence, work, friendship, and family are indicators of everyday contacts. Differences between these indicators are important because place of residence and work are not always a matter of choice, whereas friendships and family are much more so. Still, these four indicators give us a sense of the Dominican ways of being in Providence.

Chapter 2 shows that Dominicans live close to other Dominicans, but they also share the urban space with Latinos generally. The maps presented in that chapter indicate that in the southern part of the city, in the area around Broad Street, Dominicans constitute between 20 and 30 percent of the population. In the same areas, the proportion of Latinos in general—including Dominicans—is slightly more than 50 percent. That is, Dominicans share their residential areas with other Latinos and other groups—whites, African Americans, and Asian Americans—that together comprise the other half of that area. Dominicans are the largest group in that part of town but by no means the majority.

In terms of work, there are an important number of Dominican businesses in Providence, particularly in the southern neighborhoods of the city, but in terms of generating employment we cannot speak of an ethnic enclave. Among survey respondents, only 8.8 percent reported having a Dominican supervisor and only 13.8 percent reported having mostly Dominican coworkers. In both cases, the modal answer was white. Dominicans work primarily in the mainstream economy, alongside other Latinos, immigrants from other parts of the worlds (mostly from West Africa and East Asia), and white ethnics (Portuguese are mentioned most often in workplace descriptions).

Dominicans live among other Dominicans, but their everyday activities lead them beyond the boundaries of the Dominican community and into contact with other Latinos, other minorities, and with white Americans. Their ways of being transcend their ways of belonging. This is a favorable situation for the formation of emergent ethnic identities, in this case, panethnic identities (Yancey, Ericksen, and Juliani 1976).[11]

Family and friendships are important anchors of Dominican life. Dominicans invest in socializing with their extended families, an important venue for Dominican identity and cultural practices. Yet the ethnic world does not encompass the full scope of Dominican relationships. Among survey respondents, 37.2 percent said that most of their friends were Dominicans, but 44.2 percent reported having friends from all groups. In the qualitative interviews, most also reported having friends from all ethnoracial groups. In the 2000 Census, half the married second-generation Dominicans in Providence were married to or cohabiting with other Dominicans. That proportion is high but also means that half of the second generation is marrying outside the group, mostly with other Latinos and with African Americans.

Interestingly, none of the people interviewed who were married to Dominicans said that they had looked for a Dominican spouse. Alberto, for example, is married to another second-generation Dominican. He admitted that it makes things easier because of shared cultural elements and because it is easier for their respective families to communicate, but he said that his marrying another Dominican was a matter of luck rather than something he had planned or sought.

Claudia's story highlights the lack of correspondence between ways of being and ways of belonging. Her mother is Dominican and her father is from another Latin American country. She is the only Latina in the office where she works. Most of her friends are Puerto Rican. Her former husband and father of two of her three children was a white American. Only the father of her third child was Dominican, and they do not live together. She volunteers for a nonprofit that advocates for low income people. Because of her volunteer work, she is recognized by many people in Providence who often approach her in the street asking for help. To avoid that, she moved to a small town where most of the population is white. In sum, her everyday interactions and social networks encompass the general population of Providence and Rhode Island. Yet, she strongly identifies as Dominican and wants to pass that identity to her children.

Claudia's situation suggests an important point. Integration into the broader networks of city life does not lead to erasure of ethnic identity. Theorists of assimilation often look at trends in intermarriage and the reduction of residential segregation as indicating a blurring of group boundaries. This chapter, however, suggests that the boundaries of a group can become blurred, in terms of the group's ways of being, without erasing the boundaries of belonging. The dynamics of cultural classification and symbolic identification have a degree of autonomy from other practices of everyday life.

INCORPORATION AND IDENTITY

The Dominican identity choices both challenge the definition of what it means to be an American and expand the societal debate over the boundaries and the conditions of group belonging. Dominicans see themselves as part of American society but cannot, or do not, claim the American label because they perceive it to refer only to white Americans. Dominican and panethnic identities emerge as the identity alternatives in the encounter with American racialization. Both identities are imbued with ethnic and racial connotations because they are forms of claiming a place in a multiethnic, multiracial, multicultural, racially stratified society.

The choice of Dominicans, and other immigrant groups, to maintain their identity differentiation has generated a nativist reaction, perhaps best articulated by Samuel Huntington's book on American identity that renews the call for Anglo-conformity as the goal of assimilation (2004). The work reflects the anxiety of a society that is seeing its own self-definition in the process of change. The stratified ethnoracial incorporation approach argues, however, that the Dominican and panethnic identities of first- and second-generation Dominicans are not a form of anti- or unassimilationist identities. They are the result of the process of becoming American.[12] Much like the West Indian immigrants that Mary Waters (1999) and Milton Vickerman (1999) described, Dominicans have to create their identities within a racialized system of ethnic classification. They have identity choices, but those choices are limited by the boundaries imposed by the mainstream's ethnoracial categories.

CHAPTER 7

Transnational Identities

Self-identification as Dominican is one of the main identity choices of first- and second-generation Dominicans in Providence. Embracing a strong ethnic identity is one of the elements in the process of incorporation into the American racialized society—a process I call stratified ethnoracial incorporation. That Dominicans choose a Dominican ethnic identity may seem rather obvious, but in itself does not tell us much about group formation. The construction of ethnicity in the context of migration always makes reference to a place of origin, but as Vivian Louie showed in her comparison of second-generation Chinese and Dominicans, the symbolic frame of reference of the group's identity can be focused mostly on the local ethnic community or oriented toward the country of origin (2006).

In this chapter, I explore the symbolic boundaries of Dominican identity, the practices linked to this identity, and the organizations that bring into being a Dominican community in Providence. The analysis focuses on the local and transnational components of the symbolic Dominican identity and the practices that it inspires. The transnational perspective has shown that migration does not entail breaking ties with the country of origin. Immigrants maintain emotional attachments with the place they came from and establish a dense web of networks that link the places of origin and reception (Basch, Glick-Schiller, and Szanton Blanc 1994; Glick-Schiller 2004; Levitt and Glick-Schiller 2004).

Moreover, transnationalism is not a new phenomenon. Transnational practices and networks were pervasive in previous waves of migration (Foner 2005).

For Dominican immigrants—as well as other immigrant minorities—transnational linkages are reinforced by the encounter with racialization (Glick-Schiller 2004; Itzigsohn and Giorguli-Saucedo 2002; Portes, Haller, and Guarnizo 2002). Yet it is not enough to assert that first- and second-generation Dominicans maintain relations with their country of origin. Variation in the forms of transnational identity and transnational engagement can be wide. It is in the forms that identities and group practices take that the agency of migrants and their children is asserted in forging a place for themselves in American society. The presence of transnational linkages presents people interested in studying migration with three important questions: First, what is the scope and intensity of transnational identities and practices among the first and the second generation? Second, what kind of community emerges out of transnational linkages? Third, what is the relationship between transnationalism and incorporation? This chapter addresses these questions.

TRANSNATIONAL COMMUNITIES AND INCORPORATION

Early research on Dominican migration already pointed to the presence and importance of ties between migrants in New York City and the Dominican Republic (Georges 1990; Grasmuck and Pessar 1991; Guarnizo 1994). Yet it is Peggy Levitt's book *Transnational Villagers* that best describes and analyzes the shape and characteristics of the Dominican transnational community (2001). Levitt studied the lives of the people from Miraflores, a small Dominican town close to the city of Bani. Mirafloreños, however, are spread out between the Dominican Republic and Jamaica Plains. The transnational community Levitt describes is crisscrossed by a number of tensions.

Levitt painted a nuanced picture of changing cultural orientations and social relations, one in which the local hierarchies and authority structures are replaced by new hierarchies and authority structures that have emerged from the migration process (2001). She showed, for example, that the flow of resources from Boston increased the resources available to the educational system in Miraflores, but at the same time transnational migration created perverse incentives for young people in Miraflores to drop out from the educational system. Social mobility is no longer linked to education, but to migration. In addition, the resources sent by emigrants and the skills they learn abroad increase their ability to negotiate with the Dominican state. But this has not led to a more transparent relationship between citizens and state authorities. Instead, the state, realizing that Mirafloreños do not depend heavily on clientelistic ties, abandons them to their own efforts. *Transnational Villagers* describes the development of a relationship of dependency between nonmigrants and their migrant kin. There is a new hierarchy of economic power and status in the transnational village, and migrants are at the top. These changes can sometimes empower the people she describes, but can also disempower them. Moreover, class also matters within the transnational community. Differential access to the benefits of transnational migration is determined in part by premigration class positions.

Levitt's work also addresses the relationship between transnationalism and incorporation. Migrants invest in transnational linkages out of their attachment to the country of origin but also as a reaction to the barriers they encountered in the process of incorporation. Levitt described how people from Miraflores see themselves as white within the racial hierarchy of the Dominican Republic, but when they come to the United States they encounter discrimination and realize that because American society is racialized they cannot become fully American. Their response is deeper attachment to Miraflores and the possibility it offers of reclaiming whiteness. The transnational effort, however, takes a toll on the migrants' ability to stabilize their economic and social position in the host country, creating tensions within the transnational community and incentives for people to concentrate their efforts in the new country. Levitt showed that at the same time that immigrants create symbolic and practical links with their country of origin, they also enter the institutions and adopt the worldviews of the receiving society. In Nina Glick Schiller's formulation, incorporation and transnationalism are simultaneous processes (2004; Levitt and Glick Schiller 2004).

The tensions and new hierarchies Levitt described are present in other transnational communities as well. Recent work on the democratizing and developmental effect of Salvadoran home town associations shows that the political intervention of migrants in their towns of origin helps break down the power of old elites and can also result in social and economic benefits for those who remain in El Salvador. At the same time, migrants and nonmigrants do not always see eye to eye. When there are differences of vision between them, it is the migrants' ideas that have the upper hand because the migrants are the ones who control the flow of resources. Also, the socioeconomic benefits of the immigrants' action are distributed unequally, in line with the preferences and social ties of those who migrated (Itzigsohn and Villacrés 2008; Waldinger, Popkin, and Magana 2008).

These works focus mainly on the transnational participation of the first generation. The recent ethnography by Robert Smith, *Mexican New York,* addresses the extent and effects of transnational practices on the second generation (2006). Smith examined the transnational life of the people of Ticuani, a small *municipio* in the Mixteca region in southern Puebla. Much like the Mirafloreños Levitt described (2001), the people from Ticuani are dispersed between Puebla and New York City. Smith argued that there is a strong participation of the second generation in transnational life, although this claim is based on estimations and not on concrete numbers.[1] He clearly showed, however, that transnational connections and activities touch the lives of first- and second-generation people from Ticuani.

Smith emphasized the importance of the life cycle in transnational participation. He asserted that children do not like very much to travel to Ticuani, but that as they grow up and reach adolescence Ticuani becomes meaningful to them. It is a place to negotiate their ethnic and gender identities. As they grow up and acquire the obligations of adults, they have less time to participate in transnational life, but still travel to Ticuani for important events such as baptizing their children, to build houses, or just to take family vacations in their place of origin. Like Levitt and Glick-Schiller before him, Smith concluded that transnationalism and incorporation are simultaneous processes. He added, though, that transnational life is not only a consequence of but is also a context for assimilation. The opportunity to assert themselves in a positive way in Ticuani can help youngsters withstand negative assimilation pressures (Smith 2006).

Smith's work also attempts to conceptualize the multiplicity of forms of transnational engagement, in which some people invest time and energy and others only participate casually. Early research adopted an expansive framework to the study of transnationalism, a framework that encompasses symbolic frames of reference and all forms of activities that link migrants to the country of origin (Basch, Glick-Schiller, and Szanton Blanc 1994). This framework proved too loose to yield understanding about the structure of transnational practices. In reaction, other scholars have proposed focusing on specific transnational practices, particularly entrepreneurial or political activities, that demand an intense and constant involvement of migrants in their countries of origin (Portes, Haller, and Guarnizo 2002). This framework, however, leaves out important aspects of the transnational lives of immigrants.

For Smith, transnational life includes those practices that regularly link migrants and their children to the home country, but is also embodied in social structures and identities in which the lives of immigrants and their children are embedded. In Smith's formulation, the intensity of involvement in transnational life is stronger than participation in voluntary associations and less strong than what he referred to as membership in natural communities. This is an interesting attempt to go beyond those who embraced a too-expansive conceptualization of transnational activities and those who proposed a too-focused approach. But Smith's formulation is vague and does not capture the different forms of transnational involvement found in different communities.

To capture the multiplicity of forms, I distinguish between a transnational symbolic framework in the construction of identities and different forms of participation in transnational activities. Among the latter, I differentiate between broad and narrow. Broad transnational activities imply "sporadic physical movement between the two countries, a low level of institutionalization, or just occasional personal involvement," whereas narrow practices "involve a regular movement within the transnational geographical field, a high level of institutionalization, or constant personal involvement" (Itzigsohn et al. 1999, 323). Examples of broad activities are sending remittances to or sporadic involvement in the life of the town or village of origin. Examples of narrow transnationalism are membership in organizations that focus their activities in the country of origin or regular involvement in business or politics there. The distinction between broad and narrow transnationalism represents a continuum of practices rather than a dichotomy and is a useful analytical tool to differentiate between migrants who engage in only occasional transnational activities and those who are more invested in transnational networks and thus constitute the backbone of the transnational social field. The distinction thus moves beyond the vagueness I identified in Smith's formulation.

The analysis in this chapter is different from Levitt's and Smith's work in that I focus only on transnational identities and practices as they take place in the United States. In fact, my analysis is from the perspective of transnationalism's relationship to incorporation and breaks down into four sections: the contemporary political context, the boundaries of identity, the transnational practices that Dominican immigrants engage in, and the constitution of an ethnic community.

TRANSNATIONAL STATE POLICIES

Transnational identities and practices are the result of the desire of immigrants to maintain ties with their country of origin and the obligations they feel toward their families there. Yet, of late, the promotion of transnational linkages has also become state policy. Analysis must therefore take the actions of the sending state into account. Smith, for example, showed that the governor of the state of Puebla has opened an office in New York to keep links with Poblano migrants and formed a special unit of the State Judicial Police to deal with public security issues. The latter include the travel of gang members from New York to Ticuani (Smith 2006).

The Dominican state has also taken a proactive policy of reaching out to the migrant community. Until the early 1990s, the Dominican government ignored the migrants and their communities. During the second half of that decade, however, it recognized both the rights of migrants to hold dual citizenship and to vote abroad. In 2004, Dominican migrants across the world were for the first time able to exercise their voting rights. These changes were in part an answer to the mobilization of migrant organizations demanding recognition and inclusion within the Dominican political community. They were also a response to political and economic developments that took place within the Dominican Republic (Itzigsohn 2000; Sagas and Molina 2004).

During the 1990s, Dominican politicians realized the importance to the national economy of securing the continuous flow of migrant remittances. Remittances are one of the main sources of foreign exchange for the country and an important subsistence mechanism for a large number of people. Dual citizenship allows migrants to keep their attachment to their place of birth and at the same time have a more stable position in the country of reception so that they can keep sending money to their country of origin.[2] At the same time, the 1990s was a period of democratization and consolidation of competitive elections in the Dominican Republic. Under these conditions, migrant communities could leverage their economic power to gain rights to which they have long aspired. The convergence of national economic dependence on the money that emigrants send home and the emergence of political competition explains the change in the Dominican state policy toward the migrant community.

In recent years, the Dominican state has taken the initiative in building transnational ties with Dominican communities abroad. It has promoted a new type of organization, the Consejos Consultivos de la Presidencia para los

Dominicanos en el Exterior (CCPDE, the Presidency's Consulting Councils for Dominicans Abroad). The goal of the CCPDE is to look for ways to integrate migrants into a national development policy. CCPDE members are volunteer community leaders and representatives. Consulting councils have been established in several locations in the United States and other countries where there is a Dominican presence.[3] The coordinator of the activities of all the consulting councils is a member of the Dominican government with the rank of secretary of state.

The Dominican government, through the CCPDE, has engaged Dominican organizations abroad in a process of popular consultation to reform the Dominican constitution. In September 2006, Leonel Fernandez, the president of the Dominican Republic, met representatives of migrant organizations at the City University of New York's City College and asked them for their feedback on two constitutional issues that affect the relationship between migrants and the Dominican state.[4] The first issue is the automatic extension of Dominican citizenship to the children of migrants. Today, the children of immigrants can claim Dominican citizenship but must do so when they reach eighteen years of age. The second issue is the creation of parliamentary representation for Dominicans abroad.[5] The Fernandez administration supports both ideas, and they will most likely become part of the new constitution.

Another transnational group, the Fundación Global Democracia y Desarrollo (FUNGLODE), was also involved in organizing the consultation with migrant organizations. FUNGLODE is a nonprofit think tank created by President Fernandez after the end of his first term in office (1996–2000). FUNGLODE created a sister organization in the United States, the Global Foundation for Democracy and Development, with offices in Washington and New York City. Both are nonprofits independent of the government, but Fernandez is the honorary president of both and the person who guides their activities. This active policy of reaching out to the migrant community is accompanied by a discourse, which Fernandez promoted, on the need to build a new understanding of the nation suitable for the circumstances of the twenty-first century. This new national imaginary embraces the migrant communities as part of a transnational Dominican nation.[6] Yet, as the following analysis indicates, the imagined transnational nation is a project that is not likely to become hegemonic in the migrant community. For all their transnational attachments, Dominican immigrants are becoming part of American society.

Table 7.1   Transnational Attitudes in Providence

	Second Generation	First Generation
Dominican Americans are part of the Dominican nation.	95 (79.2)	52 (85.2)
Dominican Americans should help the Dominican Republic.	95 (79.2)	56 (91.8)
Dominican Americans should participate in Dominican politics.	66 (55.0)	40 (65.6)
Dominican Americans are as Dominican as those who live in the Dominican Republic.	71 (59.2)	47 (77.0)

Source: Author's compilation based on survey of first- and second-generation Dominicans.
Note: Numbers represent agreement with statement. Percentages in parentheses.

THE BOUNDARIES OF DOMINICAN IDENTITY

Empirical research indicates that first- and second-generation Dominicans indeed build their ethnic identity through the use of a transnational frame of reference (Kasinitz et al. 2008; Sagas and Molina 2004; Torres-Saillant and Hernández 1998). The question remains, however, how different generations and classes differ in their understanding of the transnational boundaries of the group.

Table 7.1 illustrates the construction of symbolic transnational boundaries. The first and second rows show that a large majority of both the first and the second generation agree that Dominican migrants are part of the Dominican nation and that they should help the Dominican Republic. Not surprisingly, the proportion is higher among the first generation, but these views are also embraced by almost 80 percent of the second. The bottom rows of the table show agreement with the statements that Dominicans in the United States should participate in Dominican politics and that they are as Dominican as those who live within the Dominican Republic. The level of agreement with the second two statements, however, is considerably lower than the level of agreement with the first and second. Both generations display a strong sense of attachment and obligation toward the country of origin. At the same time, that fewer respondents agree with the statements about participation in Dominican politics and the similarity between Dominicans in the United States and in the Dominican Republic suggests a sense of differentiation within the transnational community. It also points, as Levitt suggested (2001), to limits to the transnational commitment among both the first and the second generations.

Earlier chapters of this book describe the internal class stratification within both the first and the second generations. The main form of stratification is between those who enter middle-class occupations—those in the lower salariat and the petite bourgeoisie—and those who become part of the service and manufacturing working classes. Both groups are incorporated into American society, but those who enter middle-class occupations represent the normative expectation—held by American society, by scholars who emphasize assimilation, and by immigrants themselves—regarding the incorporation trajectory of immigrants. We can say that this group is closer to the American mainstream in terms of both its structural position and accepted social expectations. Hence we can expect the identities of middle-class Dominicans to be more strongly oriented toward the United States.

Table 7.2 presents this expectation. It shows that for the first generation, transnational orientations are slightly more widespread among the working class.[7] This suggests that access to the American mainstream leads to a small decline in the transnational construction of identity. These findings provide some support for the assimilation approach: the more successful a person is in the country of reception, the less that person embraces a transnational identity. Nevertheless, transnational orientations are quite widespread within the middle class. More than two-thirds of the first-generation middle-class respondents adopt such a framework.

Furthermore, there is an exception to the pattern of a stronger transnational orientation in the working class. The middle class are more likely to agree that Dominicans should help the Dominican Republic. This agreement may be related to greater access to resources that can be used to help the country of origin. Incorporation into the middle class does seem to diminish the transnational orientation of first-generation Dominicans, but only in a matter of degree rather than as a break with the transnational frame of identity.

In the second-generation sample we found a different pattern. Transnational orientations toward helping the Dominican Republic or participating in Dominican politics are more prevalent among working-class respondents. Middle-class respondents are more likely to agree with statements that emphasize belonging to the Dominican nation. That is, those who are more integrated in the American mainstream have a stronger attachment to the transnational

Table 7.2   Transnational Attitudes by Class and Generation

	Dominican Americans Are Part of the Dominican Nation	Dominican Americans Should Help the Dominican Republic	Dominican Americans Should Participate in Dominican Politics	Dominican Americans Are as Dominican as Those Who Live in the Dominican Republic
Second generation				
Lower salariat, petite bourgeoisie	16 (88.9)	14 (77.8)	8 (44.4)	12 (66.7)
Working class	44 (81.5)	45 (83.3)	37 (68.5)	29 (53.7)
Students	26 (76.5)	24 (70.6)	15 (44.1)	21 (61.8)
Not working	9 (64.3)	12 (85.7)	6 (42.9)	9 (64.3)
First generation				
Lower salariat, petite bourgeoisie	14 (77.8)	17 (94.4)	12 (66.7)	14 (77.8)
Working class	28 (90.3)	28 (90.3)	22 (71.0)	25 (80.6)
Students	4 (66.7)	5 (83.3)	2 (33.3)	3 (50.0)
Not working	6 (100.0)	6 (100.0)	4 (66.7)	5 (83.3)

Source: Author's compilation based on survey of first- and second-generation Dominicans.
Note: Numbers represent agreement with statement. Percentages in parentheses.

symbolic elements of their Dominican identity. The students' stories reinforce this conclusion. Students are making their way into the mainstream of American society, and their pattern of agreement with the statements resembles that of middle-class Dominicans.

These results fit nicely with those presented in chapter 5, indicating that the second-generation middle class reported more incidents of discrimination and were more critical of American society than the working class. As that chapter explains, those who are more embedded in the mainstream encounter more daily experiences of discrimination. These daily encounters with discrimination and racialization lead first- and second-generation Dominicans to turn to their country of origin as a basis for a positive understanding of self. The result is the development of a transnational orientation in the building of identity. This transnational orientation is not unassimilatory but instead a response to everyday life in America.

THE PRACTICE OF TRANSNATIONALISM

I have tried to demonstrate that first- and second-generation immigrants adopt a transnational frame of reference in their understanding of Dominican identity. The approach followed in this book, however, expands the analysis of identity to include the practices built on identity labels. It is therefore necessary to explore whether adopting transnational identity frameworks also entails involvement in transnational practices. Previous research on first-generation Dominican transnationalism suggests that narrow transnational engagement is limited to a core transnational group, but that most migrants participate in broad transnational activities (Itzigsohn et al. 1999; Itzigsohn and Giorguli-Saucedo 2002). The study of New York City second generations reported in *Inheriting the City* found that second-generation Dominicans had the highest rate of transnational participation, with the highest rate of people who have lived six months or more in the country of origin, who ever sent remittances, and who visited the country of origin four times or more (Kasinitz et al. 2008).

Table 7.3 presents survey data on participation in transnational activities by first- and second-generation Dominicans in Providence. The first two columns look at the proportion of first- and second-generation respondents who send remittances or travel to the Dominican Republic, both forms of broad transnational participation. As expected, the first generation is much more engaged in these practices than the second. Slightly more than half of

Table 7.3   Transnational Practices Among Dominicans in Providence

	Second Generation	First Generation
Send remittances	28	32
	(23.3)	(52.5)
Travel to the dominican republic	87	57
	(72.5)	(93.4)
Economic transnationalism	9	13
	(7.5)	(21.3)
Social transnationalism	29	30
	(24.2)	(49.2)
Political transnationalism	3	10
	(2.5)	(16.4)
Overall transnationalism	33	37
	(27.5)	(60.7)

Source: Author's compilation based on survey of first- and second-generation Dominicans.
Note: Numbers reflect responding in practices. Percentages in parentheses.

the first generation sample sends remittances, versus slightly less than one-quarter of the second generation who do so. This, however, is quite high for people born and raised in the United States. Visits to the Dominican Republic are widespread among both generations, though not surprisingly more so among the first generation (90 percent) than among the second (70 percent).[8]

Traveling to the Dominican Republic—similar to traveling to Ticuani in the Smith account (2006)—is an important element in transnational identity formation among the second generation, but can also show the boundaries of transnational belonging. Doris's story illustrates this point. We met Doris in chapter 6. She is nineteen years old, was born in New York City, and is studying for a professional degree at the Community College of Rhode Island. She traveled to the Dominican Republic for the first time a year before I interviewed her. Her perception of life there is telling: "Ok, I was like, you know, I knew that Dominicans were a little crazy but they're very crazy over there. . . . They had speed limits, they had names [but] they do not go by that. They have their own rules, they do what they want and, ahhh, it's just . . . I don't know. It was crazy."

She says that she really liked the Dominican Republic and that after three weeks there she did not want to come home. She definitely wants to go there again, but only on vacation. She does not see herself living there. Her explanation shows well the importance and the limits of transnational belonging: "I don't know, when I went over there I would be like 'I don't see myself living here' because I speak more English than Spanish. And then all my cousins and relatives all speak English but the ones who went with us from here, New York, they knew English so we would speak English but then I would feel bad because my other cousins [could not speak it]. You know, they would make fun of us and be like, 'oh, you, you Americans.'"

Her relatives called her gringa, a term she did not like: "I was like 'I'm not a Gringa, I just speak English, so I have to speak in English.' And they were like 'yeah, but you're Dominican, you're supposed to know how to speak more Spanish than English.' But over there we speak more English because we're always at school, always speaking English and we go home our parents speak both languages so I speak English and Spanish."

Getting to know the Dominican Republic was an important experience in Doris's life. Before the trip she could not travel because her mother's financial situation was not good, but also because she was not particularly interested. Her family in the Republic insisted that she visit, however, and paid for her ticket so she, her mother, and her New York relatives traveled there for three weeks. Her first trip introduced her to a world to which she now feels strongly connected. She had a good time with her cousins and greatly enjoyed her stay. Yet, at the same time, the trip made painfully clear her sense of American belonging. She experienced the limits of belonging in the jokes over language use. Those were meant to be funny, but they also established a boundary.

Table 7.3 presents indicators of economic, social, and political transnational practices. Economic transnational activities include taking merchandise to the Dominican Republic, investing in a business there, or buying a house, land, or other property. Social transnationalism includes being a member of an organization that sends monetary support to the Dominican Republic,[9] traveling to the town of origin to participate in local celebrations, and being a member of a social or sport club that maintains regular ties with the Dominican Republic. Political transnationalism includes contributing money to political campaigns in the Dominican Republic and being a member of a Dominican political party. These practices are narrower forms than sending remittances or traveling to the Dominican Republic. Respondents were asked if they had engaged in any of these activities in the last five years. The positive responses to each of these items are summed up into measures of economic, social, and political transnationalism. The measure of overall transnationalism is the sum of the positive responses to all forms of engagement in transnational practices.

The most common form of participation is social transnationalism. These are transnational activities that link people in the country of reception and the country of origin through mutual help or participation in local festivities. These activities are based in a sense of solidarity and common group belonging between people born in the same place with the same heritage. Almost half of the first-generation respondents participated in this form of transnationalism and close to a quarter of the second generation did so. The table shows that economic transnationalism—that is, entrepreneurial activities carried out by migrants in the country of origin—is the province of only a small group of immigrants (Portes, Haller, and Guarnizo 2002). Only one-fifth of the first-generation sample invested in business or properties in the Dominican Republic, and less than a tenth of the second generation did so.[10] As Portes and his collaborators assert, becoming a transnational entrepreneur is a specific economic strategy of incorporation followed by a limited group of first-generation immigrants (Portes, Haller, and Guarnizo 2002). Political transnationalism is even more limited activity among both generations. Given the current Dominican state policy of inclusion of its diaspora in the political sphere, it is interesting that only 16 percent of the first generation is actually involved in Dominican politics. This low level of engagement contrasts with the relatively high proportion of respondents who agree that Dominican immigrants should participate in Dominican politics.[11]

The importance of the political participation of migrants in the country of origin is highlighted by Smith, who showed that the political action of migrants was important to open up the political game in Ticuani (2008). As we mentioned earlier, however, studies of the political participation of Salvadoran migrants show that migrant political participation can create a number of tensions between the immigrants and those who remain (Itzigsohn and Villacrés 2008; Waldinger, Popkin, and Magana 2008). Intense participation of migrants in the politics of the country of origin is the realm of only a committed few.

In his analysis of Latino politics in New York City, Michael Jones-Correa argued that the attachment of first-generation Latino immigrants to dual citizenship is the result of the barriers to political incorporation they encounter in the United States (1998). This was indeed the case for those who over the years mobilized to obtain dual citizenship and the right to vote abroad. They achieved both objectives in the mid-1990s and in 2004 were able to participate in the U.S. presidential election for the first time. In 2004, there were 42,527 registered Dominicans in the United States, of which 30,118 voted (70 percent turnout). In 2008, the number of registered Dominican voters in the United States more than doubled to 96,779, and the number who voted grew by two-thirds to 52,522 (54 percent turnout).[12]

The number of emigrants participating in the Dominican elections has grown impressively between the two electoral cycles. Yet it is small given the Dominican population in the United States. The 2006 American Communities Survey estimates that population at 1,217,160 people, of whom 731,806 are foreign born. The number of registered and actual voters is therefore rather small.[13] There is an apparent contradiction in that, despite the hard-earned right to vote abroad, as well as the right to dual citizenship, only a few people exercise either.[14] I have argued elsewhere that for most people the two demands in fact indicate more a yearning for recognition from the Dominican state than a desire for political involvement (Itzigsohn 2007).

For most migrants, transnational involvement is mostly social and is linked to the idea of making a concrete difference in the life of people in the country of origin. Grace Diaz, introduced in chapter 2, is a good example. A first-generation Dominican, she is the state representative for district 11 in South Providence and intensely engaged in local politics. Before she became state representative, she was part of a campaign to create a union of daycare providers—she herself is such a provider. The attempt was blocked by the governor, but the organizing experienced propelled Diaz to the state house. Diaz was always political. In the Dominican Republic, she was for many years a member of the Dominican Revolutionary Party (Partido Revolucionario Dominicano, or PRD) and a candidate to the Santo Domingo city council. Yet when I asked her if she were involved in Dominican politics she said that in 1994 she had already decided to sever those ties. She explained that she did so because she realized that in the Dominican Republic politicians steal as much as they can and are not concerned with the education and welfare of the population.

Instead, she works with an organization of Hispanic firefighters, which has two goals. The first is to increase the number of Latinos in fire departments. The second is to connect fire departments in the United States with their counterparts in Latin America, particularly in the Dominican Republic, where conditions are decidedly poor. Diaz notes that she is very satisfied that she can do work that has social significance without having to involve herself in Dominican politics.

A look at transnational participation by class provides clues to the relationship between transnational participation and incorporation into the mainstream. Table 7.4 presents the survey results comparing transnational participation by class and generation. Among the first generation, those who are more incorporated into the mainstream—that is, those who are part of the lower salariat and the petit bourgeoisie—participate more in transnational activities.[15] In part, this is expected, given that transnational participation demands resources and those who occupy higher class positions have more resources at their disposal. These results, however, contradict the expectations of assimilation theory. This theory anticipates that those who are more incorporated in the American mainstream will be more detached from the country of origin. This, however, is not the case. For the first generation, incorporation and transnational participation are simultaneous (Levitt and Schiller 2004).

The second-generation sample presents a different picture in that it is those in the working class who participate slightly more. The overall picture, however, is that transnational participation is more or less even across classes and students. In all class groups, between 20 and 30 percent of the respondents engage in some form of transnational activity. For the second generation, then, participation is not the function of the resources of incorporation that it is for the first generation. The results also indicate that transnational participation—as opposed to identity—is also not the result of exclusion, at least not of class exclusion.

To summarize, both first- and second-generation Dominicans build their identities using transnational symbolic elements. There are big generational differences, however, in terms of participation. Among the first generation is a core of people engaged in recurrent and institutionalized transnational practices and a large circle who participate occasionally with less commitment. The broader the practices, the larger the proportion of people who participate. For the first generation, transnational ties are concomitant with incorporation. Those who are better off and have resources participate more.

For the second generation, participation is considerably more limited. Here, too, is a core of people who engage regularly in transnational practices. This is an important group, representing between 25 percent and 30 percent of the survey respondents. But this core is smaller and less intensively engaged in transnational activities than the first generation. Furthermore,

Table 7.4 Transnational Practices

	Remittances	Visits	Economic	Social	Political	Overall
Second generation						
Lower salariat, petite bourgeoisie	3 (16.7)	10 (55.6)	1 (5.6)	4 (22.2)	0 (0.0)	4 (22.2)
Working class	19 (35.2)	43 (79.6)	3 (5.6)	15 (27.8)	3 (5.6)	16 (29.6)
Students	5 (14.7)	25 (73.5)	3 (8.8)	7 (20.6)	0 (0.0)	9 (26.5)
Not working	1 (7.1)	9 (64.3)	2 (14.3)	3 (21.4)	0 (0.0)	4 (28.6)
First generation						
Lower salariat, petite bourgeoisie	11 (61.1)	18 (100.0)	6 (33.3)	11 (61.1)	7 (38.9)	14 (77.8)
Working class	15 (48.4)	28 (90.3)	6 (19.4)	13 (41.9)	1 (3.2)	15 (48.4)
Students	1 (16.7)	5 (83.3)	1 (16.7)	2 (33.3)	0 (0.0)	3 (50.0)
Not working	5 (83.3)	6 (100.0)	0 (0.0)	4 (66.7)	2 (33.3)	5 (83.3)

Source: Author's compilation based on survey of first- and second-generation Dominicans.
Note: Numbers reflect those who engage in transnational practices. Percentages in parentheses.

transnational practices are limited to this group. The second generation experiences transnationalism mainly as a symbolic frame for the construction of identity.

Claudia and Miguel, whose stories were told in chapter 4, illustrate these differences in transnational involvement among the second generation. Both Claudia and Miguel are second-generation Dominicans and identify strongly with the Dominican Republic. Yet they have very different histories of engagement in transnational activities. Claudia grew up hearing stories about the Dominican Republic from her mother and her aunts and uncles. She self-identifies as Dominican and has developed a strong emotional attachment to everything Dominican. Yet, although she is twenty-eight years old, she has never traveled there, nor does she engage in any transnational activities. Her case is one of a strong transnational identity without transnational practices. Claudia's case is perhaps extreme because she has never been to the Dominican Republic—she hopes to travel there sometime soon with her children—but the survey data suggest that her lack of involvement is typical for the second generation.

Miguel is different. Miguel identifies as Dominican and he travels often to the Dominican Republic. He does not plan to live there, but he has built a concrete attachment to the country by buying a house in the town his parents came from. He also researches and writes on the Dominican migration experience. Miguel represents a minority, those for whom transnational practices continue in the second generation. Still, that does not mean that he does not invest in American life. We have already seen how he is keenly aware of the need to empower Dominicans in the United States.

In spite of the differences between them, Claudia's and Miguel's stories clearly illustrate Smith's assertion that transnational involvement can have positive effects on incorporation (2008). Smith emphasizes the importance of the Ticuani experience in the positive assertion of Mexican identity of second-generation youngsters in New York City. This is embodied in the case of Miguel, who has spent time in the Dominican Republic, has bought land there, and studies the Dominican migration experience. Claudia, on the other hand, does not engage in any form of transnational activity. In her case, however, the transnational identity framework has helped her assert herself in American society. Although she has not traveled to the Dominican Republic, the emotional attachment to her mother's country has given her elements to construct a positive and proactive identity in the United States.

TRANSNATIONALISM AND GROUP FORMATION

The ethnic organizations Dominicans create are an expression of their identities. These organizations also create a public space in which these identities are asserted. People familiar with immigrant communities have a sense of the presence of a lively organizational life. In the survey of first- and second-generation Dominicans, however, the percentage of membership in Dominican organizations is actually small. Only 17 percent of the sample indicated that they are members of a Dominican organization. This percentage, however, masks an important generational difference. Among first-generation respondents, the figure is 33 percent but among second-generation respondents it is only 9 percent. Creating and maintaining ethnic organizations is mostly a first-generation activity.[16]

The impact of those who participate in organizations, however, is larger than their number. The adoption of identity labels indicates a feeling of group belonging, but it is through ethnic organizations and collective action that the sense of belonging is transformed into a group that affects the lives of its members as well as the place in which they live. Community organizations are involved in all aspects of immigrant lives, from the provision of information and services, through community advocacy, to the creation of ties with the country of origin (Cordero-Guzman 2005). To be sure, not everyone who joins an organization is necessarily committed to its identity or goals. Some may join because their friends are members, others because they enjoy immersing themselves in community projects, or for any number of other reasons. Yet joining a voluntary organization involves time and effort. The people who consistently commit their work to sustain voluntary organizations do so because they identify with the mission of the organization. The people who join and keep alive Dominican ethnic organizations are committed to act on their Dominican ethnic identity.

Dominican organizations in general have both a local and a transnational orientation. One example is the Hispanic firefighters organization that Grace Diaz describes. They work both to bring Latinos to fire departments in the United States and to help firefighters in the Dominican Republic. Although this is a panethnic and not a strictly Dominican organization, this duality characterizes also the work of most Dominican organizations. At the same time, it is possible to distinguish between those organizations that focus their efforts in building ties with the country of origin, and those that invest most of their energy in community building and empowerment in the United States.

The most typical transnational organization is the home town association. These are formed by groups of people from the same locality who organize in the country of reception to participate in the social, economic, and political life of their place of origin. Levitt has described this type of association in her ethnography of people from Miraflores in Boston (2000). A few associations in Providence were established by immigrants from the same Dominican town—Monte Plata and La Romana, for example. the presence of such groups, however, is not widely felt and the activities are mostly limited to financial aid fundraising events, and they do not reach the level of intervention Levitt described. The reason is probably in numbers, because there is no critical mass of people from any particular locality to sustain high levels of organizational transnational involvement. In addition to specific aid to home towns, there have been community-wide aid campaigns at times when the Dominican Republic was hit by natural disasters. When events such as hurricanes or floods hit the island, Dominicans in Providence—and elsewhere—have mobilized quickly to send food, clothes, and money to people in need.

In Providence, the most visible and active transnational organizations are political and cultural. Dominican political parties are key transnational organizations. Their origin in the United States is linked to the start of Dominican migration in the 1960s. After the 1965 invasion of the Dominican Republic, the United States succeeded in establishing a friendly government on the island under Joaquin Balaguer. To reduce the internal political pressure, Washington gave visas to those who were disgruntled with the Balaguer government. As Dominicans began to settle in New York, they established branches of their political organizations. Almost all Dominican parties have a presence in New York City. In Providence—as in other small cities—it is mainly the two largest parties, the Dominican Liberation Party (Partido para la Liberación Dominicana, or PLD) and Dominican Revolutionary Party (Partido Revolucionario Dominicano, or PRD), that have established organizations, and a small group affiliated with the third largest Dominican political group, the Reformist Social Christian Party (PRSC).

As shown in table 7.3, only a few immigrants are actually members of these parties—16.4 percent of the first-generation respondents engage in political transnationalism. They nevertheless have a very visible presence in community life, one expressed in organizing migrants to participate in both Dominican and American politics. The party machines become particularly active at elections time. They gather financial support for the party candidates and try to convince voters in the Dominican Republic—and since the 2004 election also in the United States—to vote for their party. The Dominican parties are organizations of first-generation immigrants who were socialized politically in the Dominican Republic and oriented toward that political system. Despite this transnational orientation, however, they also promote political participation among Dominicans in American politics.

The Dominican parties provide an experienced cadre of political activists for Dominicans who run for local elections or for candidates supported by the Dominican community. Members of the Dominican political parties were instrumental, for example, in the election of Leon Tejada as the first Dominican state representative. He was elected in 2001 to represent district 11 and was unseated by Grace Diaz, who relied much more heavily on locally oriented activists, in 2005. Dominican political party activists also collaborated in the first mayoral victory of David Cicilline in 2002.[17]

The other significant transnational organization present in Providence is a cultural one, the Instituto Duartiano de Rhode Island (the Duartian Institute of Rhode Island). Its goal is to promote knowledge of Dominican history and culture and is mostly a first-generation organization.[18] In 2001, a group of first-generation Dominicans organized a committee to petition the city for a place to build a monument to Juán Pablo Duarte and to raise funds for it. In 2004, the monument was inaugurated.[19] In the process of lobbying for the monument, the committee established relations with the Instituto Duartiano in New York, whose members suggested creating a similar organization in Rhode Island. For that purpose, members of the organizing committee traveled to the Dominican Republic to ask permission from the Instituto Duartiano in Santo Domingo to open a Rhode Island branch.[20]

The Instituto Duartiano de Rhode Island is a transnational cultural organization, a branch of a Dominican organization engaged in the construction of a specific Dominican national discourse and historical memory. Yet, whereas the Dominican institute is interested only in maintaining the memory of Duarte, the Rhode Island branch aims also to reach out and promote Dominican identity among the Dominican youth growing up in the state. To that end, the institute organizes talks about issues of relevance to Dominicans in the United States and maintains ties with other Dominican organizations in the country. It was the only organization from Rhode Island invited to participate in the consultation with migrant organizations organized by President Fernandez to discuss the reform of the Dominican constitution.[21]

As mentioned earlier, the Dominican government is proposing two constitutional reforms that specifically concern Dominican migrants. First is that the children of immigrants get Dominican citizenship at birth. Second is parliamentary representation for Dominicans abroad. All the organizations present at the meeting supported the first proposal and the majority supported the second. The minority who opposed it argued that expanding Dominican political competition into the United States would in fact weaken the efforts of the local communities for political empowerment. The Instituto Duartiano of Rhode Island agreed with the minority position, noting that the right to vote abroad was enough and that the Dominican community needed to concentrate its political energies on the American political system.

Transnationally oriented organizations focus their activities on the country of origin but cannot escape the fact that their members live in the in the United States and therefore also participate in local organizational efforts, mainly in the political realm. In the same way, locally oriented organizations build community and seek empowerment in the United States, but at the same time their organizational efforts are informed by a transnational identity framework.

The largest local ethnic organization in Providence is the Club Juán Pablo Duarte (CJPD), primarily a first-generation social club.[22] It is also sometimes involved in activities oriented toward promoting immigrant incorporation, such as citizenship and ESL (English as a Second Language) courses and voter registration. These activities, however, are not permanent features and depend on the specific interest of the club authorities, who are elected each year. Oriented towards the local community, the club also embraces a transnational identity framework. In its main meeting room is a picture of Juán Pablo Duarte flanked by both the American and the Dominican flags. The club also celebrates the Dominican independence and organizes cultural events related to the Dominican Republic. It brings speakers from the Dominican Republic to participate in local events, and links its sports activities with sport clubs in the Dominican Republic. In its activities we see how the building of a local immigrant community is based on the transnational identity framework that people embrace.

The most important local Dominican organization is Quisqueya en Acción (Quisqueya in Action, or QIA),[23] founded in the late 1980s by a group of young Dominicans, some born in the United States and some in the Dominican

Republic. State Senator Juán Pichardo was one of these youngsters and recalled how the group came to be formed:

> As I grew up and went to high school it became very important for young people like myself at that time to continue to identify with our culture. Being young, our culture back then was el merengue, the festivals. Out of that we established an organization called Quisqueya en Acción. The head of that was Margarita Cepeda, and I was one of those young persons [who] kept it going for many years, and continue to do so to maintain our identity as Dominicans, [because] we young people were . . . also looking into the future that we [would] not continue our culture if we didn't ground ourselves, and . . . to empower young people in the Dominican community. And so we embarked in providing that base—culture, heritage, and dance.

Quisqueya en Acción, then, was the result of a decision by young Dominicans looking for ways to express their identity and their roots. Pichardo's words reflect the importance that the assertion of identity has for young people. In chapter 4, we saw that this was one of the elements that helped young working-class Dominicans successfully navigate the public school system and complete their education.[24] Quisqueya en Acción has now been engaged in the work of building identity and community for young people for two decades.

Quisqueya en Acción is the most important local organization because it organizes the main Dominican event in the city, the Dominican Festival. Every August, several thousand first- and second-generation Dominicans gather in Roger Williams Park for a day of celebration. In recent years, the festival has included a parade of floats along Broad Street. The festival also marks the Dominican public presence and is visited by most city and state politicians, who make the most of the occasion to appear before an ever-growing constituency. But the festival is first and foremost an occasion for Dominicans to assert and celebrate their identity. Quisqueya en Acción organizes two other yearly events—a banquet that serves as a fundraiser and a pageant. The winner of the pageant becomes the queen of the Dominican Festival. In recent years, the organization has also launched a college preparedness program aimed at increasing the Latino rate of college attendance by mentoring immigrant high school students through the application process.

Quisqueya en Acción promotes the strengthening of Dominican identity in the United States but uses the transnational identity framework to define that identity. Festival performances involve Dominican dances and music and the main attraction is almost always an important musical group from the Dominican Republic, though on a few occasions the main attraction has been Dominican groups from New York City. The Dominican flag appears prominently at the festival and there are constant references to the country of origin.

An important role that Quisqueya en Acción has filled is to socialize young Dominicans into organizational life and community activism. Several of the activists who spearheaded Dominican involvement in local and national politics came from its ranks. Pichardo links his decision to go into politics directly to the experience and insight he gained through his work in the organization. He and several other Rhode Island Dominican activists were involved in the foundation of the Dominican American National Roundtable (DANR). Pichardo explained that the goal of the organization is to have "a voice at the national level on issues just as we are doing at the local level: on economic well-being, on being counted in the census, on immigration." DANR is involved in voting registration efforts, leadership development, and lobbying American policymakers on issues that concern the Dominican community.[25] In 1999, the third DANR national conference took place in Providence, organized by people linked to Quisqueya en Acción. The 2008 national conference was also held in Rhode Island.

Although the organization's voice is directed mainly toward American policymakers, it also maintains a connection with the Dominican authorities. Representatives of the Dominican government have participated in the annual meetings. In addition, delegations of the roundtable have traveled to the Dominican Republic to meet with Dominican authorities. Pichardo explained the rationale of this connection:

> The roundtable is set out to have the interests of Dominicans here in the United States. However, we also know that it cannot avoid having that relation with the country because it's all interrelated . . . when you have policies that are detrimental to families here in the United States it will impact the island. Economically, as you know, *remesas* are the number two source of economic revenue for the country. So if we have a cold here, in the Dominican Republic they have a flu, because of the financial implications. That is why now the Dominican Republic will be seeing and it will continue to see very difficult financial times.

The goal of the Dominican state in its dealing with DANR is to enlist the Dominican community support for political initiatives of interest to the Dominican Republic. The links with DANR are part of the Dominican state strategy to build transnational ties with migrant communities. The people involved in DANR also have an interest in maintaining a dialogue with the Dominican authorities and in lobbying for issues that concern the Dominican Republic, but for reasons that are not always the same as those of the Dominican state.

The support for the Central American Free Trade Agreement (CAFTA) is a case in point. The Dominican government was keenly interested in CAFTA's being approved by the U.S. Congress and that the Dominican Republic was included in its terms. CAFTA-DR was indeed ratified by Congress and signed into law in 2005. DANR also took a position favorable to the ratification of CAFTA, but for reasons that concern the Dominican community in the United States rather than the interests of the Dominican state. In speaking with a person in Providence who has been involved in the roundtable, I was offered an explanation for DANR support and advocacy for the Central American Free Trade Agreement:[26] "If there are more and better jobs in the Dominican Republic there is going to be less migration. Dominican migration comes not from political but from economic reasons. So the roundtable is not trying to limit migration, but if there are better jobs in the Dominican Republic that has an effect also on Dominicans here."

The reason that better jobs there would affect Dominicans here is that migrants make a great effort to send remittances to their families. This form of transnational engagement, as Levitt clearly showed, is costly for many low-income Dominicans (2001). Improving the economic situation of Dominicans in the Dominican Republic can thus help improve that of Dominicans here. I personally doubt that CAFTA will produce the desired results, but the interesting point is that advocacy for the Dominican Republic is conducted for the benefit of Dominicans here. Also, DANR representatives participated in the meeting between President Fernandez and Dominican organizations described, and the DANR representative opposed the Fernandez proposal to give congressional representation to Dominicans abroad, arguing that it could create divisions within the Dominican community and hamper efforts to promote local empowerment.

All Dominican organizations embrace the transnational identity frame. This is not surprising given that the same frame informs the identities of both the first and the second generations. But all the organizations also have to deal with the demands of life in the United States. Locally oriented organizations are sometimes wary of the effects of the extension of Dominican-based disputes into community life. Even for transnational organizations, the reality of life in the United States leads them to dedicate part of their efforts to local empowerment. Senator Pichardo eloquently articulated the need for Dominicans to direct their efforts toward local empowerment: "I was born in the Dominican Republic but I grew up here, I am an American, I have accepted that, I'm here."

DOMINICAN TRANSNATIONAL IDENTITY

At this point we can return to the three questions posed at the start of the chapter. First, what is the scope and intensity of transnational identities and practices among the first and the second generations? The chapter shows that both first and second generations embrace a transnational identity framework. This framework, however, leads to different levels of transnational practices across the generations. The first generation as a whole embraces broad transnational practices. At the same time, a core of people are deeply engaged in narrow forms of transnationalism. Among the second generation, the level of transnational participation decreases and is restricted to a limited group of people. Transnationalism among the second generation involves mainly the adoption of a transnational framework in the construction of identity. In other words, in the first generation both the ways of belonging and the ways of being are transnational. Among the second generation, the ways of belonging are transnational but the ways of being are focused on the place of residence.

The second question asks what the shape of the Dominican transnational community is. The chapter shows that one of the key features of transnationalism in the last decade is the active intervention of the state in encouraging the transnational loyalties of the migrant community.[27] The migrant community, however, is indeed involved in transnational linkages but independently and selectively. Dominican migrants participate in relatively large numbers in social activities but much less so in economic or political activities. Dominican immigrants and organizations are also very active in building institutions for local community life and local political and economic empowerment. They demand recognition from the Dominican state but are not that interested in investing in Dominican politics. Transnational communities—as well as identities—are not homogenous and encompass conflicting and often contentious interpretations of the common elements around which they organize.

Finally, how do incorporation and transnationalism shape the Dominican experience? The analysis in this chapter indicates that transnational participation and incorporation are not opposing processes but simultaneous ones. This simultaneity is expressed differently across generations. For the first generation, the simultaneity appears at the individual level, where those who are more incorporated into American life are also more involved in transnational practices, and at the organizational level, where transnational organizations are involved also in local empowerment efforts.

In the second generation, the simultaneity appears as an apparent break between ways of belonging and ways of being. On the one hand, the second generation embraces a transnational frame of identity. On the other, its actions are oriented mainly toward establishing a place in American society. The break between transnational identities and local practices is only an apparent one, because second-generation transnational identities do not indicate a failure to assimilate. They are a reaction to the encounter with American racialization. Transnational identities are the result of the pattern of stratified ethnoracial incorporation described in this book.

The analysis of this chapter highlights two additional important points. First is the importance of distinguishing analytically between the symbolic construction of transnationalism and the concrete practices that sustain a transnational social field—that is, between an expansive and a focused understanding of transnationalism. If one focuses only on identities, one is likely to conclude that transnational participation is much more widespread than it is. Second are the limits of transnational participation. Dominicans have a documented high level of transnational involvement (Kasinitz et al. 2008; Louie 2006). But it is precisely this that makes the case important, because Dominicans can be thought as marking an upper limit of transnational engagement. For all their transnational involvement, the main efforts of first- and second-generation Dominicans are oriented toward local community building and empowerment.

CHAPTER 8

Panethnic Identities

Dominicans embrace a panethnic identity. When they are asked in surveys to define their identity, their main answers are variations of panethnicity: Hispanic, Hispano, Hispana, Latino, Latina. These identities, however, are quintessentially American. They are not part of the repertoire of identity choices that immigrants bring with them. Latino or Hispanic panethnicity is an identity that emerges from social life and social practices in the United States. As they incorporate into American society, Dominican immigrants and their children learn that they are categorized as Hispanic or Latino by mainstream society and thus adopt this label to refer to themselves.

The rise of panethnicity is, then, a consequence of stratified ethnoracial incorporation. External categorization, however, is just the beginning of the process of identity and group formation. Dominicans and other Latinos embrace panethnic identity and use it to start collective projects, build organizations, and mobilize politically. Dominicans appropriate the externally defined panethnic labels and use them to construct a community in their own terms. This chapter analyzes the ways in which Dominican immigrants participate in the construction of a Latino community in Providence.

PANETHNICITY

The emergence of panethnic identities poses a number of questions for people interested in ethnic formation. Can peoples with such diverse national histories, racial formations, and histories of migration as the various Latin American immigrants be considered one group? If so, is panethnicity anything more than an instrumental tool used to participate in American ethnic politics? Elsewhere I have reviewed the literature and the debates on Latino identity (Itzigsohn, Giorguli, and Vazquez 2005; Itzigsohn 2004). My argument is that this is a form of emergent ethnoracial identity. As William Yancey and his colleagues asserted, the rise of ethnicity in America is rooted in the everyday encounters that take place in neighborhoods and workplaces in American cities (Yancey, Ericksen, and Juliani 1976). Among Latin American immigrants and their children, coming together in urban areas, coupled with external classification, gives rise to a sense of panethnic belonging. This shared identity has both ethnic and racial meanings and transcends instrumental goals.

Yet that a group embraces an identity does not tell us much about the type of practices that are anchored on this identity. This chapter examines the ways in which different practices of first- and second-generation Dominicans help build a panethnic community. The analysis is based on a modified version of the anthropologists Milagros Ricourt's and Ruby Danta's model for the study of the emergence of Latino panethicity (2003). These authors identified four dimensions of panethnic formation. The first, called experiential panethnicity, refers to everyday interactions between Latinos in neighborhoods, schools, and workplaces. For example, immigrants from the same region may settle close to each other and help each other based on the commonalities created by a shared origin without necessarily adopting a common identity label. The second dimension, called categorical panethnicity, appears when people start to use panethnic labels for self-identification. The third dimension, institutional panethnicity, emerges when people build social, cultural, and political organizations anchored around panethnic labels. The fourth dimension, ideological panethnicity, points to articulated ideological discourses concerning Latino identity and community.

This model is useful for two reasons. First, following the Yancey, Ericksen, and Juliani emergent ethnicity model (1976), Ricourt and Danta argued that we ought to look for the roots of panethnicity in the everyday lives of immigrants and their children. Second, Ricourt's and Danta's model allows us to differentiate analytically among the forms and expressions that panethnic identities and practices can take. Panethnicity is not just a label people can embrace or reject. It also entails various discourses of self-identification tied to complex sets of individual and organizational practices. Some of those practices, such as political coalitions, can have an instrumental character, but even those practices, to be effective, demand the previous existence of categorical panethnic self-identification.

My analysis departs from Ricourt's and Danta's in two ways. First, I see experiential panethnicity, that is, the forms of solidarity that emerge in common urban life, as a precondition for the emergence of Latino identities and communities rather than as a dimension of panethnicity. Furthermore, the emergence is also fostered by the social practices of classification in the United States. The federal and state governments see immigrants from the Spanish-speaking countries of Latin America and the Caribbean as one group and relate to them accordingly. Similarly, political parties, the educational system, and private corporations all relate to this group of immigrants as Latinos, helping in that way to bring the group into being.

The second point on which my analysis departs from Ricourt's and Danta's is that I look at political panethnicity as a dimension of analysis separate from institutional panethnicity. There are two reasons for this. First, political participation is seen as a particularly important indicator of incorporation. Political mobilization implies a stronger commitment to participation in the life of the receiving country than other forms of institutional panethnicity. Second, it is through political mobilization that a group acquires a voice in public life and attempts to influence the larger social context in which the process of incorporation unfolds.

The analysis is divided into three sections, each addressing a different aspect of Latino panethnic community formation. Because I demonstrated in chapter 6 that Dominicans widely embrace categorical panethnicity, I start with an examination of institutional panethnicity. It is in the collective projects that people undertake that a diffuse sense of group belonging is transformed into a panethnic community. I then focus on panethnic political organization and mobilization, and lastly I look at the extent to which first- and second-generation Dominicans embrace ideological panethnicity.[1]

INSTITUTIONAL PANETHNICITY

Categorical panethnicity is part of the identity repertoire of Dominicans. Chapter 6 indicates that a majority of Dominicans use panethnic labels for self-identification. Similarly, among the participants in the Latino National

Survey, all first- and second-generation respondents answered affirmatively to the question, "Do you consider yourself Hispanic or Latino or a person of Spanish origin?" Here I examine the ways in which categorical panethnicity becomes institutional panethnicity. Latino organizations are the backbone of this process of group formation. It is through the work of panethnic organizations that a community emerges. We review three cases that illustrate the involvement of Dominicans in the formation of Latino organizations and the way in which such organizations create a Latino community and public space. The first looks at a radio station, the second at an immigrant workers organization, and the third at a cultural association.[2]

Latino Broadcasting

Media is an important factor in the formation of identities. What people see in television or hear in the radio influences the ways in which they think about themselves (Davila 2001). At the local level, the main forms of ethnic media are newspapers and radio. I focus on radio because it has a greater impact in the daily lives of people. Latino newspapers in Providence are published once a week and it is not clear whether they are widely read. Radio, on the other hand, is present in people's daily routines at work, on the way to work, and at home. Dominicans have played a central role in the development of Latino radio.

Currently—spring 2009—there are three Spanish-language radio stations in the Providence area. The oldest is Poder 1110, a Dominican-owned and managed AM station that transmits from dawn to dusk. The owners, Tony Mendez and Zoilo Garcia, were among the first people to engage in Latino radio in Providence.[3] They started making their own Spanish-language programs in an English-language station and slowly built up their own station. Of the stations that have begun transmitting in Spanish in the area, Poder 1110 is the only one that has stayed on the air over time. Another founder of Latino radio in Providence is Hugo Adames, a well-known Dominican radio personality known by the nickname of El Monseñor de la Salsa (Salsa's Monsignor) because of his knowledge of this musical style. Hugo Adames ran for many years La Inconfundible 1220, an AM station that transmitted afternoons and nights until it was bought out by a national chain and closed in 2005.[4]

A second Spanish-language station in Providence is an FM station that took the name of Latino Public Radio. The founder and general manager is a Dominican entrepreneur named Reynaldo Almonte. The president and public face of the radio is one of the most prominent and respected local Latino activists, Pablo Rodriguez, who is Puerto Rican. The third and newest station in the area is Latina 100.3, an FM band that transmits continuously. Hugo Adames has a salsa program at this station. The three radios appeal to the diverse Latino public, which is clear from their names: Latino Public Radio and Latina 100.3 both assume the existence of a Latino public and at the same time create it.

I focus here on Poder 1110 because it is the oldest station, one with deep roots in the community, and the one most clearly identified as Dominican. The station regularly transmits news from the Dominican Republic and pays attention to Dominican issues in the United States. Several—but certainly not all—of its broadcasters are Dominicans, and their programs make constant references to Dominican culture and history and use Dominican linguistic expressions. At the same time, the radio presents itself as a Latino station—the staff includes people from several Latin American countries, the musical programming appeals to the Latino audience in general, and the station gives wide coverage to the issues that affect Latinos locally and nationally.

The community-building work of the station, however, goes beyond promoting a panethnic identity framework. For example, when community-based organizations need to provide public information or to call for the mobilization of the community, they approach the radio station to spread their word and reach a large number of people. When there is a need to organize community solidarity or to raise funds for a community purpose, people use the radio microphones to ask for help. Also, during election campaigns, the station includes in its programming political analyses by Latino commentators and interviews with Latino candidates, and it endorses efforts to promote voter registration and political participation among Latinos.

Poder 1110 exemplifies how Dominican media entrepreneurs following their own business project promote the creation of a panethnic public discourse and a panethnic community. If Dominicans did not embrace categorical panethnicity, the station would not reach that audience. The station could also choose not to open its microphones to community organizations and their causes. Ultimately, whether the owners of the radio embrace a Latino identity framework for their programming because they understand that the way for a Spanish-language radio station to flourish in a city like Providence is to embrace a panethnic discourse or because they are engaged in community building is irrelevant. Most likely, their choice is based in a combination of these two reasons.

My own knowledge of the owners indicates that they are genuinely invested in empowering the local Latino community. The point is that the programming of the station addresses Dominicans as both Dominicans and Latinos, and also brings other Latinos in touch with Dominican cultural practices. In adopting a Latino framework for its programming, and in addressing community concerns and promoting community causes, Poder 1110 builds on and reinforces categorical panethnicity and helps construct institutional panethnicity.

Workers' Rights

The second case I address is an organization created to defend immigrant workers' rights. It was initially known the United Latino Workers Committee and later changed its name to the United Workers Committee (UWC, or Comité de Trabajadores Unidos in Spanish) as it expanded its membership to include non-Latino workers, mainly Cape Verdeans. Created by Mario Bueno, a second-generation Dominican activist, the UWC operated within a larger nonprofit services agency called Progreso Latino.[5] The UWC was, simultaneously, a program within a nonprofit services organization and a grassroots organization in itself. As a service program, the UWC helped immigrant workers address specific complaints, succeeding on numerous occasions to reverse workplace abuses. As a grassroots organization, the UWC failed in its initial goal to organize workers in the workplace, but it succeeded in mobilizing community members to hold state agencies accountable in the enforcement of the few labor protections that are written into the law. The UWC also participated in campaigns for the increase of the state minimum wage and for legislation to protect the employees of temporary employment agencies. This organization served mostly first-generation, often undocumented immigrants because they are the most vulnerable to workplace abuse. But the membership included established documented immigrants and a few second-generation activists. Because its offices were established in Central Falls, over time the majority of its members came to be Colombians, but Dominican activists were central to its creation and its activities.[6]

This was a small organization that at no point comprised more than thirty active members. Yet, through the services it provided and the labor rights campaigns it organized, it helped organize Latinos as a collective actor. In this sense, the effects of its action were much more significant than simply bringing a small group of people into an organization. The UWC was terminated as a program and as an organization in 2006 as a result of a Progreso Latino financial crisis, but it left a legacy of a large number of people socialized into community action and a practice of defending immigrant workers' rights that was continued by other local organizations.[7]

Latino Theater

The third case is a local nonprofit association dedicated to the promotion of Latino theater in Providence. The Educational Center for Arts and Science (ECAS) was founded by Nancy Patiño, an Ecuadorian teacher and community activist. Its initial goal was to develop after-school programs for Latino students in public schools—in other words, an education services organization. Despite some success, because of its limited financial resources ECAS suffered the fate of many nonprofits that cannot consolidate themselves over time. The organization then changed its mission to focus on the promotion of Latino and Latin American theater. The person responsible for this transformation was Francis Parra, a local Dominican theater actress and director.

Since 2000, ECAS has organized a Latino theater festival every March, staging plays from local directors working with amateur actors from the local community and bringing professional Latino theater companies to perform in the state. Its biggest success was the presentation of the theater adaptation of Mario Vargas Llosa's *La Fiesta del Chivo,* a novelized version of the killing of Dominican dictator Rafael Trujillo. The play, staged by Repertorio Español, a New York–based theater company, performed in front of a full house of several hundred people who seldom go to the theater. ECAS has also put together several theater workshops for low-income young Latinos. ECAS activities bring people from different Latino groups together through a common interest in theater, providing them with a space for cultural production and cultural expression. In this way, the action of a small nonprofit cultural association contributes to Latino identity and community formation.

There is a strong element of contingency in the emergence of these organizations. In a different place, we might find that people put their energies into very different panethnic projects. What these cases illustrate are the ways in which Dominican entrepreneurs and social and cultural activists—together with their counterparts from other Latino groups—participate in building panethnic institutions and organizations, rather than or in addition to ethnic organizations. Through these organizations, Latinos come together and act as a group. Through them also, Latinos acquire a social and cultural presence in the city and a Latino public space is formed.

These three cases are only a small sample of a much larger field of organizational forms that construct panethnicity in everyday life. Another area is religious life. Catholic and evangelical churches are an important arena of panethnicity because they appeal to Latinos as a group rather than to the various ethnic groups separately. For Dominicans who go to college, Latino student organizations are a powerful promoter of panethnic identity and community.

The panethnic community, however, encompasses important sources of difference within it. Although the emergence of organizational life creates community, it also reflects class faultlines within the emerging group. The ethnic media points to the emergence of a business sector that identifies itself as Latino and depends also on the presence of Latino businesses that buy advertising and on a Latino customer base. The community service organizations are one area of employment for the growing professional stratum, the lower salariat described earlier in the book. The struggle for immigrant workers' rights points to the presence of a large working class that is often undocumented and is exposed to workplace abuse.

POLITICAL PANETHNICITY

Political participation is a central aspect in the study of immigrant incorporation. Political incorporation is special because it demands a high level of engagement with the institutions of the receiving society. It is through political mobilization that a panethnic group becomes an actor in its place of residence. Indeed, voting and civil and political rights loom large in the consideration of first-generation Dominican immigrants in Providence. Among the first-generation respondents to the Latino National Survey, 32 percent of those who are American citizens asserted that they became a citizen "to be able to vote." Among those who are not citizens, 22.5 percent said that being able to vote would be a reason to become a citizen. In addition, 28 percent of those who are citizens answered that they naturalized "to have legal, political, or civil rights" or "so people would not treat me unfairly." Among those who are not citizens, 37.5 percent indicated that this would be their reason to naturalize.

At the national level, Dominicans have created their own organization—the Dominican American National Roundtable—to advocate on issues that are important to their community, but at the local level they have incorporated into the political process as Latinos.[8] The decision of Dominicans and other Latino political activists to organize and run for office on a panethnic base rather than on an ethnic or national base is, on the one hand, an instrumental choice. Given the way in which all Latinos share the urban space, Dominican candidates—and, for that matter, all Latino candidates—need to mobilize people on a panethnic base to get elected. As Nicole Marwell showed in her analysis of second-generation Dominican politics in two areas of New York City, the choice of political strategies and identities has a great deal to do with the demographic character of the electoral districts (Marwell 2004). Yet without the widespread acceptance of categorical panethnicity, this instrumental choice would be ineffective.[9] The ability to appeal to a constituency as Latinos presupposes the presence of that form of identification.

Dominicans in Rhode Island Politics

At the time of this writing—fall 2008—there are four Dominican elected officials in Rhode Island: State Senator Juán Pichardo, State Representative Grace Diaz, Providence Councilperson Miguel Luna, and Providence Councilperson León Tejada. All were elected from Providence districts and wards, making Providence, along with New York City, the municipality with the largest number of Dominican elected officials in the country.[10] The path to gaining a political presence in Rhode Island politics, however, demanded a great effort of community mobilization. During the early 1990s, there were some attempts by Dominicans to run for office in Providence, but it was only in 1996 that they began to participate in large numbers in the local political process.

That year, a young Dominican named Victor Capellán ran, unsuccessfully, in the Democratic primaries to become state representative. Capellán came to the United States as a young boy and grew up in Providence, graduating from the Providence public schools and the University of Rhode Island. He was a member of Quisqueya en Acción and his candidacy brought into politics a new generation of young Dominicans linked to that organization, young Latinos who knew Capellán from his youth in Providence, and other Latinos and Latinas who were looking for ways to participate in local politics. Indeed, Capellán's campaign manager was Juán Pichardo. The two had been close friends since the days when both were involved in the formation of Quisqueya en Acción and both entered politics together.[11]

Capellán tried twice to become state representative, losing both times by very low margins to Joseph Almeida, current president of the Minority Legislative Caucus. Yet the enthusiasm generated by his campaigns and his very close defeats indicated to first- and second-generation Dominicans that it was possible to be elected to office. Since then, the number of Dominicans participating in politics and running for office has grown steadily. León Tejada was elected state representative for Providence's district 18 in 2000, was reelected in 2002, but was unseated by Grace Diaz, who is also Dominican, in 2004. Diaz became the state representative of the district that is known now as district 11. In 2006, Diaz was reelected and Tejada elected to the Providence city council. In 2002, Latinos won their largest electoral victory so far with the election of Juán Pichardo to the state senate for district 2.[12] Also in 2002, Miguel Luna was elected to represent ward 8 in the Providence city council, his second attempt to win that office, to which he was reelected in 2006. All the districts and wards in which Dominicans were elected are in the southern part of the city, where the Dominican population is concentrated.

This wave of increasing political participation brought about another initiative that consolidated Latino politics in the state. In 1998, a group of Latino activists, many of whom had participated in the Capellán campaigns, created the Rhode Island Latino Political Action Committee (RILPAC). RILPAC became a tool to generate support for Latino candidates and for putting Latino issues on the agenda of non-Latino elected officials. RILPAC has strengthened the presence of Latinos in local politics as mainstream politicians aim to obtain the organization's support. Through its endorsement process, RILPAC is able, to a certain extent, to hold mainstream politicians accountable on issues of importance to the Latino community. In 2002, the people involved in RILPAC created the Rhode Island Latino Civic Fund (RILCF) as a broader organization oriented to increase Latino political education and participation in civic life. RILPAC's goal remains to impact the political process through the endorsement of candidates and the raising of issues that affect the Latino community. RILPAC and RILCF have become important instruments in the mobilization of Latinos in the Rhode Island political process.

Paths to Political Participation

It is often argued that political parties facilitated the political incorporation of European immigrants in the late nineteenth and early twentieth centuries, that the political machines took it upon themselves to recruit immigrants into local politics (Dahl 1961; Wong 2006). The political scientist Steven Erie, however, demonstrated that the role of political machines in mobilizing immigrants was exaggerated (1988). Looking at Irish political machines before World War II, Erie showed that they mobilized only people of Irish origin. After World War II, the political machines included white ethnics but excluded

African Americans and Latinos. Furthermore, Erie argued that, contrary to what is commonly thought, the Irish political machines hindered rather than promoted the social mobility of Irish immigrants and their offspring (1988).

Today's political parties engage in mobilizing their political base rather than in expanding their ranks and bringing new people into politics. Nevertheless, people with the ambition to run for office need to be recruited. Political campaigns also demand resources. One such resource is people who are willing to knock on doors, make phone calls, stuff envelopes, review voter lists, and so on. Another, of course, is money. Fundraising efforts, however, also demand people who can organize events and have connections with potential donors. The role of recruiting and mobilizing immigrants into the political arena is today filled by community organizations (Bloemraad 2006; Cordero-Guzman 2005; Sterne 2003; Wong 2006).[13] This is certainly the case in Rhode Island, where the rapid pace of increasing political representation is sustained through the action of a dense web of community organizations (Uriarte 2006). The study of second generations in New York City also found that political participation is related to engagement in other kinds of civic organizations (Kasinitz et al. 2008).

We can see the importance of community organizations in the path to political participation of Senator Pichardo and Representative Diaz, both of whom were first introduced early in this volume. Juán Pichardo was born in the Dominican Republic and came to New York City with his family when he was nine years old. Five years later his mother moved to Providence, where he finished middle school and high school. As a youngster he was one of the group that created Quisqueya en Acción. He recalled that at the beginning the emphasis of the group of young people linked to the organization was in promoting Dominican culture among the youth, but with time, they started to pay attention to the political and socioeconomic predicament of the community. He elaborated: "As the year progressed we saw also the inequalities that we had in our city and our state. And that inequality was lack of voice in government, lack of resources coming in to the city, and that at least we could feel that government was responding to us. Whether there was on education or whether there was the elected officials or where there was responding to the ills of society, how to counter poverty. So those were some of the issues why I got into politics."[14]

The group that initially worked with him in his campaigns—as well as in Capellán's campaigns—was composed, in part, of people he knew from his work in Quisqueya en Acción and other local organizations he came to know in his many years in Providence. The people who created RILPAC also mobilized to get Pichardo elected.

Grace Diaz came to the United States as an adult. She worked in several jobs until she opened her own home daycare center. In this capacity, she became one of the leaders of an effort by daycare providers to create a union to negotiate, with the state, the conditions of their work. That effort had the strong support of some local progressive unions, linked to Jobs with Justice. Diaz said in our interview that she did not have plans to run for office. She did so because the group of child care providers asked her to do so. Her goal as a candidate was to provide a voice to this group in the state house and there to advance their goal of achieving recognition from the state as a negotiating unit. The support for her campaign came from the group that was behind the unionization drive.

Similarly, the campaigns of León Tejada and Miguel Luna were rooted in community organizations. In his first campaign to the state house, León Tejada built on his ties with the Dominican Revolutionary Party, which mobilized it members to help him. Interestingly, he was also able to gather the active support of members of the other major Dominican political party, the Dominican Liberation Party. These two groups are most of the time bitter rivals, but they united in working together to elect Tejada.[15] Miguel Luna received the support of Direct Actions for Rights and Equality (DARE), a local activist grassroots organization that mobilizes low-income people to struggle for social justice and against racism. He also received the support of the progressive unions in the city.

At the city and state levels, Dominicans entered the political field through the ranks of the Democratic Party.[16] In 2003, the Democrats tapped Melba de Peña, a young Dominican activist who directed many local electoral campaigns, to be the party's executive director. DePeña, who like Capellán and Pichardo came to the United States at an early age, grew up in Providence, and was also linked to Quisqueya en Acción, filled that position for three years (2003–2006).[17] Grace Diaz is currently the vice president of the Rhode Island Democratic Party. One might assume that the Democratic Party reached out to Latinos. This, however, would be an inaccurate impression.

It is indeed true that Latinos have managed to occupy positions within the Democratic Party. Latinos have been elected to district and ward committees as well as to elected office. Latinos have pushed open, to a certain extent, the doors of the Democratic Party, but they have done so as a result of their own mobilization and through the strength of their own organizations, not as a result of party outreach. As Michael Jones-Correa pointed out about the relationship of the Queens' Democratic Party and the local Latino community, the political parties reach out to those who are already mobilized, they are not in the business of integrating immigrants into the political game (1997). It is participation in ethnic or panethnic community life, and not the action of the mainstream institutions (in this case the political parties), that leads to participation in mainstream political life.

Moreover, not all of the Rhode Island Democratic party is reaching out to immigrants. Indeed, Democratic state representatives from areas of the state without a strong presence of immigrants are notorious for trying to pass strong anti-immigrant bills in the state legislature. Those bills address only undocumented immigrants but they constitute an attack on the entire immigrant community. Diaz has said that those who pursue anti-immigrant bills are not real Democrats, but the fact remains that they are long-term Democratic incumbents.

Competition and Cooperation

Participation in community organization is the base on which Dominican—and Latino—political participation is built. This mode of political incorporation, however, carries the potential cost of generating interethnic competition. In places like Providence, where immigrant groups often occupy the same urban space as African Americans, the political incorporation of immigrants often comes at the cost of hard-fought positions occupied by blacks not so long ago. At the same time, Latinos and African Americans often confront a similar predicament: the need for good jobs, affordable health care, and access to a quality education. This situation can then lead to both the rise of interethnic tensions in fighting for political positions and also to the emergence of relations of cooperation (Jones-Correa 2001; McClain and Tauber 2001). This ambiguity is reflected in the answers to the Latino National Survey. A large majority of first-generation Dominicans, 73.3 percent, and ten out of eleven second-generation respondents answered that, for Latinos, doing well depends some or a lot on African Americans doing well. At the same time, 71.1 percent of first-generation and seven out of eleven second-generation respondents asserted that there was competition in the election of group members to public office.

The entry of Latinos to the Rhode Island political field has indeed been, to a certain extent, at the expense of African Americans. León Tejada in his first election to the state legislature and Juán Pichardo indeed unseated African American incumbents. But the entry of Dominicans—and other Latinos—to the political realm is not only at the expense of African Americans. Miguel Luna unseated a long term white incumbent. And Grace Diaz unseated León Tejada who later on got elected to the Providence city council on an open ward. Moreover, each of them had to fight off challenges by both African Americans and other Latino candidates. The politics of south Providence has become an arena for intergroup and intragroup competition. Furthermore, as the number of Latinos in neighborhoods outside of south Providence grows, they will increasingly challenge established white incumbents.

The recent history of changes in the boundaries of the state senate districts illustrates the sources of conflict and the possibilities of cooperation between Latinos and African Americans. In his first unsuccessful run for the senate, in 2000, Pichardo ran against a long-term white incumbent. He explained that he ran that year because he knew that the senate districts would be affected by the redistricting and downsizing of the legislature mandated by referendum. He hoped that by winning that year he could help protect two senate seats for minorities after the redistricting. He was defeated by a small margin. In 2002, the limits of the districts were redrawn in such a way that he had to compete against Senator Charles Walton, an eighteen-year incumbent and the only African American senator. Pichardo considered it very unfortunate that he had to run against Walton and admits that his defeat of Walton was devastating for many people in the African American community.

In 2004, as a result of the settlement of a lawsuit against the 2002 senate map brought by African American organizations, the state senate districts were redrawn again. The lawsuit, based on the Voting Rights Act, argued that the 2002 map diluted the voting power of African Americans by dividing the Providence south side into two districts.[18] The 2004 map created a new district with a high proportion of African American and Latino population.[19] It also divided Pichardo's district and forced him to get acquainted with a new constituency. In spite of this, he supported the new district because it meant the addition of another minority legislator to the senate.

In the 2004 elections, the campaign in the new district pitted an African American candidate, former State Representative Harold Metts, and a Latino candidate, Pedro Espinal, a Dominican entrepreneur and political activist, against one another. Pichardo remained neutral in that race, to the extent that he hardly went into the new district during the elections, but remarked that he "always thought that to [ensure] balance it should be an African American" who is elected in that district. Metts did in fact win that race. In statements made to the local paper, he recognized the existence of divisions between the African American and Latino communities because of competing aspirations, but added that neither African Americans nor Latinos can pursue their agendas separately and that they need to work together (Smith 2004). Pichardo agreed that Metts's victory was good in that it compelled Latinos and African Americans to cooperate politically. They are now both part of the minority caucus. In 2008, Pichardo and Metts were the only ones to vote against the budget in the senate because the cuts in it deeply affected both constituencies.

Pichardo described the collaboration between Latinos and African Americans in the state house as a sign of political maturity. He is currently the vice chair of the Minority Legislative Leadership Caucus. The chair is State Representative Joseph Almeida, who twice defeated Victor Capellán in the run for state representative. Pichardo noted that ten years ago, when he directed Capellán's campaigns, Almeida was a foe, but that they now work well together.

Diaz, also a member of the Minority Legislative Caucus, says that Latinos and African Americans in the legislature work together to benefit both communities. She too became a good friend of Almeida and admires him for the determination with which he defends all the communities of South Providence. Diaz added that in March 2008, when Rhode Island Governor Donald Carcieri came out with an executive order that state agencies should collaborate with the federal Immigration and Customs Enforcement (ICE) agency in identifying undocumented migrants, Almeida strongly opposed it, aligning himself with the Latino elected officials and community organizations.

There is a tension between the need of both communities to acquire a voice and a presence in the political arena and the common interests that derive from their similar positions in the American stratification system. It would be a mistake to argue that both communities should focus on their common interests and abandon their aspirations for a public presence. In a racialized society, the need for recognition and the assertion of identity is not one that can be overlooked. Furthermore, the political mobilization of minorities springs from community life and is galvanized by the presence of political entrepreneurs and activists who belong to the group.

In their pursuit of recognition of their presence in the United States, Latino politicians and organizations promote a policy based on identity and ethnic group mobilization. In fact, the present ethnic community base of political incorporation may not be very different from the past, in that the political machines of old also emerged out of clubs, churches, and other ethnic organizations (Erie 1988; Sterne 2003). This is a tried and true strategy and is necessary to address the invisibility and marginalization caused by racialization. This policy, however, inevitably brings different minority groups into direct competition because of their geographic proximity in wards and districts. It also distances minority politicians and activists from working and poor whites who do not experience racial exclusion but are excluded on a class basis.

This perhaps would not be the case if the Democrats and the Republicans were membership-based parties or if unions were strong. The two parties, however, are geared to running candidates and getting out the vote in electoral periods rather than to mobilizing people into day-to-day politics, and unions have been losing membership and strength for decades. The current strategy of unions to regain their power interestingly involves dropping their historical anti-immigration stand and reaching out to immigrants.

Nevertheless, given that working and poor Latinos, African Americans, and whites overlap to a large extent in their needs and demands, it would be a mistake to overlook the concrete and potential forms of collaboration that exist in pursuing a common agenda. This is the dilemma that Latino elected officials as well as grassroots activists confront. On the one hand, they mobilize people based on their shared ethnic or panethnic identity. On the other, they need to build broad coalitions with other groups that confront a similar predicament, coalitions that need to transcend the identity base of political mobilization.

Working Family Politics

As the sociologist Agustín Laó-Montes asserted in his analysis of Latino social movements, Latino politics cover a wide range of political positions, from conservative to radical (2001). Here I examine the politics of two of the four Dominican elected officials—State Senator Juán Pichardo and State Representative Grace Díaz. Of course, electoral politics does not exhaust the arc of political options open to Dominicans. Grassroots mobilization and activism is also an important arena of political engagement (Laó-Montes 2001). I choose to emphasize electoral and legislative politics because of their importance in the literature on political incorporation and because these are the areas in which Dominicans in Providence have invested the most in search of empowerment.

I focus on the legislative work of Pichardo's and Diaz's politics because it illustrates the possibilities and the limits of addressing stratified ethnoracial incorporation. I assess the type of politics they pursue. Is it their presence that matters? Is it about securing resources for their districts or their ethnic groups, in what would be a reenacting of sorts of old machine politics? Diaz believes that one of her main achievements is that people in her district trust her. She finds being able to intervene on behalf of the people in her district when they are wronged by a public office deeply satisfying. It is very important to her for the people in her district to know that there is someone in office that they can turn to for help. Pichardo also emphasizes that one of the things he likes about being in office is that he can solve problems for people. Both Pichardo and Diaz are proud of their ability to bring resources to their district. Both also asserted that through legislative grants and other sources of funds they channel to their district they keep programs and organizations going. Both emphasized that they bring money for organizations belonging to all ethnic groups in their district. Pichardo also pointed to the importance of empowering his constituency by getting members of the district to sit in state boards.

To be sure, having elected officials has increased the sense of belonging and the public confidence of Dominicans and Latinos in general. Alejandra, whose story is in chapter 4, said that the political participation of Latinos has changed the ways in which the mainstream looks at them. She has worked as a volunteer in a few electoral campaigns of Latino candidates and stressed that because of their involvement in the political life of the state Latinos are seen as a group that contributes positively to society. Alejandra's interest in politics came from her parents, who are members of a Dominican political party. Alejandra also follows Dominican politics closely. Claudia also emphasized the importance of Latino political participation and said, half jokingly, half seriously, that she would like to run for office in the future. When she was growing up, she was not interested in politics, but that changed with a visit to the welfare office in which she met a member of a community nonprofit. Since then she has been doing voluntary work for that organization. That work sometimes involves attending meetings in the state house, and those meetings made her aware of the importance of having people who are responsive to community concerns there. The other three people whose stories I also narrate in chapter 4—Luisa, Carlos, and Miguel—belong to the not-so-small group of people who are disenchanted with or simply detached from the political arena.

Helping constituents and channeling funds to the district are indeed important elements of any district-based electoral politics. If this were all that these two elected officials did, it would not be much in terms of addressing ethnoracial and class exclusions. For a broader scope of Latino politics, we need to look instead at their legislative agendas. Alberto, introduced in chapter 6, emphasized the importance of legislative work. When he was in his early twenties, he believed in grassroots activism and did not pay much attention to electoral politics. He acquired a fondness for community organizing after participating in church-based groups as a teenager. After several years of community work, however, he realized the importance of having people in the inside who are willing to address the needs of the community. Today he thinks that to bring social change it is necessary to know how to play within the political system. Yet, hearing Pichardo and Diaz speak about their legislative work, it becomes clear that they confront difficult obstacles in advancing their legislative agendas.

Diaz noted that establishing an office for a civil rights advocate in the Office of the Attorney General is one of her main legislative achievements. She says that it is not a very big step, but it is a small step in the right direction. She adds to this her work to raise the state's minimum wage, and her work on legislation aimed to regulate, at least a little, in her own words, the operation of temporary employment agencies. These agencies employ a high percentage of the migrant work force in Rhode Island. She also worked in the House of Representatives to pass the law regulating subprime mortgages. This was the bill that Pichardo was most proud of. He also mentioned as one of his achievements cosponsoring a law that judges must explain to those who want to plead nolo contendere the potential implications of doing so. Pichardo pointed out that many immigrants did plead it without realizing the implications and suffered the consequences.

If we look at the legislation that both Diaz and Pichardo have been involved in, we do see items that affect immigrants specifically, but mostly legislation on behalf of all working families. Whether it is the minimum wage, temporary employment agencies, or subprime lending, their concern is with laws that can improve the living conditions of their constituents, who are for the most part the working class and the poor. Pichardo articulated a four-point agenda to deal with the problems of the community.

The first is the need to create a stable financial situation for working families: "We need to attract more jobs that support . . . working families. Others may say, okay, we want high quality jobs, high-end jobs, but the fact is that [the] majority of my constituents are Latinos here, their education level is not high, [and] therefore we need to attract more jobs that can sustain a family." The second important issue, Pichardo said, is health care—the knowledge that parents can take their children to the doctor and not wait until they have to run to the emergency room reduces their stress and increases the stability of working families. Ultimately, Pichardo added, it is less costly for society to provide adequate health care up front because those who rely on the emergency room are typically sicker when they get there and need more care to get well. Eventually everybody ends up paying for it. The third issue is the need to provide working families with a financial education so that they can save and buy a home they can afford without falling victim to predatory lending. The fourth element is education. "When you put these things together," Pichard noted, "a family can buy a home, purchase more things, add to their quality of life, and eventually provide a household in which a child can flourish."

Both Pichardo and Diaz follow similar policies, policies geared to improve the livelihood of working families, and as we saw earlier in this volume, working families constitute the bulk of immigrant families. Pichardo believes, though, that the state is going in the opposite direction. He mentioned in particular the deep cuts in the coverage for child health care included in the budget, cuts that led him to vote against it. I asked how it is possible to provide health-care coverage for children in an age of increasing cuts. His answer was clear: "People who make over $200,000 or $250,000 should be able to contribute a little bit more so we don't have kids with less health coverage. . . . I don't know in my district anyone who makes over $250,000. In my family I don't know anyone who makes over $250,000. Surely, we all would want to have that problem, that we are making $250,000. Even then I think we would want to do the right thing, and that is to pay a little more to help provide health coverage . . . because we will all pay for it."

The agenda Pichardo proposed depends on political decisions about the collection and use of public resources. Are these changes feasible? "One of the biggest frustrations I see in office is that change doesn't come as fast as I would want [it] to," Pichardo remarked. "When you are on the outside you want things changing quickly and unfortunately there is a process, but my people cannot wait."

At the same time, Pichardo has not lost his optimism. He believes that Latinos and non-Latinos are advocating for almost the same thing, which he defines as making sure that "families have a very safe secure financial future for their children and for themselves." He believes that once other people realize that Latinos are a diverse group and no different than anyone else they will embrace the changes needed to address the Latino predicament.

Diaz has a bleaker take on this question. She believes that what she, Pichardo, and the people in the Legislative Minority Caucus do is very important because it has concrete effects on people's lives, but it is not nearly enough. They are a minority and their numbers are not enough. She did not know when she agreed to run for public office what being a state representative entailed. She did not realize that she would have to be ready to work twenty-four hours a day, seven days a week on behalf of a community with seemingly endless needs. She sometimes feels very lonely in her efforts. Ultimately, in different ways, both Pichardo and Diaz reflect the challenge of Latino politics, which is how to transcend and create broad coalitions that can push forward policies that benefit working families and the poor.

IDEOLOGICAL PANETHNICITY

Dominicans and Latinos have acquired a considerable political presence in Providence and in Rhode Island. This process of panethnic political incorporation, however, does not tell whether and to what extent individual Dominicans adopt a panethnic political ideology, defined here as the belief that political alignment and participation should be along Latino lines. This is the last dimension of the analytical model used here. The survey provides some answers to the question and the results suggest that despite the strong Latino mobilization effort and its electoral success, there is only limited support for ideological panethnicity.

Respondents were presented with two statements about Latino political involvement. The first claimed that when Latino candidates run against non-Latino candidates Dominicans should vote for the Latino simply because the candidate is Latino. This is a strong form of panethnic political identity that endorses voting automatically along panethnic lines. Table 8.1 shows that only 31 percent of the first generation and 17 percent of the second generation—a minority of both samples—embrace this strong version of ideological panethnicity.

The second statement asserted that Latino politicians represent the interest of Dominicans better than their non-Latino counterparts. This weaker form of identity politics is based on the belief that someone familiar with the everyday experience of immigrants and their children is better suited to understand and represent their interests. Whereas the previous statement implied an emotional attachment based on common identity, this statement implies an instrumental support based on the idea that common experiences may generate similar understandings of the situations that immigrants and their children

Table 8.1   Ideological Panethnicity

	Dominicans should vote for Latino candidates because they are Latinos	Latino politicians represent interests of Dominicans better than non-Latino politicians
Second generation	21	56
	(17.5)	(46.7)
First generation	19	23
	(31.1)	(37.7)

Source: Author's compilation based on survey of first- and second-generation Dominicans.
Note: Numbers reflect those agreeing with statement. Percentages in parentheses.

confront. Grace Diaz stressed this point, explaining that she is passionate in her work on the issues that affect the community because as an immigrant and as a single mother who had to work hard all her life she understands the predicament of those in a similar situation.

The proportion of respondents who support this weaker, instrumental form of ideological panethnicity is higher than those who agree with the stronger version, but is still a minority position. Almost 50 percent of the second-generation respondents and 38 percent of the first-generation sample agree with the statement. The results of the Latino National Survey support these findings. A large majority of first-generation respondents, 68.8 percent, and eight out of eleven second-generation respondents answered that it is somewhat important or very important that a candidate is Latino. An even larger percentage, however, 96.7 percent of the first-generation respondents and all the second-generation respondents, argued that is somewhat important or very important that a candidate share their positions on issues.

The in-depth interviews throw light on the low support for ideological panethnicity. In my conversations with first- and second-generation Dominicans, I found two basic positions on this issue. The first articulated the weak form of ideological panethnicity observed in the survey responses. Respondents expressed their support for panethnic political mobilization and sympathy for Latinos running for office. They emphasized, however, that their vote depends on the viewpoints of the candidate rather than on their ethnicity. They argued that because Latino candidates are immigrant or of immigrant origin they would probably have a closer understanding of the issues that affect Dominicans. They added, however, that this cannot always be assumed, and that it is important to know what candidates stand for on important issues. This position shows a high level of political sophistication.

The second position was detachment from political involvement. In this case, respondents were suspicious of the ability of politicians—Latinos and non-Latinos alike—to make changes for good in their lives. In particular, they were suspicious of their intentions and their honesty. The limited support for ideological panethnicity is explained by a combination of political maturity, as Pichardo suggested—paying attention to the positions of the candidates rather than to her or his origin—and political disenchantment—the belief that politicians are dishonest and that politics are a waste of time.

Political mobilization takes place along Latino lines because the drive and enthusiasm necessary for political participation spring from community organizations and because of the sense, expressed in several interviews, that Latino politicians better understand the Latinos' situation. Nevertheless, the lack of a strong ideological form of panethnicity found in the responses to the survey and in the qualitative interviews indicates that, at least among Dominicans in Providence, the broad coalitions that are necessary to push for a politics of working families are possible.

The last topic to address is the relationship between class and ideological panethnicity. The survey results are presented in table 8.2. The relation between class and ideological panethnicity is weak for the first generation and almost absent for the second generation. Class does not seem to be a factor in determining the presence and form of panethnic ideologies.

In the first-generation sample, there are similar levels of agreement, with a strong version of panethnic political identity for middle- and working-class respondents. Close to one-third of middle- and working-class first-generation respondents argued that they would vote along panethnic lines. The pattern is different for the weaker form of panethnic political identity—the idea that Latinos can better represent the interests of other Latinos. The support for this position is stronger among middle-class first-generation respondents. For the first generation, panethnic political sympathies seem to be related to mainstream incorporation. Those who have done better stake their political future on panethnic politics.

The second-generation pattern is different. On the one hand, the support for automatic panethnic voting is low across all classes, and only somewhat stronger among working-class respondents. On the other hand, there is similar and relatively strong agreement between working- and middle-class respondents on the

Table 8.2   Ideological Panethnicity by Class and Generation

	Dominicans should vote for Latino candidates because they are Latinos	Latino politicians represent the interests of Dominicans better than non-Latino politicians
Second generation		
Lower salariat, petite bourgeoisie	2 (11.1)	9 (50.0)
Working class	11 (20.4)	26 (48.1)
Students	4 (11.8)	13 (38.2)
Not working	4 (28.6)	8 (57.1)
First generation		
Lower salariat, petite bourgeoisie	6 (33.3)	11 (61.1)
Working class	10 (32.3)	9 (29.0)
Students	0 (0.0)	0 (0.0)
Not working	3 (50.0)	3 (50.0)

Source: Author's compilation based on survey of first- and second-generation Dominicans.
Note: Numbers reflect those agreeing with statement. Percentages in parentheses.

second statement. Class seems to have a limited effect on the panethnic political positions of the second-generation sample. It is not clear from these results—and it is an issue for further research—whether second-generation Dominicans are more attuned to the weak form of panethnic ideology or are simply disillusioned with the possibilities of effecting change through politics. Probably both reasons are important in explaining their pattern of answers.

MULTILAYERED PANETHNICITY

In the urban Providence context, Dominicans share social spaces—residence, work, education—with other Latino immigrants and their children, making the city a fertile ground for the emergence of panethnicity. As with previous generations of immigrants, everyday life in American cities creates new forms of identification. In addition, the American mainstream categorizes Spanish-speaking Latin American and Caribbean immigrants and their children as Latinos (or Hispanic). As a result, first- and second-generation Dominicans in Providence embrace categorical panethnicity, identifying as Latinos and seeing a common predicament across the various Latino groups. The pervasiveness of panethnic identities and their continuation across generations is, therefore, not a failure of assimilation. Becoming American means becoming Latino.

Dominicans, however, appropriate this label creatively and engage in panethnic collective action and institution building. As with ethnic organizations, the number of people involved in this endeavor is small, but the effect of their action is to create a Latino public space and to strengthen categorical panethnicity. Dominicans have also been very successful in promoting panethnic politics and gaining public office. The chapter, however, identifies a tension in the Dominican political strategy. For Latino politics to be effective in addressing stratified racialized incorporation, they need to address both racialization and class exclusion. The problem is that these two have contradictory demands. The former calls for an assertion of identity, which carries the potential for tensions with other groups, and the latter calls for building broad coalitions. Not recognizing the need for a sense of identity is not realizing the everyday exclusionary impact of racialization and the ethnic community roots of political participation. But emphasizing only the assertion of identity means giving up on the possibility of addressing class exclusions. Addressing class exclusions is critical to transforming the politics of the ethnic group into a politics of working families, bringing together different minority groups as well as whites. The challenge for Dominican—and Latino—activists and organizations is to be able to play this contradictory political game and participate in the building of ample coalitions that can change the political direction of the last several decades.

PART IV

Conclusion

CHAPTER 9

Becoming American

It is a Sunday afternoon in August and thousands of people are gathered in Roger Williams Park. On the stage, youth groups perform Dominican music and dances as well as contemporary youth music such as reggaeton and hip-hop. Thousands of people sit on the park's rolling lawn watching the performances. Many wave Dominican flags. Here and there a flag from a different Latin American country can also be seen. On the far edges of the lawn are numerous booths of local eateries, mostly selling Dominican food. The day is the Dominican Festival, a celebration of Dominican identity that marks the strong presence of Dominicans in Providence. In between performances elected officials and local personalities, both Latino and non-Latino, go on stage to salute the community. The festival highlights the extent to which Dominicans have become part of the local social and political scene: within three decades Dominicans have acquired a central presence in the cultural and political life of the city. The festival celebrates Dominicans becoming Americans.

This volume shows that the process of becoming American follows the pattern of stratified ethnoracial incorporation. The socioeconomic position of Dominicans in the American social structure is characterized by three elements. The first is a marked improvement of the second generation over the first. The second is the emergence of a class bifurcation in the occupational insertion of the second generation between those who secure middle-class occupations and the majority, which becomes part of a multiracial and multi-ethnic working class concentrated mainly in the service sector. As chapter 3 shows, this pattern of internal class stratification is more pronounced among women than among men. The third element is that Dominicans become part of an ethnoracial system of stratification. This means that although mobility is considerable, the pattern of internal stratification of Dominicans is closer to that of other minority groups than to white Americans.

This book shows the persistent effects of race and class on immigrant incorporation. Chapter 3 notes that at the lower end of American stratification there is a multiracial working class concentrated mainly in service occupations where minorities, immigrant and native alike, are overrepresented. There is, no doubt, some mobility and middle-class formation within the Dominican and other minority populations. The majority, however, become part of the American working class. The first generation joins to a large degree the remaining manufacturing sector and the second is concentrated mainly in the services working class. Indeed, the American stratification system is a racialized class system characterized by internal stratification within all ethnoracial groups, but the pattern of stratification is tilted downward for minorities compared to the white population.

Concerning identity formation, the United States expects immigrants to assimilate and largely abandon their group identities. Contemporary American culture embraces a mild form of multiculturalism that celebrates symbolic identities, but groups are expected to shed their ethnic attachments and identify as Americans. Stratified ethnoracial incorporation, however, creates ethnoracial differentiation. It leads to the emergence of new ethnic and panethnic identities and to new forms of group formation. Consequently, first- and second-generation Dominicans embrace Dominican and panethnic labels as their forms of identification.

The Dominican identity in the United States is constructed using a transnational symbolic framework. This is common to both the first and the second generations. The difference is that the lives of the first generation are, in different degrees, also transnational, whereas the lives of the second are much more focused on the United States. In other words, the ways of belonging and ways of being of the first generation coincide, but do not in the second generation.

Panethnicity is a distinct American emergent identity with ethnic and racial meanings. It is a form of group positioning in the American racial classification system and constitutes a foundation for organizations and communities.

The political empowerment of Dominicans, at least at the local level, also takes place along panethnic lines. This creates tensions with other groups, particularly African Americans, because they share urban space and compete for elected offices. At the same time, as chapter 8 shows, the politics developed by Dominicans in Providence has a strong component addressed to the needs of working families that creates possibilities for building coalitions with other groups.

Immigration and the emergence of new ethnoracial identities are changing the American racial classification system and there is no consensus about the direction of the ongoing changes. Scholars working from the assimilation perspective suggest that a redrawing of racial boundaries to make them less pervasive and poignant is slowly taking place. One scenario posits a redefinition of the boundaries of whiteness to include Asian Americans and part of the Latino migration (Alba 2005; Prewitt 2004). Another posits the dilution of whiteness into a multiracial nonblack category and the redrawing of the racial boundaries into nonblacks and blacks (Perlmann and Waldinger 1997). Either of these two scenarios leaves most Dominicans—together with other Caribbean immigrants, most Mexican Americans, most of the Central American immigrant population, and of course, African Americans—out of the racial mainstream. These populations would remain on the other side of the new racial divide. An expansion of the boundaries of whiteness or of multiraciality will not solve the problem of the color line—as W. E. B. DuBois famously framed it more than a hundred years ago—it will simply redraw that line. Such a transformation would just repeat the story of early twentieth-century Americanization, which, as Nathan Glazer pointed out, kept blacks—and we should add, minority immigrants—outside of the American mainstream (Glazer 1993).

Working from a racial formation perspective, Eduardo Bonilla Silva proposed a different scenario—a tripartite, Latin American–style, racial stratification system (2004). In it, some Asian Americans groups with high socioeconomic status, as well as light skin Latinos, will be assigned an "honorary white" status and would constitute a buffer group between whites, and a collective black subject composed of African Americans, dark-skin Latinos, Native Americans, and Asian Americans with low socioeconomic status. This scenario allows for the redrawing of the boundaries of whiteness suggested by assimilation scholars, but emphasizes the pervasiveness of racial difference at the core of the American system of stratification. The tripartite scenario proposed by Bonilla Silva coincides with the broad outlines of the racialized class stratification system portrayed in this volume.

Yet the analysis of the Dominican experience suggests a more complex scenario. Two more factors need to be taken into account to understand the contemporary experience of minority immigrant incorporation. First is class stratification within the different components of Bonilla-Silva's black collective subject. The class and the racial systems are correlated but they do not overlap. Second, there is no collective black subject at the level of group formation and collective action. Latinos share a structural position and living conditions with African Americans, but separate themselves in terms of identity formation and group organization. Recognizing this pattern is critical when thinking about the possibilities of collective action for common ends.

To summarize the theoretical argument developed in this book, then, the stratified ethnoracial incorporation approach builds on the findings of both the new assimilation approach and the segmented assimilation approach, but goes beyond them. From the first, it takes the emphasis on the mobility of the second generation, mobility that takes place through entering the mainstream institutions of American society. There is no indication, however, of a process of convergence between the children of immigrants and the white American mainstream. The available evidence on mobility discussed in chapter 2 indicates that the racialized character of the stratification system is sturdy (Hertz 2005; Mazumder 2005). Furthermore, although Dominicans do experience mobility and acculturation, ethnoracial difference does not disappear. As shown in chapters 5, 7, and 8, the middle class develops critical views of the encounter with American society and also embraces transnationalism and panethnicity.

From segmented assimilation, the stratified ethnoracial incorporation approach focuses on different paths of incorporation. This volume, however, emphasizes the fact that the second generation is joining the services working class rather than the more marginalized sectors. Both processes take place, but the former is more important in understanding the incorporation of immigrant generations, though less poignant as a social issue. The stratified incorporation approach also emphasizes mobility through entering mainstream institutions rather than through ethnic enclaves.

Another element that distinguishes the stratified approach is the place of the American social structure in the analysis of immigrant incorporation. Both the new and the segmented assimilation approaches see the American social structure as a context into which different groups with different characteristics incorporate. As Min Zhou and Carl Bankston explained, the study of the assimilation of immigrants takes the structure of American society as a given, focusing in turn on the elements that help immigrants adapt to it (1988). This take on American society is embodied in the concept of context of reception that Alejandro Portes and Rubén Rumbaut proposed (1996).

The focus of the stratified ethnoracial incorporation approach is on how the American social structure shapes the incorporation of immigrant generations. It goes beyond the concept of context of reception in looking at the general trends of mobility and stratification in American society to explain the past and likely future trajectories of Dominican—and other immigrant—generations. Of course, the social, human, and economic capital of an immigrant group matter. The human and economic capital of a group determine the point of entry into the social structure of the receiving society and its social capital affects how much individuals can rely on the group in the process of incorporation. Yet the argument proposed here is that once a group enters the American social structure, the broad structural trends overcome group dynamics. As a result, the future position of immigrants in American society—as the trajectories of immigrants in the past—depends more on the evolution of the American economic structure and on which forces become hegemonic in politics than on the characteristics of the group. In this way, the study of immigrant incorporation is the study of American society.

Dominicans arrive in the United States without economic resources or high levels of education. Furthermore, those with higher education have a difficult time translating their Dominican credentials into occupational mobility in America. The analysis of Dominican incorporation therefore shows the experience of a group that enters the labor market at its lower end, does not have many resources, and is also racialized. The volume would be very different if its focus were on a group that arrived with significant economic capital or with education credentials recognized by American employers. The path of incorporation of Dominicans sheds light on the dynamics of stratification and mobility at the bottom of American society. The analysis of the encounter of Dominicans with American material and symbolic stratification highlights the class and racial faultlines of U.S. society.

To emphasize the power of the social structure, however, is not to deny the agency of immigrants. As chapter 4 shows, individual immigrants try to make the best of a difficult situation and the result is mobility. And, as analyzed in chapter 8, Dominicans also act collectively to improve their predicament through the political system. The point this book makes, however, is that the general trends of mobility in American society are such that, other things being equal, the third generation will likely continue the present pattern of ethno-racial and class stratification rather than close the gap with the mainstream. Of course, the key to the statement is "other things being equal," and social processes are rarely so. To understand how things can be different, it is useful to look at past processes of incorporation. A detour to the past can throw light on the possibilities of change in the future.

IMMIGRANT INCORPORATION
THEN AND NOW

Warner's and Srole's *The Social Systems of American Ethnic Groups* is useful because of its detailed predictions on the process of assimilation of different immigrant groups, predictions that can be compared with the actual process of immigrant assimilation (1945). Warner's and Srole's research in Newburyport was conducted in the first half of the 1930s and the book was published in 1945, the period immediately previous to the large transformations that led to the assimilation of the children of southern, central, and eastern European immigrants. The book therefore shows us how that process of incorporation looked like at the time it was going on.

Warner and Srole thought that the pace of assimilation of immigrants depended on their racial and cultural distance from the white Anglo-Protestant mainstream of those days. To analyze this process, they proposed a typology of five racial groups, further dividing these according to the cultural distance of each of the ethnic groups that composed it from Anglo-Protestants. Each of the types was expected to assimilate at a different pace.

The first group they called the Light Caucasoid type, composed of western European immigrants, such as French, Dutch, and Germans, and others of European origin such as Canadians, French Canadians, and Australians. This group was expected to assimilate quickly, which for Warner and Srole meant between one and six generations. The second group was the Dark Caucasoid, and included southern, central, and eastern Europeans—such as Italians, Armenians, Portuguese, and Jews—as well as Near-Eastern Christians and European Muslims. Part of this group was expected to assimilate in a moderate span, which for Warner and Srole meant more than six generations. Jews and European Muslims, because of their cultural distance from the Protestant mainstream, were expected to assimilate at a slow pace, which Warner and Srole defined as "a very long time in the future which is not yet discernible" (1945, 292).

The third group they called the Caucasoid Mixtures, describing it as "the mixed bloods of Latin America"—an ethnoracial group, that is, one defined by both cultural and racial distinctiveness (1945, 291). Warner and Srole argued that once the cultural distinctiveness was lost, the lighter skin members of the group could assimilate at a slow pace. The dark-skin members of the group, on the other hand, would become a semicaste or assimilate into that formed by black Americans. The fourth and fifth racial types were Asians and blacks. Their fate was a caste system and they were not expected to assimilate until the American social order changed, "gradually or by revolution" (1945, 292). Warner and Srole put Puerto Ricans within the black category rather than the Latin American racially mixed groups.[1]

Looking back six decades later, the most striking element is the speed with which southern, central, and eastern European groups assimilated. In the 1940s, Warner and Srole expected Italians to assimilate in more than six generations, and Jews, in a nondiscernible future. Yet, within the span of one generation from the publication of their book, white ethnicity would take the form of symbolic ethnicity. The incorporation of previous immigrant generations took place in the context of two broad social transformation. First was economic expansion and policies of social inclusion. Second was a blurring of the ethnoracial boundaries that had separated the white ethnic groups from the American mainstream. The speed of assimilation of European groups, then, was the result of a process of large-scale structural upward mobility and cultural change that Warner and Srole could not have predicted.

After World War II, America experienced unprecedented economic growth and social mobility—the golden years of American economic expansion. This expansion was accompanied by two sociopolitical trends that guaranteed that the fruits of economic growth reached broad segments of society. The first was the expansion of unions and unions' political leverage. The unions' strength translated into higher salaries and the expansion of health and pension coverage to unionized sectors. The second development was the political hegemony of what can be called the Democratic New Deal coalition. From the 1930s to the late 1960s, the Democratic Party shaped the orientation of social policies in the United States. The different Democratic administrations introduced policies to fight poverty and social exclusion, such as Social Security and later Medicare and Medicaid, and to expand mobility opportunities, such as the GI

Bill. It was the combination of the power of unions that guaranteed a middle-class lifestyle to wage workers and the social integration policies promoted by the federal government that created the American middle-class society into which the children of southern, central, and eastern European immigrants assimilated. This process of rapid economic growth and mobility made it possible for the boundaries of whiteness to become porous at a much faster pace than these two scholars thought they would.

The second major transformation was the blurring of the ethnic and racial barriers that differentiated the children of European immigrants from the white American mainstream. The assimilation of white immigrants was accompanied by an expansion of the white category to include southern, central, and eastern Europeans in addition to Anglo and northern Europeans and to encompass Catholics and Jews in addition to Protestant groups. Marginalized immigrant groups became white ethnics and their ethnicity became symbolic, that is, it became an identity that can be worn in public celebrations and relished in the privacy of the home, but does not structure the daily life of the members of the group or affect their encounters with mainstream institutions.

The speed and scope of these changes support the argument that the racial system is unstable and that racial boundaries can be blurred. Yet the experiences of European and minority immigrants were not similar to one another. The Warner and Srole typology showed that European groups were racialized, but not in the same way as Latin Americans, Caribbeans, Asians, and blacks. The racial boundary between southern, central, and eastern Europeans and the white mainstream was considered porous. The children of European immigrants were expected to assimilate very slowly but assimilate nonetheless. Minorities were expected to be part of a caste system until the American racial system changed radically. Whereas Warner and Srole were wrong about the pace of assimilation of European immigrants, they were right in arguing that the assimilation of minorities depended on a major social and political transformation of American society.

The transformation they posed occurred with the civil rights movement, a mass-based social movement that brought down the legal exclusion system based on race. The civil rights movement pushed open—albeit partially—the doors of economic opportunity for racial minorities and made open expressions of racism in mainstream culture unacceptable. Only the mass mobilization of large numbers of people could achieve such a thing. It is important to remember that although the civil rights movement was spearheaded and led by African Americans, there were at the same time massive mobilizations of Chicanos, Puerto Ricans, and Native Americans demanding their own recognition and inclusion. The movement also had the sympathy of segments of the white population.

As a result of the civil rights movement, avenues of mobility opened up for minority groups. Since then, the country has seen the emergence of minority middle class and minority elites in all walks of life. One of the most notable changes is that large segments of the Asian American population entered the upper strata of American society, to the point that the aggregate average socioeconomic indicators for some Asian American groups are equal or better than those of the white population. This is a remarkable change given that in the mid-1940s Warner and Srole saw Asian American groups as an excluded caste group. The rapid economic and social incorporation of Asian Americans is one of the main points in arguing that a process of blurring of racial boundaries is underway. Nevertheless, as impressive as the Asian American process of upward mobility indeed is, it is important to remember that the aggregate indicators hide a situation of class stratification and inequality (Kwong 1996). Moreover, middle-class Asian Americans are still undergoing processes of ethnoracial identity formation (Kibria 2002; Min and Kim 1999).

The mass mobilization of minorities in the 1960s, in fact, left a truncated agenda in terms of socioeconomic equality of opportunity. The civil rights movement opened mobility avenues for minorities through affirmative action programs in education, equal employment policies, and the elimination of openly racist practices in hiring. As argued by Kasinitz and his colleagues in *Inheriting the City,* the civil rights movement led to the formation of an institutional field that allows for the partial mobility of minorities and immigrants. The policies and institutions it inspired, however, have been under constant attack for the last three decades. Furthermore, since the 1980s, structural economic trends have been toward increasing social inequality (Massey 2007). The reduction of employment in manufacturing since the late 1970s created urban areas of extreme poverty in cities that had a manufacturing economic base. This process strongly affected black and Puerto Ricans communities in the Northeast and Midwest. It also deeply affected the process of Dominican socioeconomic incorporation (Hernández 2002; Wilson 1996).

The truncated economic equality agenda of the social movements of the 1960s created the stratified ethnoracial incorporation system that characterizes the position of Dominicans—and other native and migrant minorities—in

American society. Within this system, upward mobility is possible for segments of minority populations, creating internal class stratification within all minority communities. Nevertheless, even though minorities have progressed within the American class system and achieved middle-class status, the minority middle classes still confront racialization (Lacy 2004; Pattillo 2005). Minorities cannot escape racialization in everyday life and in their dealings with social institutions.

A DIFFERENT FUTURE?

The analysis of the process of assimilation of past immigrant generations shows that the path of incorporation of minority groups depends on the racial and class structure and on the political dynamics of the country. Therefore, to think about the possibility of a different future, one in which the children of Dominican immigrants—and the children of other minority immigrants, as well as African Americans—achieve equality of opportunity with the American mainstream and one in which racialization is not an element of everyday life, we need to pay attention to the economic structural trends and, in particular, to political developments.

Trying to predict the trends of the American economy is a particularly risky endeavor. As I finish writing this book, the country is immersed in the deepest financial and economic crisis since the Great Depression. The likely course of this crisis is hard to predict at this point, creating a great deal of uncertainty concerning the future of America's economy and social structure. A prolonged recession scenario will certainly reduce opportunities for mobility and threaten the stability of the existing middle classes. Furthermore, under a situation of increased economic competition for scarce opportunities, ethnic and racial tensions may increase, both between whites and minorities but also between different minority groups that compete in the labor market. Yet, even if the country were to come up relatively quickly and relatively unscathed from the current crisis, without a change in the dynamics of racialization and in the political orientation of the country, a return to growth will reproduce the existing patterns of class and racial inequality.

The future trajectory of the children of immigrants will be determined by the political dynamic of the country, not by the passing of generations. The convergence of the children of Dominicans—and the children of other native and immigrant minorities—and the white mainstream, if it is to happen, demands a new transformation of the American social and cultural order. It demands an economic transformation to reduce the growing inequalities of the last three decades, a political transformation to create equality of opportunity for all and in that way address the racialization of the class system, and a cultural transformation to address the pervasive forms of everyday racialization. The challenge for progressive change is to build a coalition that brings together people from all groups behind a politics that addresses the needs of working families. The union support for the immigrant rights movement and the mass demonstrations for immigrant rights that took place in 2006 seemed for a while to be a prelude to such a movement. Yet what we are witnessing now is a large anti-immigrant backlash in American politics, a turn that makes a broad alliance of working people difficult.

As I finish this volume, the country has just elected its first African American president. The election of Barack Obama to the presidency is a momentous event. It represents the culmination of the process of change that began with the civil rights movement. It is notable in this regard the strong support he gathers among young people. The generations that grew up after the civil rights movement seem to accept with ease the idea of an African American reaching the presidency of the United States. Not only the young, however, voted for Obama; an important element of his victory is that he managed to secure votes across class and racial lines.

Yet, as momentous as the election of Obama to the presidency is, racialization and racial structural inequalities are not going to disappear because he is the president. The election of Barack Obama is an enormous step in the struggle for racial equality but not the end of it.[2] Racial boundaries are changing, but they have proven in the past to be rather sturdy. After all, the emergence of minority elites in all walks of life—in the cultural industries, sports, politics, the military, the academy, and also the economic system—is part of the post–civil rights movement stratified ethnoracial social structure. Opening opportunities for the struggling middle class was a central theme of the Obama campaign. It remains to be seen whether he will be able to implement policies to reverse the trend toward growing inequality. For this to happen, the progressive part of the broad coalition that elected him needs to put pressure on his administration to advance in the direction of inclusiveness and expansion of opportunities to all.

Dominicans in Providence participated in the making of the historic 2008 election. The southern Providence constituencies voted in large numbers in spite of the fact that no one doubted that Rhode Island would vote for Obama and that there were no competitive races for local offices. They voted because they wanted to participate in shaping the future of the country and because they understood that voting is the way to guarantee that their voice will be heard in the political arena. The analysis of Dominican political participation in Providence shows that they have achieved a measure of electoral success at the state and city level. Their political mobilization was key to gaining mainstream recognition for the group and directing resources to the poorer parts of Providence. The limit of this type of politics is that it has not—at least not yet—been able to build a broad coalition to address the dynamics of racial categorization and class exclusion. Dominican elected officials in Providence work with other minority elected officials to pursue an agenda that improves the lives of working families, but they have not been able so far to build the political coalition that would propel that agenda. Such a coalition, to be effective, has to be multiracial; it has to involve immigrant and native minorities and parts of the white working and middle classes.

The obstacles in building such a broad progressive coalition for change are large and well known. Political mobilization is based on the particular identities and interests of different groups. Different minority groups often encounter each other as competitors in the labor market and for access to social goods, and as such each may prefer to try to mobilize and improve its position by itself. A broad coalition for progressive change also has to overcome the pervasive effects of racism and white privilege that have historically divided the white working class from minority groups. To build such a political coalition is not easy and success is certainly not guaranteed. Yet only such a movement can bring the political and cultural changes that will allow for the full integration of the children of Dominican immigrants—and other immigrant minorities—into the mainstream. Otherwise, the passing of generations will only repeat the pattern of stratified ethnoracial incorporation.

NOTES

CHAPTER 1

1. In fairness to Gordon, setting Anglo-conformity as the end point of the assimilation process was for him an empirical assessment, not a normative statement.

2. That I point to the inaccurate predictions of Warner and Srole about the speed of assimilation of different ethnic groups does not mean that I intend to dwell on the error. In fact, I use their book as an anchor for my argument because they were alone in the assimilation tradition in bringing the color line to the center of an analysis of ethnicity.

3. The class structure of post-industrial societies is further analyzed in chapter 5.

4. I develop this conceptual framework in chapter 6.

5. Although several years old, these data are still the best we have for the analysis of relatively small groups, such as Dominicans in Providence. I tried to pull together several yearly samples of the Current Population Survey (CPS) or the American Communities Survey (ACS) but the number of Dominicans in Rhode Island included in those surveys was very low, even after pooling together different years. As a result, the analysis showed obvious holes (for example, in the proportions of people who abandoned school or in the occupational distribution). Those surveys can be used to analyze socioeconomic trends in places where the Dominican population is large, such as New York City, because the number of Dominicans included in the sample is large enough, but in places with small populations to begin with, such as Rhode Island, only the census allows us to look at specific groups.

6. Because they are unique cases in each of their capacities—that is, there are no other Dominican state senators or representatives—and because they are public

personalities, I cannot conceal their identities and so use their names when I quote them or talk about them.

CHAPTER 2

1. The number of Dominicans reported in the 2000 Census was 764,945, but there was a broad consensus among scholars that this number underestimated the number of Dominicans in the United States. In all the analyses of census-based data throughout the book, I use my own estimates. I used the 5 percent PUMS files of the 2000 Census. I started the process identifying those who self-identified as Dominican in the Hispanic Census question. Then, I examined those who answered Hispanic but did not specify a nationality. I identified two groups within this population: those who were born in the Dominican Republic and those who reported Dominican ancestry (I did not include those who reported mixed Dominican ancestry, but this was a very small group). I added these two groups to the number of those who self-identified as Dominicans. For the United States as a whole, this sum yielded 995,726 people—a number very close to the Pew Hispanic Center estimate. Following a different methodology, Pew estimated that there were 938,316 Dominicans in the United States in the year 2000 (Suro 2002). I repeated this procedure to estimate the number of Dominicans in Providence, New York City, and Lawrence, and also in Rhode Island, Massachusetts, New York State, New Jersey, and Florida.

2. The towns north of Providence are agglomerated in the 2000 Census PUMS into PUMA5 400. Being familiar with the state, I know that the Dominican population is concentrated in Central Falls. If we could isolate the data for Central Falls, the weight of the Dominican population would be much higher, but this is impossible to do using PUMS data.

3. I discuss the process of local political empowerment of Dominicans in chapter 8.

4. Juán Pichardo, interview, July 16, 2008.

CHAPTER 3

1. Of course, each of these categories could be disaggregated. One could differentiate between mainland and island-born Puerto Ricans. The Latino category is very broad and incorporates too many different migration histories. Blacks can be separated into African Americans and black immigrants, and their children. This effort would produce more accurate, yet more cumbersome, tables. For this comparison, which is to establish the overall position of Dominicans in Providence's socioeconomic structure, the more aggregate categories are enough.

2. The tables in this chapter present data on those between twenty-four and sixty-four years of age. Labor market studies usually look at people between twenty-five and sixty-four. Given the small number of second-generation Dominicans, I lowered the cut-off age for the analysis. The analytical choice is to focus on people of working age who are likely to have completed their education and started working. At twenty-four, those who went to college are likely to be out of it and working and those who did not go to college have already worked several years.

3. To avoid overwhelming the reader with tables and numbers, I do not include this data in table form, but the results are available upon request.

4. People working within the segmented assimilation approach call this strategy selective acculturation and emphasize its positive effects for the mobility of the second generation (Portes and Rumbaut 2001).

5. The other second-generation groups included in the New York study are Russian Jews, West Indians, Chinese, and South Americans.

6. Because the analysis is based on the census's 5 percent PUMS, the information in this section corresponds to the Massachusetts PUMA 700, which includes, in addition to Lawrence, Andover, and Methuen (it is not possible to isolate Lawrence within this database). Most Dominicans in this area live in Lawrence, so I refer to it by that name, but the data refers to an area and a population larger than the municipal boundaries of Lawrence.

7. These results are perhaps obvious to anyone familiar with American statistics on racial inequality, yet, it is important to document them in the light of portrayals of American society as color-blind.

8. To avoid overwhelming the reader with tables, I do not present the data for New Jersey and Florida.

9. I conduct a partial version of this exercise in chapter 4, where I look at the class transitions among a small sample of Dominicans in Providence.

10. The authors pooled the 1996 to 1999 samples of the Current Population Survey for a cross-sectional comparison of three generations of Mexican Americans (Bean and Stevens 2003). Their analysis suffers from the same problems as the one I conducted—cross-sectional data and no information about parent-children educational and occupational transitions—but the deeper generational composition of the data allows these researchers to compare cross-sections of the second and third generations (in fact, they have no way of distinguishing between the third and further generations), something I cannot do given the young age of the Dominican second generation.

11. This research is of a technical complexity that I cannot address in this book. To summarize, Bhashkar Mazumder matched data on the participants in the Survey of Income and Program Participation with data from the Social Security Administration summary earnings records (2005). This dataset allows Mazumder to compare intergenerational income differences across several years. He showed that when averaging the incomes of parents and children over a large number of years, the intergenerational elasticity equals 0.6. In lay terms, this means that other things being equal, a 10 percent difference in parents' income translates into a 6 percent difference in children's incomes.

12. Tom Hertz's numbers are different from those of Mazumder because Hertz relied exclusively on the Panel Studies of Income Dynamics, he used different measures, and compared income over a lower number of years (2005). Hertz's results are a measure of income differentials using "age adjusted log family income" (again, the technical complexity of the analysis goes beyond what I can address in this book). Yet, the results of Hertz and Mazumder for the whole population are not so different, and they are consistent in showing a much less mobile society than the popular view imagines. Hertz's article has the advantage of comparing the differences in the intergenerational transmission of income between the black and white populations.

CHAPTER 4

1. López posited two reasons for the fact that girls are doing better than boys (2003). The first has to do with their different school experiences. School authorities perceive boys as being more threatening than girls and therefore subject boys to more disciplining. As a result, the boys' school experience becomes particularly burdensome and alienating. The second reason that girls do better in school has to do with gender socialization. López argued that girls are socialized into taking on household duties whereas boys are left alone without much supervision or responsibilities. This gives girls a structure and discipline in everyday life that helps them in dealing with school life, a structure and discipline that boys lack.

2. I am simplifying and slightly modifying Stanton-Salazar's argument. Stanton-Salazar embeds his analysis of networks within the concept of social capital. In my opinion, emphasizing the analysis of the class differences in networks is enough and the concept of social capital does not add much to it.

3. I present information on Latinos rather than on Dominicans because the publically available information from the Providence School Department and from

the Rhode Island Department of Elementary and Secondary Education is not disaggregated by national origin. Nevertheless, in the previous chapter we saw that although there are differences between second-generation Dominicans, other Latinos, and Puerto Ricans, the broad picture for all Latinos is similar.

4. Information about the Providence School Department is available online at http://www.providenceschools.org/dept/news/facts.html.

5. The table was constructed using publically available information provided at the website of the Rhode Island Department of Elementary and Secondary Education (Available at: http://www.ride.ri.gov/applications/statistics.aspx). I chose the 2005–2006 academic year because it was the latest for which RIDE provides the information presented in the table.

6. The choice of year makes a difference though. In 2007, Feinstein High School was upgraded to adequate yearly progress.

7. Following the accepted practices in the presentation of qualitative research, I have changed the names of the respondents and blurred details of their lives that can identify them. I have also omitted the names of the schools and organizations mentioned in the narratives to protect the privacy of the people I have interviewed.

8. The interview with Alejandra was in Spanish, the quotations are my translation.

9. Luisa and Alejandra attended different high schools.

CHAPTER 5

1. This notion of class draws from the work of contemporary neo-Weberian and neo-Marxist analysts of stratification (Breen 2005; Erikson and Goldthorpe 1992; Wright 2005b).

2. Given that employees always retain a measure of autonomy in the performance of their duties, Goldthorpe argued that the form of employment relationship chosen is given by efficiency considerations: which form of employment guarantees the possibility of monitoring work and the loyalty and commitment of the employee to the goals of the organization. In those cases in which the monitoring of work is simple and there is no high specificity of assets needed to conduct the job, a labor contract is used. On the other hand, when monitoring is difficult or the assets necessary to carry the job are specific, a service relationship arises (Goldthorpe and McKnight 2004). Richard Breen criticized Goldthorpe approach for relying too much on considerations of efficiency and leaving out the ability of workers to negotiate their working conditions (2005). This criticism is correct, but the role of workers agency can be incorporated into the

causal understanding of the different types of working relations without invalidating the basic distinction, as the specific elements of the employment relation are often determined by negotiations between employers and employees.

3. The model draws inspiration from Weber's approach, in which classes are groups that command similar resources in the labor market and class position has an effect on the economic conditions of life of people in different classes.

4. He has also developed an eleven- and a four-classes model that are in fact a more detailed and a more synthetic version of the seven-class model. Which is the more appropriate one depends on the analytical needs that arise from the question one is interested in.

5. The survey asked what the job of the respondent is, what the respondent does at work, who the employer is, whether the respondent is a permanent or a temporary employee, whether the job requires a certain level of education, and how long the respondent has been at the present job.

6. In single-parent households or in households where only one parent was employed, the household was assigned to the class of that parent. In two-parent households, if the two parents were in the same class, then that was the class of the household. If at least one of the parents was in the salariat, the household was assigned to that class. If one of the parents was in the blue-collar working class and the other was in the services working class the household was assigned to the services working class.

7. This analysis is different from the mobility research reported in chapter 2. The latter uses data on the income of parents and their children over a long period (Hertz 2005; Mazumder 2005). As I mentioned in that chapter, there is no available data that will allow me to conduct that type of analysis for the Dominican second generation. In the survey used here all the information comes from the respondent.

8. This is a common strategy. The seven-classes model is a heuristic model, one of several possible ways of classifying classes for analysis.

9. As shown in table 3.5, 38.6 percent of the Dominican second generation in Providence work in middle-class occupations, most of them in class II managerial positions. Nationwide, the percentage of people in this stratum is 35.9, and again, most of them work in class II occupations.

10. A comparison of the mean earnings of each of these groups in the sample shows that the mean earnings of respondents in the lower salariat and the petite bourgeoisie are higher than those in the manufacturing working class, which in turn are higher than the earnings of those in the services working class. These differences are statistically significant.

11. This category is broad, including the unemployed and those who are not in the labor force. As a result, there is not much I will be able to say about it.

12. Included in this table are only those cases with valid information on current occupation and parents' occupation when the interviewee was age sixteen.

13. The reason to focus on the mobility of the second generation is that the mobility trends of the first generation—which often show downward mobility with respect to their parents—are the result of the migration experience and the difficulties in acquiring a new language, transferring skills, and getting educational credentials recognized. The mobility experiences of the first generation are unique. To understand the incorporation of immigrants, then, we need to look at the second generation (and beyond). The reason to focus on people who are twenty-four or older is—as explained in chapter 3—that by age twenty-four people who did not go to college have acquired some work experience, and those who have gone to college, unless they pursued graduate studies, are in the labor market.

14. There are another seven students in the sample but no information about their class of origin.

15. There were 101 Dominicans from Providence included in the New England segment of the Latino National Survey. Ninety were of the first generation and the remaining eleven were of the second generation.

16. Because the results were so uniform across class and generation, I did not include them in the table, but they are available on request.

17. People were asked to answer in a scale of 1 to 5, in which the latter was strongly agree and the former strongly disagree. I combined the answers of those who answered that they agree or strongly agree. The table presents the percentage who answered that they agree or strongly agree with the statement.

18. One-quarter of Providence Dominicans who participated in the Latino National Survey reported discrimination. Among this group, 41 percent responded that they were being discriminated against for being Latinos and 76.2 percent reported that the people who discriminated against them were white.

19. As with the previous question, the numbers in this table show the percentages of people who agree or strongly agree with the statements.

CHAPTER 6

1. Debates on national identity are global as immigration is a global phenomenon (for a comparative assessment of debates and policies generated by large-scale migration, see Joppke 1999, 2005).

2. The structural relation between the multiple identities of the self has been addressed in social psychology through the concepts of salience and centrality (for a review of these concepts, see Sellers et al. 1998; Stryker and Serpe 1994; for a discussion of the relative importance of the available social categories of identification and the networks to which a person belongs in structuring identities, see Deaux and Martin 2003).

3. This understanding of identity is by no means agreed upon by all who work in this field, but it seems to me to be the most productive to make sense of my research findings. In proposing it, I rely on recent work in social psychology (see Ashmore, Deaux, and McLaughlin-Volpe 2004; Deaux and Martin 2003; Sellers et al. 1998; Stryker and Serpe 1994; and the writings of anthropologist Richard Jenkins 1997).

4. The five questions were phrased as follows. General identity question: "If you have to fill a form that asks how do you identify, what would you write?" Open-ended ethnic identity question: "Could you please tell us what is your ethnicity? That is, if you had to fill out a form indicating to which ethnic group you belong, what would you write?" Open-ended racial identity question: "Could you please tell us what is your race? That is, if you had to fill out a form indicating your race, what would you write?" These three questions were open ended and did not limit the choice of answers. Closed racial identity question: "Could you please tell us what is your race? That is, if you had to fill out a form indicating your race, what would you write?" Question about how the respondents think mainstream Americans see them: "How do you think mainstream Americans see you in terms of race?" The last two questions offered three possible answers: black, white, and other. If the respondent chose the third answer, they were asked to specify what they meant. The questions were spread out throughout the questionnaire to avoid a situation in which people give similar answers to the different questions because the questions were close to each other and were perceived to be asking about the same thing. Indeed, as we will see, there was not much superposition in the answers to the five questions.

5. The table in fact reduces the number of labels Dominicans use as some panethnic combinations, different mixed-race answers, and various non-racial self descriptions were combined under common labels.

6. This answer encompassed those who answered Hispanic and Hispana or Hispano. I lumped these together because whether in English or in Spanish they are used in the same way. I also included in this category a handful of hyphenated answers that started with Hispanic because they refer to a similar understanding of panethnicity.

7. The importance of language in the formation of Dominican identity is covered in chapter 5.

8. This by no means invalidates the survey results or surveys in general as a methodology for the research of identity. It does point out, however, to the need to complement survey research with qualitative and ethnographic research methods.

9. Of course, the family ideal is one thing and the actual working of families is another. Dominicans indeed have close attachments to their parents, relatives, and siblings; they send large amounts of money to help relatives in the Dominican Republic and invest time in socializing with their extend families. At the same time, I talked with elderly first-generation Dominicans who complained that the second generation is Americanized and does not take care of the elderly as people in the Dominican Republic do (or, at least, as they believe that people in the Dominican Republic do). Also, in spite of the emphasis on respecting the elderly, first-generation Dominican parents often tell how difficult it is to control their children in the United States. On the other hand, I've heard second-generation people complain that their relatives in the Dominican Republic are only interested in remittances and not in family per se.

10. Several of my respondents insisted that because Latinos are multiracial the panethnic label is not racial and should not be used that way. Yet they recognized the fact that people indeed do use it in a racial sense.

11. I return to this topic in chapter 7, where I show that Dominicans incorporate into Providence's social and political life through the formation of panethnic organizations and panethnic activism.

12. The sociologist Tanya Golash-Boza called this process racialized assimilation (2006).

CHAPTER 7

1. Smith first described Ticuani as being a small county with a population of fewer than 2,000 people. On page 8, however, he asserted that according to his estimations, between 100 and 150 youngsters and 300 to 400 adults travel to Ticuani every year. These numbers, he wrote, constituted at least 10 percent of all Ticuani immigrants in the United States. The minimum number of visitors according to these estimations is therefore 400, and this represents at least 20 percent of the size of the municipio mentioned earlier. In fact, Smith never makes clear his estimation of the size of the population of the Ticuanense transnational community. Furthermore, based on his estimation that 10 percent of the population returns each year, Smith said also that 30 to 40 percent of the population returns

over a period of three years. This may be so, but only if no one returns year after year.

2. Until the approval of dual citizenship, many immigrants were reluctant to naturalize because they did not want to lose their Dominican citizenship.

3. In the United States, consulting councils have been established in New York, New Jersey, Massachusetts, and Puerto Rico—but not, at the time of this writing, in Rhode Island.

4. The Dominican government held consultations with different sectors of Dominican society, asking for feedback from each sector on constitutional reform issues that directly affected them.

5. Several countries with large migrant populations, including Italy, Colombia, and Cape Verde, have already created mechanisms for parliamentary representation of their migrant communities.

6. This twenty-first-century understanding of the nation seems fairly close to nineteenth-century romantic notions of the nation rooted in blood.

7. The table uses the class categories delineated in chapter 4. Because of the small number of cases, the working-class category includes both services and manufacturing. Also because of the small number of cases, the nonworking category includes the unemployed, those who are not in the labor market, those on welfare, and those who have retired, making the results for this group at best difficult to interpret.

8. The Latino National Survey presents a similar picture of extended engagement in broad transnational practices. Among the first-generation Dominicans included in this survey 66 percent have visited the Dominican Republic in the last three years and 57.2 send remittances at least once a year—although only 35.9 percent send remittances once a month or more. Furthermore, 67.4 percent are in touch with friends and family in the Dominican Republic at least once a month.

9. I included this item in the measure of social rather than economic transnationalism because the latter refers to entrepreneurial activities, and organizations that send money to the town of origin of their members usually do so to develop social or community projects.

10. Among the first-generation respondents to the Latino National Survey, 17.8 percent own a house in the Dominican Republic and 4.4 percent own land there.

11. Among the first-generation respondents to the Latino National Survey, only 4.4 have contributed money to candidates in the Dominican Republic since com-

ing to the United States, but 61.6 percent believed that it is appropriate for Dominicans living in the United States to cast a ballot in the Dominican national elections.

12. Worldwide, the number of registered people in 2004 was 52,440, out of which 35,042 voted. In 2008, the number of registered voters tripled, reaching 154,789, and the number of voters was slightly more than twice those who voted in 2004, with 76,713 Dominican migrants casting their votes abroad. The numbers of registered and actual voters can be found in the website of the Junta Central Electoral, the state agency that organizes and supervises the elections in the Dominican Republic.

13. Among the LNS first-generation respondents, 15.6 percent have voted in Dominican elections since their migration to the United States. Only 5.5 percent, however, have cast their vote in the United States. The rest probably traveled to vote in the Dominican Republic before voting in the United States was an option. It is important to remember, however, that the Latino National Survey was conducted before the 2008 elections.

14. In this, the development of broad political transnationalism is quite similar in the Dominican and the Mexican cases (Itzigsohn 2007).

15. There are also high percentages of nonworking people who engage in transnational practices, but given the low numbers and the heterogeneity of the category, we cannot reach conclusions regarding this group.

16. First-generation respondents in the survey are also more involved in non-Dominican organizations. Approximately 30 percent of the first-generation sample reported membership in a non-Dominican political party, union, or community organization, versus only 15 percent of the second-generation sample. These results point, on the one side, to the incorporation of the second generation into American life as a larger proportion is involved in non-Dominican organizations than in Dominican ones. On the other hand, the results suggest that incorporation into American life leads to a decline in civic involvement, because first generation respondents are more involved in both Dominican and non-Dominican organizations than second-generation respondents.

17. I return to this topic in chapter 8, when I analyze the process of incorporation of Dominicans into Rhode Island's local politics.

18. Juán Pablo Duarte was the main hero of Dominican independence and many organizations are named after him.

19. The monument to Juán Pablo Duarte was a first in efforts of local Latino communities to establish a symbolic presence in the city. In 2006, as a result of

efforts by local Mexican American organizations, a monument to César Chávez was inaugurated.

20. The Instituto Duartiano in Santo Domingo is dedicated to the preservation of the memory of Juán Pablo Duarte. It runs a museum in what was Duarte's house in the old colonial neighborhood of Santo Domingo. The Santo Domingo Institute is a civic association with its own board of directors but receives its budget from the Dominican government.

21. This encounter is described earlier in this chapter.

22. There are several Dominican sport leagues in Providence. Many are independent leagues and not related to any particular organization.

23. Quisqueya is a Taino name for the island that the Dominican Republic shares with Haiti.

24. The assertion of identity is, of course, not enough for navigating the school system and can also sometimes have negative effects. The key element to explain the school experience, as asserted in chapter 4, is the encounter with institutional agents that open or close doors of mobility (Stanton-Salazar 1997). But the positive assertion of ethnic identity, such as was done by Quisqueya en Acción, can help youngsters to succeed in an institutional context often experienced as hostile.

25. The comparative references used to explain the role of this organization are the Cuban and Jewish lobbies. Cubans and Jews are seen as ethnic groups that have successfully acquired a voice in American policy.

26. The individual quoted has already been introduced in this book and is deliberately not identified in deference to personal privacy.

27. This is true for the Dominican Republic as well as for other migration states such as Mexico, El Salvador, and Cape Verde (Itzigsohn 2000; Itzigsohn and Villacrés 2008; Smith 2006).

CHAPTER 8

1. The analysis of each of these dimensions of panethnicity fits the model of analysis of identity that Richard Ashmore, Kay Deux, and Tracy McLaughlin-Volpe proposed, described in chapter 6 (2004). Categorical panethnicity corresponds to the analysis of self-categorization. Institutional and political panethnicity correspond to the analysis of behavioral involvement in practices that are anchored in categorical panethnicity. Finally, the study of ideological panethnicity fits the analysis of the content and meaning of identities.

2. I focus on the latter two organizations because I know the cases well through personal involvement.

3. I use the real names of people because the narrative is based on the description of events in the public domain.

4. Another of the pioneers of Latino radio in Providence was Franklyn Navarro, a Colombian entrepreneur who ran several radio stations that had a strong presence in the city until the late 1990s, when he returned to Colombia.

5. Progreso Latino is one of two Latino service agencies in the state. The other is called CHISPA (Center for Hispanic Policy and Advocacy). Latino nonprofit service agencies are critical in forging panethnic identities. Latin American immigrants who come to these agencies learn that they have access to their services because they are Latinos.

6. The first Colombian migrants, who came to the state recruited to work in the textile mills in the early 1960s, settled in Central Falls. For years, this town was the place of concentration of Colombians in the state. This is no longer the case because Colombians have been moving into Providence and Pawtucket and the Mexican and Guatemalan populations have grown rapidly in Central Falls. Yet, the heritage of the Colombian concentration in Central Falls is seen in the town's political representation of Latinos.

7. Part of the staff of the former UWC rebuilt it as an independent grassroots organization called Fuerza Laboral.

8. The story of Latino political mobilization in Rhode Island has been documented by local political activist Tomás Avila in a book that compiles the principal documents and journalistic notes on the topic between 1996 and 2006 period.

9. Indeed, 65.6 percent of first-generation respondents to the Latino National Survey, and seven out of eleven of their second-generation counterparts, answered that in areas such as government services and employment and political power and representation, Dominicans have either some or a lot in common with other Latinos.

10. There are three other Latinos elected to office in the Providence–Central Falls area. One is State Representative Anastasia Williams, from Panama, the first Latina elected official in the state, who has represented district 9 in South Providence since 1992. The second is councilman Luis Aponte, from Puerto Rico, who represents ward 10, also in South Providence, since 1998. The third is Central Falls councilperson Eunice de la Hoz, a Colombian elected to the city council in 2006. For many years, Central Falls had another Colombian on its council, Ricardo Patiño, who was the first Latino elected official in that city. Colombians' history in Central Falls gives them the knowledge and the organization necessary to enter the local political system.

11. Today Victor Capellán is the president of the National Executive Board of the Dominican American National Roundtable.

12. This was the largest victory because senate districts are larger that city wards and house districts. Hence, to win elections for the senate, a larger organizational effort is needed.

13. To be sure, political parties were not the only important actor in the political incorporation of immigrants. Community organizations always played a role in this process (Sterne 2001). Yet, what is different today is the virtual absence of political party involvement in the mobilization of immigrants (Wong 2006).

14. Juán Pichardo, interview, July 16, 2008.

15. I do not know the organizational base for his later campaign to city hall. It may have also relied on Dominican political party activists.

16. In 1992, Juan Francisco, a Dominican pastor, ran unsuccessfully for state representative in the Republican primary. He is one of a small group of Latinos who have tried to run for office as Republicans.

17. After she resigned her position with the Democratic Party, she was hired to direct the Human Relations office of the city of Providence.

18. When the 2002 map was unveiled, Latino organizations also introduced a lawsuit arguing that the redistricting diluted the Latino voting power. This lawsuit was withdrawn. Only African American organizations pressed on with their lawsuit.

19. The Rhode Island senate never admitted wrongdoing in the drawing of the 2002 maps. In 2004, however, the retirement of two powerful incumbents allowed the senate to redraw the district boundaries without affecting any powerful stakeholders and avoiding the costs of the legal battle.

CHAPTER 9

1. It is interesting to point out that the Warner and Srole racial typology included intermediate groups beyond the black and white distinction and that they used the concept of ethnoracial group.

2. Similarly, the election of women to the prime minister position or the presidency in many countries has been very important in the struggle for gender equality but has not ended gender economic disparities or violence and discrimination toward women.

REFERENCES

Alba, Richard D. 2005. "Bright vs. Blurred Boundaries: Second-Generation Assimilation and Exclusion in France, Germany, and the United States." *Ethnic and Racial Studies* 28(1): 20–49.

———. 1985. *Italian Americans: Into the Twilight of Ethnicity.* Englewood Cliffs, N.J.: Prentice Hall.

———. 1990. *Ethnic Identity: The Transformation of White America.* New Haven, Conn.: Yale University Press.

Alba, Richard D., and Victor Nee. 2003. *Remaking the American Mainstream: Assimilation and Contemporary Immigration.* Cambridge, Mass.: Harvard University Press.

Anderson, Elijah, and Douglas S. Massey. 2001. *Problem of the Century: Racial Stratification in the United States.* New York: Russell Sage Foundation.

Aparicio, Ana. 2006. *Dominican-Americans and the Politics of Empowerment.* Gainesville: University Press of Florida.

Ashmore, Richard D., Kay Deaux, and Tracy McLaughlin-Volpe. 2004. "An Organizing Framework for Collective Identity: Articulation and Significance of Multidimensionality." *Psychological Bulletin* 130(1): 80–114.

Auyero, Javier. 2003. *Contentious Lives: Two Argentine Women, Two Protests, and the Quest for Recognition.* Durham, N.C.: Duke University Press.

Basch, Linda G., Nina Glick Glick-Schiller, and Cristina Szanton Blanc. 1994. *Nations Unbound: Transnational Projects, Postcolonial Predicaments, and Deterritorialized Nation-States.* New York: Gordon and Breach.

Bean, Frank D., and Gillian Stevens. 2003. *America's Newcomers and the Dynamics of Diversity.* New York: Russell Sage Foundation.

Beck, Sam. 1992. *Manny Almeida's Ringside Lounge: The Cape Verdean's Struggle for Their Neighborhood.* Providence, R.I.: Gávea-Brown Publications.

Bloemraad, Irene. 2006. *Becoming a Citizen: Incorporating Immigrants and Refugees in the United States and Canada.* Berkeley: University of California Press.

Bonilla-Silva, Eduardo. 2004. "From Bi-Racial to Tri-Racial: Towards a New System of Racial Stratification in the USA." *Ethnic and Racial Studies* 27(6): 931–50.

Bowles, Samuel, and Herbert Gintis. 1976. *Schooling in Capitalist America: Educational Reform and the Contradictions of Economic Life.* New York: Basic Books.

Breen, Richard. 2005. "Foundations of a Neo-Weberian Class Analysis." In *Approaches to Class Analysis,* edited by E. O. Wright. Cambridge: Cambridge University Press.

Brooks, Clem, and Jeff Manza. 1997. "Social Cleavages and Political Alignments: U.S. Presidential Elections, 1960 to 1992." *American Sociological Review* 62(6): 937–46.

Brubaker, Rogers. 2000. "Beyond 'Identity.'" *Theory and Society* 29(1): 1–48.

Bryce-Laporte, Roy S., and Delores M. Mortimer. 1983. *Caribbean Immigration to the United States.* Washington, D.C.: Research Institute on Immigration and Ethnic Studies, Smithsonian Institution.

Burawoy, Michael. 1998. "The Extended Case Method." *Sociological Theory* 16(1): 4–33.

Candelario, Ginetta. 2007. *Black Behind the Ears: Dominican Racial Identity from Museums to Beauty Shops.* Durham, N.C.: Duke University Press.

Conley, Patrick T., and Paul Campbell. 2006. *South Providence.* Charleston, S.C.: Arcadia Publishing.

Cordero-Guzman, Hector. 2005. "Community-Based Organizations and Migration in New York City." *Journal of Ethnic and Migration Studies* 31(5): 889–909.

Dahl, Robert. 1961. *Who Governs? Democracy and Power in an American City.* New Haven, Conn.: Yale University Press.

Davila, Arlene 2001. *Latinos, Inc.: The Marketing and Making of a People.* Berkeley: University of California Press.

Deaux, Kay, and Daniela Martin. 2003. "Interpersonal Networks and Social Categories: Specifying Levels of Context in Identity Processes." *Social Psychology Quarterly* 66(2): 101–18.

Erie, Steven P. 1988. *Rainbow's End.* Berkeley: University of California Press.

Erikson, Robert, and John H. Goldthorpe. 1992. *The Constant Flux: A Study of Class Mobility in Industrial Societies.* Oxford: Clarendon Press.

Feliciano, Cynthia, and Rubén G. Rumbaut. 2005. "Gendered Paths: Educational and Occupational Expectations and Outcomes Among Adult Children of Immigrants." *Ethnic and Racial Studies* 28(6): 1087–1118.

Foner, Nancy. 2001. *Islands in the City West Indian Migration to New York.* Berkeley: University of California Press.

———. 2005. *In a New Land: A Comparative View of Immigration.* New York: New York University Press.

Gans, Hans J. 1992. "2nd-Generation Decline: Scenarios for the Economic and Ethnic Futures of the Post-1965 American Immigrants." *Ethnic and Racial Studies* 15(2): 173–92.

Georges, Eugenia. 1990. *The Making of a Transnational Community: Migration, Development, and Cultural Change in the Dominican Republic.* New York: Columbia University Press.

Glazer, Nathan. 1993. "Is Assimilation Dead?" *Annals of the American Academy of Political and Social Science* 530: 122–36.

Glazer, Nathan, and Daniel P. Moynihan. 1970. *Beyond the Melting Pot: The Negroes, Puerto Ricans, Jews, Italians, and Irish of New York City.* Cambridge, Mass.: M.I.T. Press.

Glick-Schiller, Nina. 2004. "Transnationality." In *A Companion to the Anthropology of Politics,* edited by David Nugent and Joan Vincent. Malden, Mass.: Blackwell Publishing.

Golash-Boza, Tanya. 2006. "Dropping the Hyphen? Becoming Latino(a)-American Through Racialized Assimilation." *Social Forces* 85(1): 27–55.

Goldthorpe, John H., and Abigail McKnight. 2004. *The Economic Basis of Social Class.* London: Centre for Analysis of Social Exclusion, London School of Economics and Political Science.

Goldthorpe, John H., Catriona Llewellyn, and Clive Payne. 1987. *Social Mobility and Class Structure in Modern Britain.* Oxford: Clarendon Press.

Gordon, Milton Myron. 1964. *Assimilation in American Life: The Role of Race, Religion, and National Origins.* New York: Oxford University Press.

Grasmuck, Sherri, and Patricia Pessar. 1991. *Between Two Islands: Dominican International Migration.* Berkeley: University of California Press.

Grosfoguel, Ramón. 1997. "Colonial Caribbean Migrations to France, the Netherlands, Great Britain and the United States." *Ethnic and Racial Studies* 20(3): 594–612.

Grosfoguel, Ramón, and Chloe S. Georas. 2000. "'Coloniality of Power' and Racial Dynamics: Notes Toward a Reinterpretation of Latino Caribbeans in New York City." *Identities-Global Studies in Culture and Power* 7(1): 85–125.

Guarnizo, Luis E. 1994. "Los-Dominicanyorks: The Making of a Binational Society." *Annals of the American Academy of Political and Social Science* 533: 70–86.

Halter, Marilyn. 1993. *Between Race and Ethnicity: Cape Verdean American Immigrants, 1860–1965.* Urbana: University of Illinois Press.

Hattam, Victoria. 2004. "Ethnicity: An American Geneology." In *Not Just Black and White: Historical and Contemporary Perspectives on Immigration, Race, and Ethnicity in the United States,* edited by Nancy Foner and G. M. Fredrickson. New York: Russell Sage Foundation.

Hernández, Ramona. 2002. *The Mobility of Workers Under Advanced Capitalism Dominican Migration to the United States.* New York: Columbia University Press.

Hernández, Ramona, and Francisco L. Rivera-Batiz. 2003. *Dominicans in the United States: A Socioeconomic Profile, 2000.* New York: CUNY Dominican Studies Institute.

Hertz, Tom. 2005. "Rags, Riches, and Race: The Intergenerational Economic Mobility of Black and White Families in the United States." In *Unequal Chances: Family Background and Economic Success,* edited by Samuel Bowles, Herbert Gintis, and Melissa Osborne Groves. New York: Russell Sage Foundation.

Higham, John. 1955. *Strangers in the Land: Patterns of American Nativism, 1860–1925.* New Brunswick, N.J.: Rutgers University Press.

Hochschild, Jennifer L. 1995. "Facing Up to the American Dream: Race, Class, and the Soul of the Nation." In *Princeton Studies in American Politics.* Princeton, N.J.: Princeton University Press.

Hoffman-Guzman, Carol. 2004. "Transnationalism and Middle-Class Dominican Immigrants." In *Dominican Migration: Transnational Perspectives, New World Diaspora Series,* edited by Ernesto Sagas and Sintia Molina. Gainesville: University Press of Florida.

Hout, M., Clem Brooks, and Jeff Manza. 1995. "The Democratic Class Struggle in the United States, 1948–1992." *American Sociological Review* 60(6): 805–28.

Huntington, Samuel P. 2004. *Who Are We?: The Challenges to America's National Identity.* New York: Simon & Schuster.

Itzigsohn, José. 2000. "Immigration and the Boundaries of Citizenship: The Institutions of Immigrants' Political Transnationalism." *International Migration Review* 34(4): 1126–54.

———. 2004. "Latino Panethnicity: Assessment and Perspectives." In *Not Just Black and White,* edited by Nancy Foner and G. Fredricson. New York: Russell Sage Foundation.

———. 2007. "Migration and Transnational Citizenship in Latin America: The Cases of Mexico and the Dominican Republic." In *Dual Citizenship in Global Perspective,* edited by Thomas Faist and Peter Kivisto. New York: Palgrave Macmillan.

Itzigsohn, José, and Silvia Giorguli-Saucedo. 2002. "Immigrant Incorporation and Sociocultural Transnationalism." *International Migration Review* 36(3): 766–98.

Itzigsohn, José, and Daniela Villacrés. 2008. "Migrant Political Transnationalism and the Practice of Democracy: Dominican External Voting Rights and Salvadoran Home Town Associations." *Ethnic & Racial Studies* 31(4): 664–86.

Itzigsohn, José, Silvia Giorguli, and Obed Vazquez. 2005. "Immigrant Incorporation and Racial Identity: Racial Self-Identification Among Dominican Immigrants." *Ethnic and Racial Studies* 28(1): 50–78.

Itzigsohn, José, Carlos Dore-Cabral, Esther Hernandez-Medina, and Obed Vazquez. 1999. "Mapping Dominican Transnationalism: Narrow and Broad Transnational Practices." *Ethnic and Racial Studies* 22(2): 316–39.

Jenkins, Richard. 1994. "Rethinking Ethnicity: Identity, Categorization and Power." *Ethnic and Racial Studies* 17(2): 197–223.

———. 1996. "Ethnicity Etcetera: Social Anthropological Points of View." *Ethnic and Racial Studies* 19(4): 807–22.

———. 1997. *Rethinking Ethnicity: Arguments and Explorations.* Thousand Oaks, Calif.: Sage Publications.

Jones-Correa, Michael. 1998. *Between Two Nations: The Political Predicament of Latinos in New York City.* Ithaca, N.Y.: Cornell University Press.

———. 2001. "Comparative Approaches to Changing Interethnic Relations in Cities." In *Governing American Cities,* edited by Michael Jones-Correa. New York: Russell Sage Foundation.

Joppke, Christian. 1999. *Immigration and the Nation-state: the United States, Germany, and Great Britain.* Oxford: Oxford University Press.

———. 2005. *Selecting by Origin: Ethnic Migration in the Liberal State.* Cambridge, Mass.: Harvard University Press.

Kasinitz, Philip. 1992. *Caribbean New York: Black Immigrants and the Politics of Race.* Ithaca, N.Y.: Cornell University Press.

Kasinitz, Philip, John H. Mollenkopf, and Mary C. Waters. 2004. *Becoming New Yorkers: Ethnographies of the New Second Generation.* New York: Russell Sage Foundation.

Kasinitz, Philip, John H. Mollenkopf, Mary C. Waters, and Jennifer Holdaway. 2008. *Inheriting the City: The Children of Immigrants Come of Age.* New York and Cambridge, Mass.: Russell Sage Foundation and Harvard University Press.

Kibria, Nazly. 2002. *Becoming Asian American: Identities of Second Generation Chinese and Korean Americans.* Baltimore, Md.: Johns Hopkins University Press.

Kivisto, Peter. 2005. "The Revival of Assimilation in Historical Perspective." In *Incorporating Diversity: Rethinking Assimilation in a Multicultural Age,* edited by Peter Kivisto. Boulder, Colo.: Paradigm Publishers.

Kwong, Peter. 1996. *The New Chinatown,* rev. ed. New York: Hill and Wang.

Lacy, Karen R. 2004. "Black Spaces, Black Places: Strategic Assimilation and Identity Construction in Middle-Class Suburbia." *Ethnic and Racial Studies* 27(6): 908–30.

Laó-Montes, Agustín. 2001. "Niuyol: Urban Regimes, Latino Social Movements, Ideologies of Latinidad." In *Mambo Montage: The Latinization of New York,* edited by Agustín Laó-Montes and Arlene Dávila. New York: Columbia University Press.

Levitt, Peggy. 2001. *The Transnational Villagers.* Berkeley: University of California Press.

Levitt, Peggy, and Nina Glick-Schiller. 2004. "Conceptualizing Simultaneity: A Transnational Social Field Perspective on Society." *International Migration Review* 38(3): 1002–39.

Lieberson, Stanley. 1980. *A Piece of the Pie: Blacks and White Immigrants Since 1880.* Berkeley: University of California Press.

Light, Ivan, and Steven J. Gold. 2000. *Ethnic Economies.* San Diego, Calif.: Academic Press.

López, Nancy. 2003. *Hopeful Girls, Troubled Boys: Race and Gender Disparity in Urban Education.* New York: Routledge.

Louie, Vivian. 2006. "Growing Up Ethnic in Transnational Worlds: Identities Among Second-Generation Chinese and Dominicans." *Identities-Global Studies in Culture and Power* 13(3): 363–94.

Marwell, Nicole P. 2004. "Ethnic and Postethnic Politics in New York City: The Dominican Second Generation." In *Becoming New Yorkers: Ethnographies of the New Second Generation,* edited by Philip Kasinitz, John H. Mollenkopf, and Mary C. Waters. New York: Russell Sage Foundation.

Massey, Douglas S. 2007. *Categorically Unequal: The American Stratification System.* New York: Russell Sage Foundation.

Massey, Douglas S., and Nancy A. Denton. 1993. *American Apartheid: Segregation and the Making of the Underclass.* Cambridge, Mass.: Harvard University Press.

Mazumder, Bhashkar. 2005. "The Apple Falls Even Closer to the Tree than We Thought." In *Unequal Chances: Family Background and Economic Success,* edited by Samuel Bowles, Herbert Gintis, and M. O. Groves. New York: Russell Sage Foundation.

McCall, Leslie. 2005. "The Complexity of Intersectionality." *Signs: Journal of Women in Culture and Society* 30(3): 1771–1800.

McClain, Paula D., and Steven C. Tauber. 2001. "Racial Minority Group Relations in a Multiracial Society." In *Governing American Cities,* edited by Michael Jones-Correa. New York: Russell Sage Foundation.

Mills, C. Wright. 1959. *The Sociological Imagination.* New York: Oxford University Press.

Min, Pyong Gap, and Rose Kim. 1999. *Struggle for Ethnic Identity: Narratives by Asian American Professionals.* Walnut Creek, Calif.: AltaMira Press.

Model, Suzanne. 1991. "Caribbean Immigrants: A Black Success Story?" *International Migration Review* 25(2): 249–75.

Paige, Jeffery. M. 1999. "Conjuncture, Comparison, and Conditional Theory in Macrosocial Inquiry." *American Journal of Sociology* 105(3): 781–800.

Pattillo, Mary. 2005. "Black Middle-Class Neighborhoods." *Annual Review of Sociology* 31(1): 305–31.

Perlmann, Joel. 2005. *Italians Then, Mexicans Now: Immigrant Origins and Second-Generation Progress, 1890 to 2000.* New York: Russell Sage Foundation.

Perlmann, Joel, and Roger Waldinger. 1997. "Second Generation Decline? Children of Immigrants, Past and Present a Reconsideration." *International Migration Review* 31(4): 893–922.

Portes, Alejandro. 2006. "Paths of Assimilation in the Second Generation." *Sociological Forum* 21(3): 499–504.

Portes, Alejandro, and Robert L. Bach. 1985. *Latin Journey: Cuban and Mexican Immigrants in the United States.* Berkeley: University of California Press.

Portes, Alejandro, and Rubén G. Rumbaut. 1996. *Immigrant America: A Portrait.* Berkeley: University of California Press.

———. 2001. *Legacies: The Story of the Immigrant Second Generation.* Berkeley and New York: University of California Press and Russell Sage Foundation.

Portes, Alejandro, and Alex Stepick. 1993. *City on The Edge: The Transformation of Miami.* Berkeley: University of California Press.

Portes, Alejandro, and Min Zhou. 1993. "The New 2nd Generation: Segmented Assimilation and Its Variants." *Annals of the American Academy of Political and Social Science* 530: 74–96.

Portes, Alejandro, Cristina Escobar, and Alexandria W. Radford. 2007. "Immigrant Transnational Organizations and Development: A Comparative Study." *International Migration Review* 41(1): 242–81.

Portes, Alejandro, William J. Haller, and Luis E. Guarnizo. 2002. "Transnational Entrepreneurs: An Alternative Form of Immigrant Economic Adaptation." *American Sociological Review* 67(2): 278–98.

Portes, Alejandro, Patricia Fernandez-Kelly, and William Haller. 2005. "Segmented Assimilation on the Ground: The New Second Generation in Early Adulthood." *Ethnic and Racial Studies.* 28(6): 1000–40.

Prewitt, Kenneth. 2004. *The Census Counts, the Census Classifies,* edited by Nancy Foner and G. M. Fredrickson. New York: Russell Sage Foundation.

Ricourt, Milagros. 2002. *Dominicans in New York City: Power from the Margins.* New York: Routledge.

Ricourt, Milagros, and Ruby Danta. 2003. *Hispanas de Queens: Latino Panethnicity in a New York City Neighborhood.* Ithaca, N.Y.: Cornell University Press.

Rumbaut, Rubén G. 1997. "Assimilation and its Discontents: Between Rhetoric and Reality." *International Migration Review* 31(4): 923–60.

Sagas, Ernesto, and Sintia Molina. 2004. *Dominican Migration: Transnational Perspectives.* Gainesville: University Press of Florida.

Sellers, Robert M., Mia A. Smith, J. Nicole Shelton, Stephanie A. J. Rowley, and Tabbye M. Chavous. 1998. "Multidimensional Model of Racial Identity: A Reconceptualization of African American Racial Identity." *Personality and Social Psychology Review* 2(1): 18–39.

Smith, Gregory. 2004. "Metts Captures Redrawn Providence District." *Providence Journal,* September 15, Section C, Page 1.

Smith, Robert C. 2006. *Mexican New York: Transnational Lives of New Immigrants.* Berkeley: University of California Press.

Sokefeld, Martin. 2001. "Reconsidering Identity." *Anthropos* 96(2): 527–44.

Sowell, Thomas. 1981. *Ethnic America: A History.* New York: Basic Books.

Stanton-Salazar, Ricardo D. 1997. "A Social Capital Framework for Understanding the Socialization of Racial Minority Children and Youths." *Harvard Educational Review* 67(1): 1–39.

Sterne, Evelyn Savidge. 2003. *Ballots and Bibles: Ethnic Politics and the Catholic Church in Providence.* Ithaca, N.Y.: Cornell University Press.

Stryker, Sheldon, and Richard T. Serpe. 1994. "Identity Salience and Psychological Centrality: Equivalent, Overlapping, or Complementart Concepts?" *Social Psychological Quarterly* 57(1): 16–35.

Stryker, Sheldon, Richard T. Serpe, and Matthew O. Hunt. 2005. "Making Good on a Promise: The Impact of Larger Social Structures on Commitments." *Advances in Group Processes* 22: 93–123.

Suro, Robert. 2002. "Counting the 'Other Hispanics': How Many Colombians, Dominicans, Ecuadorians, Guatemalans, and Salvadorans Are There in the United States?" Washington, D.C.: Pew Hispanic Center.

Telles, Edward E., and Vilma Ortiz. 2008. *Generations of Exclusion: Mexican Americans, Assimilation, and Race.* New York: Russell Sage Foundation.

Torres-Saillant, Silvio, and Ramona Hernández. 1998. *The Dominican Americans.* Westport, Conn.: Greenwood Press.

U.S. Bureau of the Census. 2000. 5-Percent Public Use Microdata Sample. Washington: U.S. Bureau of the Census.

Uriarte, Miren. 2006. "Growing into Power in Rhode Island." In *Latinos in New England,* edited by Andrés Torres. Philadelphia, Pa.: Temple University Press.

Vickerman, Milton. 1999. *Crosscurrents: West Indian Immigrants and Race.* Oxford: Oxford University Press.

Waldinger, Roger, and Cynthia Feliciano. 2004. "Will the New Second Generation Experience 'Downward Assimilation'? Segmented Assimilation Re-Assessed." *Ethnic and Racial Studies* 27(3): 376–402.

Waldinger, Roger, and Bozorgmehr Mehdi. 1996. *Ethnic Los Angeles.* New York: Russell Sage Foundation.

Waldinger, Roger, Eric Popkin, and Hector Aquiles Magana. 2008. "Conflict and Contestation in the Cross-Border Community: Hometown Associations Reassessed." *Ethnic and Racial Studies* 31(5): 843–70.

Warner, W. Lloyd, and Leo Srole. 1945. *The Social Systems of American Ethnic Groups.* New Haven, Conn.: Yale University Press.

Waters, Mary C. 1990. *Ethnic Options: Choosing Identities in America.* Berkeley: University of California Press.

———. 1996. "Ethnic and Racial Identities of Second Generation Black Immigrants in New York City." In *The New Second Generation,* edited by Alejandro Portes. New York: Russell Sage Foundation.

———. 1999. *Black Identities: West Indian Immigrant Dreams and American Realities.* New York: Russell Sage Foundation.

Wilson, George. 2001. "Support for Redistributive Policies Among the African American Middle Class: Race and Class Effects." *Research in Social Stratification and Mobility* 18:97–115.

Wilson, William J. 1978. *The Declining Significance of Race: Blacks and Changing American Institutions.* Chicago: University of Chicago Press.

———. 1996. *When Work Disappears: The World of the New Urban Poor.* New York: Alfred A. Knopf.

Winant, Howard. 2004. *The New Politics of Race.* Minneapolis: University of Minnesota Press.

Wong, Janelle. 2006. *Democracy's Promise: Immigrants and American Civic Institutions.* Ann Arbor: University of Michigan Press.

Wright, Erik Olin. 2005a. *Approaches to Class Analysis.* Cambridge: Cambridge University Press.

————. 2005b. "Foundations of a Neo-Marxist Class Analysis." In *Approaches to Class Analysis,* edited by Erik O. Wright. Cambridge: Cambridge University Press.

Yancey, William L., Eugene P. Ericksen, and Richard N. Juliani. 1976. "Emergent Ethnicity: Review and Reformulation." *American Sociological Review* 41(3): 391–403.

Zhou, Min. 1992. *Chinatown: The Socioeconomic Potential of an Urban Enclave.* Philadelphia, Pa.: Temple University Press.

Zhou, Min, and Carl L. Bankston. 1998. *Growing Up American: How Vietnamese Children Adapt to Life in the United States.* New York: Russell Sage Foundation.

INDEX

Boldface numbers refer to figures and tables